# THE RIGHT TO LIVE

## By C. C. Cawley

*The Right to Live* deals with the problems created when a parent, because of his religious convictions, denies a child proper medical aid. Although basically the solution seems simple—if the parent won't call a doctor the state must do so—constitutional guarantees of religious freedom greatly complicate the issue.

Today, when medicine, religion, and law collide, three groups unlike in precept—the "true" faith healers, the Christian Scientists and the Jehovah's Witnesses—come into identical conflict with the law over their one identical act: denial of medical aid because of religious belief. A revivalist-healer only aggravates a polio victim's condition but charges against him of practicing medicine without a license are dismissed. A critically injured Jehovah's Witness refuses the blood transfusion which alone can save his life; the law does not intervene and his physician helplessly watches him die. A Christian Science "practitioner" counsels a parent to deny his diabetic child insulin; the child dies; the parent is charged with manslaughter but the practitioner goes free. Why?

This book supplies the answers, and explains how they have been worked out by the courts over a course of many years.

The author discusses in Part I some of the players in this grim drama: faith healers, Christian Scientists, Jehovah's Witnesses, and the like. Following this the author offers his explanation of faith healing in the light of present-day knowledge.

Part II traces "the historical working out of the general problem of freedom versus license." How long and how far are acts done under the claims of constitutional protection to be tolerated? At what point must they be forbidden? The history of the Mormons offers the best example of how this difficulty has been resolved, and the author offers an account of the history of their relations with the American public and the American government.

Part III discusses in specific terms areas in which medicine, religion, and law have collided. It takes up such topics as the faith healer at common law, the efforts to bring religious healers under the prohibitions of the medical practice acts, and concludes with the question: "At what point does disbelief in a religious representation become actionable fraud?" In answer the author submits a Supreme Court decision that has ruled on this matter, plus a concurring opinion, and a notable dissent by Justice Jackson.

The book's concluding part traces the developments that have led to today's interpretations, where by legal precedent the state has now reserved the right to interfere actively with parental control and religious freedom in order to guarantee the child's *Right to Live*. You will also learn what you can do should you encounter a situation similar to those described in the book. You can get help—and fast; and the author tells you exactly how to go about it.

Provocative, thoroughly researched, with 131 legal cases cited, plus appendices and 35 photographs, this book belongs on the shelves of physicians, clergymen, judges, legislators, attorneys and interested laymen.

# THE RIGHT TO LIVE

# THE RIGHT TO LIVE

by

## C. C. Cawley

South Brunswick and New York: A. S. Barnes and Company
London: Thomas Yoseloff Ltd

A. S. Barnes and Co., Inc.
Cranbury, New Jersey 08512

Thomas Yoseloff Ltd
108 New Bond Street
London W. 1, England

SBN 498 06973 7
Printed in the United States of America

to Sue
who saw it through

# Acknowledgments

Grateful acknowledgment is due to the copyright owners for:

Excerpts from the article "Science and the Supernatural" by Dr. A. J. Carlson, copyright 1931 by *Science*. Reprinted by permission of American Association for the Advancement of Science.

Excerpts from the article "The Lunatic Fringe of Religion" by Dr. Frank S. Mead, in *American Mercury* for February, 1941. Reprinted by permission of *American Mercury*, Torrance, California.

Excerpts from the editorial "Who Killed Cock Robin?" in American Journal of Public Health. Reprinted by permission of American Public Health Association, Inc.

Excerpts from the article "Seeing the Doctor, 'Quacks Can Cure Hysteria but Rarely Anything Else,'" by Dr. Walter C. Alvarez, in the Boston *Globe* for September 4, 1955. Reprinted by permission of The Boston *Globe*.

Excerpts from the editorial "Religious Liberty and Fraud" in *The Christian Century*, copyright 1944 Christian Century Foundation. Reprinted by permission from the May 10, 1944, issue of *The Christian Century*.

Excerpts from the article "The Outlaws" by Clifford Cawley in *The Christian Century*, copyright 1957 Christian Century Foundation. Reprinted by permission from the April 3, 1957, issue of *The Christian Century*.

Excerpts from the article, "Roman Catholic by Law?" by Clifford Cawley in *The Churchman* for April 15, 1957. Reprinted by permission of *The Churchman*.

Excerpts from the article "Why Do People Detour to Quacks?" by Dr. Beatrix Cobb. Reprinted by permission of Beatrix Cobb.

Excerpts from the Donna Jones account in *The Globe and Mail*. Reprinted by permission of *The Globe and Mail*, Toronto.

Excerpts from *Devils, Drugs and Doctors* by Howard W. Haggard, copyright 1929 by Harper & Row, Publishers, Incorporated. Reprinted by permission of Harper & Row, Publishers, Incorporated.

Excerpts from *The True Believer* by Eric Hoffer, copyright 1951 by Harper & Row, Publishers, Incorporated. Reprinted by permission of Harper & Row, Publishers, Incorporated.

Excerpts from *The Psychology of Adjustment* by Dr. Laurance Frederic Shaffer, copyright 1936 by Houghton Mifflin Company. Reprinted by permission of the author and Houghton Mifflin Company.

Excerpts from the article "Is Any Sick Among You?" by Clifford Cawley, in *The Humanist* No. 1, 1954 issue. Reprinted by permission of *The Humanist*.

Excerpts from the reports of the Volstad-Alvis trial in the Los Angeles *Times*. Reprinted by permission of the Los Angeles *Times*.

Excerpts from the A. A. Allen account by Ernest Y. Cox in the Sacramento *Bee*. Reprinted by permission of McClatchy Newspapers, Sacramento.

Excerpts from the article "Babies Have the Right to Live" by Clifford Cawley, in *Together* for August, 1957, copyright 1957 by Lovick Pierce (The Methodist Publishing House). Reprinted by permission of The Methodist Publishing House.

Excerpts from the article, "The Debt of Constitutional Law to Jehovah's Witnesses" by Edward F. Waite, in the *Minnesota Law Review* for March, 1944. Reprinted by permission of the *Minnesota Law Review*.

Excerpts from the editorial comment on "Seiferth" in the *Minnesota Law Review* for December, 1954. Reprinted by permission of the *Minnesota Law Review*.

Excerpts from the article "Criminal Liability in Faith Healing" by Clifford Cawley, in the *Minnesota Law Review* for December, 1954. Reprinted by permission of the *Minnesota Law Review*.

Excerpts from the Grant account in The Montreal *Star*. Reprinted by permission of The Montreal *Star*.

Excerpts from the article "Parens Patriae: The Sovereign Power of Guardianship" by Clifford Cawley, in *The New England Journal of Medicine* for November 25, 1954. Reprinted by permission of *The New England Journal of Medicine*.

Excerpts from the Willis Vernon Cole, Helen Vasko, Oral Roberts and Greet Hofmans accounts in *The New York Times,* copyright 1914, 1916, 1933, 1935 and 1956 by The New York Times Company. Reprinted by permission.

Excerpts from *An American Doctor's Odyssey* by Victor Heiser, copyright 1936 by W. W. Norton & Company, Inc. Reprinted by permission of W. W. Norton & Company, Inc.

Excerpts from the news story, "Borden Sues 'I Am' Cult Leaders," in *Publisher's Weekly* for January 4, 1941. Reprinted by permission of *Publisher's Weekly*.

Excerpts from *Mrs. Eddy* by Edwin Franden Dakin, copyright 1929 by Charles Scribner's Sons. Reprinted by permission of Charles Scribner's Sons.

# Contents

# Contents

# THE RIGHT TO LIVE

*Part I*

# THE PLAYERS

# 1
# Doctors Are for People Who Ain't Got Jesus

*Is any sick among you? Let him call for the elders of the church; and let them pray over him, anointing him with oil in the name of the Lord: And the prayer of faith shall save the sick, and the Lord shall rise him up . . .*

*—James 5:14, 15.*

*F. S. Sanchez, state's witness:* "When I got there the child was plumb raving crazy, apparently. She didn't know anybody, and was biting herself and tearing up the bedclothes, and they were rubbing her and I had to help hold her on the bed. They claimed that God had done healed her; said, 'Glory to God, it would never have another pain.' It made me so mad that I could hardly stand it, to see that child suffer like she was, and they saying that, and I said: 'Well, I hope so; but, gentlemen, that poor child!' When it had three or four more fits like it was having, but [*sic*] it was the horriblest thing I ever saw, and I just had to harness my horse and go on home."

The child, Bertha Bradley, an epileptic, had fallen into a fire during a seizure and was badly burned, but her father refused to call in a physician. His reasons:

We were trusting to the Lord for the healing of the body. I believed that I was doing all that God required me to do; I had the saints and elders pray for her, which we did twice a day, and anointed her with oil.

Sanchez, his brother-in-law, had argued for a physician:

I said, "Jim, let's have a doctor to her"; and he said, "Oh, Glory to God, all the doctor I want is Jesus; I got Jesus. He is the greatest physician of all. He has promised to do it all"; and he placed his hands on her and was praying. I said, "Jim, He ain't promised to do it all"; and he said, "Doctors are for people who ain't got Jesus." I tried to argue and persuade him, and told him I knew that Jesus was the great doctor, but there were some on earth; and he said, "Frank, I would rather follow her to the grave than to have one come in this house."

On May 30, 1918, thirty-four days after her burning, authorities from the Florida Hospital for the Insane at Chattahoochee took Bertha into custody. There she received treatment but died on June 22. James Bradley was convicted of manslaughter, but on appeal the court reversed judgment on a remarkable logic, holding that the act committed did not fall strictly within the statute.

Mark Twain, vacationing near Vienna, fell over a 75-foot cliff. He lay at the bottom, "an incoherent series of compound fractures," until he by good luck was "found by some peasants who had lost an ass." They carried him to the nearest farmhouse and summoned the only available aid, a lady from Boston, summering nearby, who was a "Christian Science doctor." She sent word that there was nothing the matter with him; that his pains were a delusion; that she would now give him "absent treatment"; and that she herself would come in the morning. After this visit, Mark Twain in desperation engaged a horse doctor, who after horse-wise diagnosis applied "energetic measures" and restored him to health.[1]

One winter evening of that same period, a friend of mine and his chum Stuart "iced" a sled-run. Next morning, Stuart's first wild descent ended with a crash and a broken leg. My friend helped carry him home, then returned to his own home to report how Stuart's father, a Christian Scientist, had refused his offer to run for a doctor. Instead, he was "demonstrating" over the boy, who lay in his bed screaming with pain. My friend's father, enraged, enlisted two sizeable neighbors and a doctor. This foursome without formality entered Stuart's house, and while the others held the father prisoner downstairs the doctor properly set the broken leg. This done, the party marched out again.

Granted, the adult Mark Twain was free to submit himself at his own risk to any mode of ministration he chose. And granted that as to children, society did not then and does not now countenance such *unauthorized* forthright action as that just described. But the state has come to assert its right to interfere more and more with the rights of parenthood and religion in its overriding regard for the child's welfare. In the last two decades, more determined than ever that infants shall not be martyred by their parents' eccentricities, our courts have legally executed child-rescue missions with a singleness of mind and a speed approaching that of the foursome above.

How many deaths do faith healers cause? For an answer we turn to the Public Health Service's yearly tottings but find listed neither *"Faith Healers"* nor *"Healers, Faith."* Here is "MALIGNANT NEO-PLASMS," but thereunder no subheading *"Deaths from cancer of the breast due to reliance on prayer cloth."* Here is "TUBERCULOSIS, ALL FORMS," but no subhead *"Deaths due to treatment of active form by Christian Science Practitioner."*[2] And here is "CERTAIN DIS-EASES OF EARLY INFANCY," but thereunder no *"Deaths due to religion-dictated denial of blood transfusion."* The answer is not to be found so easily. One hypothetical case will explain why. A child is stricken with an unfamiliar ailment. The mother resorts to prayer, then to a chiropractor, then an osteopath—I am not trying to be funny: the sequence is from the Mitchell case (Ch. 14). Finally, six months after onset of the disease, the child is taken to a competent medical doctor. From clinical tests the strange malady is identified; at once the doctor applies all known remedies. But by now the unchecked disease has pro-gressed (here I depart from *Mitchell's* happier ending) to an incurable stage. The doctor succeeds in prolonging the child's life but finally it dies. And on the death certificate he writes only two words: *"Rheu-matic Fever."* Only these two words reach the Public Health Service files. No accompanying script lists the other players' names and parts.

In the fall of 1953, in one attempt to assess the extent of denial of medical aid because of religious belief, the author engaged a newsclip-ping bureau's services for three months. This agency actually "scanned" one-fifth of all U.S. dailies, but claimed—considering the pickup by wire services from unscanned papers—a forty per cent coverage of the subject. In analyzing the resulting clippings it was necessary, first, to combine different accounts of the same event; second, to eliminate items not truly "events" but prepared discussions—for example, an excellent article by Dr. Frank G. Slaughter, some practical instructions for the amateur by Norman Vincent Peale ("7. If the real thought is positive, you will get positive and healing results") and the like; and third, to eliminate accounts of non-healing miracles—how, for example, a serviceman during a landing operation was knocked overboard and drawn down by a heavy undertow, whereupon he thought, "God's love is all around me," and promptly was washed ashore. There then remained seventeen items, or twenty *events* (counting two events for Item 4 and three for Item 7). These, summarized, were as follows:

1. *Rockland (Mass.) Standard, Oct. 22.*—According to a Christian Science lecturer here, a woman in 1940 had a growth she feared was cancer. Her doctor advised an operation, but she turned instead to

Christian Science. Soon she realized that "God had not created cancer, therefore it had never been true." This destroyed her fear, and the growth diminished and disappeared.

2. *Boston (Mass.) Record, Oct. 24.*—In George Clarke's column, "Around Boston." Sidney Bechet, "Grand Old Man of New Orleans Jazz," last year was so ill with ulcers that a drastic operation seemed inevitable, but he was cured instead by a Paris faith healer: "This man cures by personal magnetism, and about once a month he's in trouble with the law. But they can never beat him in court, it seems." Bechet has had no pain since, and is in remarkably good health. Told the "acquisition of psychological equanimity" could have helped, he looked startled, then cried: "Yes, that's it. What did you say?"

3. *Baltimore (Md.) Sun, Oct. 25.*—AP wire datelined Frankfort, Ind., Oct. 24. Mrs. Lydia Ann Eichelberger, 78, a cousin of President Eisenhower, told how, as a boy, Eisenhower had blood poisoning in his leg, was told it would have to be amputated, refused, and instead placed his faith in God. His family kept up a chain of prayers for several days, "—and then suddenly his fever went down, and the swelling became less and less."

4. *Boston (Mass.) Traveler, Oct. 27.*—AP wire datelined Vatican City. Pope Pius X's elevation to sainthood was virtually assured when the Congregation of Rites accepted as valid two miracles attributed to his intervention after his death. The miracles, verified by nine doctors who examined the records last June 18: Francesco Belsani of Naples, healed in August, 1951 of a cancer; and Sister Maria Lusa Scorcia of Palermo, Sicily, healed in February, 1952 of a virus and other ailments.

5. *Cleveland (Ohio) Press, Oct. 28.*—Mrs. Lulu Durrah, 32, asked a spiritualist leader how to cure her mother, Mrs. Rosia Bryant, 52, of a speech impediment, was advised that her mother should walk 13 paces over running water while reading the 139th Psalm aloud. After dark, on a bridge over the Cuyahoga River, the two women paced the 13 steps, back and forth, while repeating the psalm. Then the bridge— a lift bridge—started to rise. Mrs. Durrah jumped to the ground; her mother hung on. When their screams reached the operator's ears he lowered the span and Mrs. Bryant stepped safely ashore. Said Mrs. Durrah, afterwards: "I think it did help mother's speech a little."

6. *Harwich Port (Mass.) Central Cape Press, Oct. 29.*—Reporting a local Christian Science lecture. Twenty years ago, a man facing a serious hernia operation was given "Science and Health" to read. The same day, as he neared book's end, his trouble left and has never returned.

7. *Winthrop (Mass.) Sun, Nov. 7.*—Reporting a Christian Science lecture. 1) A Christian Scientist mother's baby appeared to have a

contagious disease. As required by law, she reported it to the health department. An officer came, pronounced the disease polio, and asked her to take the child to a hospital. Knowing the law did not require this, she refused, and instead applied Christian Science. Next day the baby was well. 2) A girl of three was very ill; her grandmother prayed all day with no apparent result. Then suddenly the little girl declared "God is Love!" and arose, well. 3) After an accident a young man was taken unconscious to a hospital. His doctor expected him to die without ever regaining consciousness. But when his mother called in a Christian Science practitioner, the young man promptly came to, and soon was well.

8. *Waukesha (Wis.) Freeman, Nov. 13.*—Datelined North Lake, Special. Marvin Brandt, Holy Name speaker, told how his 4-year-old son had his arm caught for 20 minutes in a mangle set at 550 degrees F. Prayers to miracle-working St. Philomena saved the boy's life and saved his arm from amputation. After 28 operations, the arm is not normal but the boy gets some use from it. "We do not take credit for this," one doctor said, "as it is truly a miracle and beyond the realm of the human."

9. *Milwaukee (Wis.) Journal, Nov. 15.*—Three pages of photos and text. More in Nov. 20 *Sentinel.* "A true and abiding faith in God is all you need to cure any illness," says evangelist-healer A. C. Valdez, Jr. The sick write their illnesses on cards and line up before the microphone. Valdez takes the card, reads the illness, sometimes "diagnoses" additional ailments which the sufferer then acknowledges present. Valdez touches the ailing portion, prays that the sufferer be healed. In each case, the evangelist's hand jerks suddenly in the prayer: "You felt that," he asks, "didn't you? Ah, there's real power here tonight!" Caption: "God has started to work in this sister's life," says Valdez after a woman rises from her wheelchair.

10. *Framingham (Mass.) News, Nov. 16.*—Christian Science lecture. An abnormal growth on a woman's face had reached alarming proportions. She turned to Christian Science and learned that her diseased condition was "as unreal as a mistake in mathematics," whereupon the growth gradually disappeared.

11. *New York World-Telegram, Nov. 23.*—"Rev." Jessie E. Curl, 63, "huna healer" and "internationally renowned clairvoyant" was arrested today on a charge of practicing medicine without a license ($5 a treatment; $1 admission to lectures). She exhibited testimonials as to having cured paralysis, deafness, and goiter, and claimed to have performed six miracles on Oct. 30. Two investigators posed as patients; one was "treated" for a heart condition by Mrs. Curl waving her right hand over the patient's body.

12. *Christian Science Monitor (Boston, Mass.) Nov. 24.*—A Christian Scientist student serving as a juror became ill the day before the case was to reach the jury. Recalling the judge's words on their first

day, advising them to sift the evidence and separate fact from fable, he "realized that the suggestion of sickness was a lie, the false evidence of material sense," and was healed in time to complete his jury duty.

13. *Eureka (Cal.) Standard, Dec. 4.*—Reporting a C.S. lecture. A woman 30 years ago suffered chronic stomach and bowel trouble and a malignant growth. Operations and years of doctoring had failed to cure her but Christian Science soon cured the stomach and bowel trouble. As to the growth: "earnestly searching her own thought to detect the obstruction to complete healing, she discovered there was lurking in her thinking a great sense of hurt and disappointment she had held because her father several years before had married a woman she had hated ever since that time." With more S&H study, the growth disappeared.

14. *Des Moines (Iowa) Register, Dec. 27.*—"Rev." Martis C. Scalf, 45, evangelist and member of the Elijah Ministry, is under investigation by the state health department to determine whether or not he is violating the medical practice act. Scalf denies being a faith healer: "I have no power at all, personally. I do no diagnosing. Give the Holy Spirit the credit." Scalf usually meets with groups in farm houses. When he prays, the Holy Spirit tells him what is wrong with a person and he relays the information—usually that the person has something serious, as heart disease or tuberculosis. He has told 600 people they had polio, and a much larger number they had cancer. He never asks for money; "free will" offerings supply his needs. One farmer with a persistent cough, told by Scalf he had cancer of the lungs, rushed to a hospital for X-rays, where doctors afterwards assured him that his lungs were perfect. Scalf maintains that: 1) at the time of his diagnosis, the farmer did indeed have cancer; but that, 2) in the interval between diagnosis and hospital, Scalf's prayers healed him.

15. *Prescott (Ariz.) Courier, Jan. 8, 1954.*—From a 3-column advertisement: "Hundreds Healed! Because They Attended A Bible Deliverance Campaign of Evangelist R. E. Henke. You Can Be Next. Now In Progress Nightly Except Saturdays. Assembly of God Church . . . Wheel chair and stretcher patients welcome (If necessary, phone for transportation). Tumors, cancers, hernias, rheumatism, deafness, lameness, eye troubles, ulcers, diabetes, heart troubles, high blood pressure, pyorrhea, asthma, kidney ailments, etc., etc. All Have Been Healed As He Prayed And Preached. Healing is not just a sideline with Evangelist R. E. Hencke, It Is Second Only To Saving Of Souls. Everyone is invited to see these miracles. His Association with THE VOICE OF HEALING Guarantees His Having a PROVEN HEALING MINISTRY."

16. *Chicago (Ill.), all papers, Jan. 14 and 15.*—Thomas Jr., first child of Thomas Grzyb, 20, and his wife Barbara, 18, was born Wednesday, January 6 at St. Anthony's Hospital with a serious

throat condition. Told the baby needed a blood transfusion, the parents, Jehovah's Witnesses, refused to allow it. The following Tuesday, the boy was operated on for an abdominal obstruction and afterwards was in a state of shock. Told their baby's life now depended on a transfusion, Thomas Grzyb said, "Our belief won't allow it. It's better to have a dead baby without the blood than a living baby with the transfusion." Their desperate doctor and hospital officials appealed to Dr. Herman N. Bundesen, Chicago Board of Health president. He petitioned Chicago's Family Court to declare the Grzybs unfit parents and make the infant a court ward so that a court-appointed guardian could legally order the transfusion. Wednesday the Grzybs were summoned to Family Court and urged, because of the baby's critical condition, to waive their right to delay the hearing one day. They refused. "If the baby dies," Barbara Grzyb said, "that is God's will. I have no fear. The blood won't make any difference. I am not going to hand him over to the court until I have to. The judge doesn't care what's in the Bible." Hearing was set for the earliest allowable time: the following morning at 9:30. The doctor stayed at St. Anthony's into the night, hoping the parents would come or telephone. They never did. Just after midnight, 8-day-old Thomas Grzyb died. At their home, early Thursday morning, Barbara repeated, "My baby, my baby!" and sobbed hysterically. Thomas told reporters, "We want more children. But if such a thing happens again, and if I am called a murderer, that is God's will. I am sorry the child died. But if it is God's will that a life be taken, it must be taken." Later, at the now meaningless hearing, they stood dry-eyed and silent while an angry judge censured them. "You held everybody else from helping the child," he said, "—while its life was ebbing away."

17. *Framingham (Mass.) Independent, Jan. 19.*—Reporting a C.S. lecture. A man in a city hospital, suffering from lobar pneumonia, had been given up by doctors as beyond cure. But after a Christian Scientist was called in, there was a remarkable change and the man recovered.

The reader will object that out of the above, only Items 5, 9, 11, 14, 15 and 16 were immediate happenings, the rest being second-hand reports of a basic event that happened anywhere from one to over thirty years previously. I agree and can only ask, How many similar to those six went unreported? How many other spiritualist-advised ladies, for example, performed antics on bridges that did *not* go up, and thus were denied newspaper immortality? But the attempted survey was a failure. Why, indeed, were those other fourteen events in our daily "news" columns? Here, however, is the clue to a different appraisal. I refer to the distinction between "spot" and "created" news. In "spot" news, the professional publicist has had no hand: much more likely than not—and this is the test—the person or organization involved did not want the event to happen, and was harmed by it. Thus, Mrs. Durrah and Mrs. Bryant (Item 5) did not want to risk their lives on a lift bridge; huna healer Curl (Item 11) did not want to be arrested; faith healer Scalf (Item 14) did not want to be investigated; and no one wanted Thomas Grzyb (Item 16) to die. These four events clearly were "spot" news.

One definition of "created" news: the reporter did not rush to the scene—he was dragged. In "created" news, a paid publicist or volunteer press bureau by shrewd planning and showmanship creates an event which the press cannot ignore. In most of the above this is no more than a speech or lecture, copies of which afterwards will be urged upon the press. But "created" news is almost always identified by its furthering a cause.

Items 1, 6, 7, 10, 12, 13 and 17, all reports of lectures by paid members of the Christian Science "Board of Lectureship," demonstrate a tried-and-true publicity device of this sect: as to total area of free advertising, they win hands down. The two Roman Catholic items are press releases, Item 8 a belabored attempt to establish a miracle and Item 4 serving up its miracles only as "merit points" for a contender to sainthood. Item 2 doubtless was an "exclusive" from Bechet's agent: the account in full concerns the "jazz professor's" opening at a local hotel. Item 3, President Eisenhower's leg, is beyond me. Was it unearthed for the "religion for all" campaign then in progress? Or was it engineered by Jehovah's Witness publicists in line with their later documentation that the President's parents once belonged to an earlier version of that organization—the familiar device of tying one's cause to prominent figures? I do not (here) question the truth of any of the above. Too, the editor protests that they are legitimate news: "something which interests many people today," and that he never could afford to replace this area, which comes to him free (of the continuous outpouring urged upon him, he uses only about 5 per cent) by his own staff's legwork. I only emphasize that such cause-favoring items must be recognized as to paternity. A final observation: the Roman Catholic items show Catholics employing medicine and surgery while praying for additional aid from the Lord. Item 16 shows Jehovah's Witnesses resorting to medicine and surgery except for blood transfusions. The Christian Science items, on the other hand, emphasize distrust of medical doctors and complete failure of their efforts—followed, upon the subject's turning to Christian Science, by quick and permanent recovery.

I should like now, to distinguish between "wonders," "miracles" in general and "faith healing" in particular. A reading of Moses' activities in Exodus 4:1–7 will help:

> And Moses answered and said, But, behold, they will not believe me, nor hearken unto my voice: for they will say, The LORD hath not appeared unto thee. And the LORD said unto him, what is that in thine hand? And he said, a rod. And he said, Cast it on the ground. And he cast it on the ground, and it became a serpent, and Moses fled from before it. And the LORD said unto Moses, Put forth thine hand, and take it by the tail. And he put forth his hand, and caught it, and it became a rod in his hand . . . And the LORD said furthermore unto him, Put now thine hand into thy bosom. And he put his hand into his bosom: and when he took it out, behold, his hand was leprous as snow. And he said, Put thine hand into thine bosom again. And he put his hand into his bosom again; and plucked it out of his bosom, and behold, it was turned again as his other flesh.

Some demonstrations of God's existence and active support, like those of Moses, differ from the stage magician's bag of tricks only in the demonstrator's aim: *to bolster the faith of his followers.* When such demonstrations no more than cause wonder, they are termed "wonders"—not "miracles."[3] Only when in addition to being "wonders" they also result in immediate personal benefit are they properly called "miracles." Thus, with his shipload of disciples imperiled, Jesus in stilling the wind and waves (Mt. 8:26) performed a *miracle.* Again, we set off miracles not involving healing from those that do. Miracles in which disease is cured by faith and prayer we call *faith healing:* "faith healers" are those who undertake to treat disease by prayer and exercise of faith. Here, also, a distinction must be made. Today, most people take their hurts to their medical doctors, but the more serious a man's illness, the more likely are he and his friends *at the same time* to pray for his recovery. (And the physician, realizing more clearly than the others the limits to his own powers, may offer up the most fervent prayer of all.) Thus, most religious people today might be called "part-time" faith healers. But certain sects undertake to treat disease *solely* by prayer. They accept God's scriptural promise to heal sickness through faith and prayer—and it logically follows that any recourse on their part to medicine would constitute the grossest act of non-faith. Accordingly, they must deny themselves and their children all of the aids of modern medical science. To complete the logic, when a member dies in spite of their prayers it is due either to his lacking complete faith or "because God willed it so." The term *faith healer,* in popular usage, has come to refer only to members of such sects, as has the all too familiar headline expression, *faith death.*

A second group prominently involved is the Christian Scientists. These would tell us that disease, at least for those in the know, is but an illusion. Where others would "cure" a disease, they by proper understanding dispel the "illusion" or "error" of disease; and it is only with a great deal of kicking and screaming that this sect is properly to be hauled into the faith healers' camp. But the Christian Scientists' troubles, quite like those of the less streamlined faith healers they so derogate, arise not in their attempt to heal by faith and prayer but over the deadly corollary—denial at the same time of medical aid.

The Jehovah's Witnesses enter the religio-medico-legal arena from a different corner. Let me emphasize that they are not at all a faith-healing sect. They believe that Jesus healed and gave his disciples healing powers, but assert that these were the last to possess such powers. They are outspoken against present-day faith healers, Christian Science, and Roman Catholic "shrines." They resort to physicians with one important reservation: because of God's commandment not to "eat blood" they refuse, live or die, to submit to a blood transfusion.

Thus three groups unlike in precept have come into identical conflict with the law over their one identical act: denial of medical aid because of religious belief. As a practical matter, society is presented with the same bloodstained package of medical, legal and public health problems by the "true" faith healing sects, the Christian Scientists and the Jehovah's Witnesses.

Two news items illustrate aspects of the subject of this book. In Canada, a critically injured woman refused to accept needed blood transfusions unless so advised by her local Jehovah's Witness leader. He advised her to refuse. She refused and died. Could the Dominion have forced administration of the transfusions? And on what ground could her leader be punished for his part in her death—or enjoined from similar counselling afterwards? In Philadelphia, a doctor warned Christian Scientist parents that if their diabetic son was not given insulin he would die. Instead, they engaged a Christian Science practitioner to treat him. He died, and they were charged with involuntary manslaughter. But does not our Constitution bar prosecution for conduct in accordance with religious belief? Or if not barred, could the practitioner who undertook to treat the child also be prosecuted as accessory to the parents' neglect or for malpractice? Moreover, with such counsellings and ministrations demonstrated to be dangerous to life, why are they not proscribed by law?[4]

The subject of this study may now be defined. It is the element common to the above incidents: *denial of medical aid because of religious belief*. This becomes a problem and approaches a dilemma because of two duties constitutionally imposed upon our federal and state governments: to promote the general welfare and to preserve religious freedom. And where medicine, religion and government collide, the dilemma is to be headed off only by compromise.

Chapters 2, 3 and 4 introduce the players in the drama of religion-inspired denial of medical aid: the faith healers, Mary Eddy and her cult, and the Jehovah's Witnesses. Chapter 2, I should note, intends no more than to present a series of persons and incidents in the continuing phenomenon of faith healing; for a thoughtful analysis of the priest-physician relationship, the former's long domination and the latter's recent freeing, the reader is directed to New York's *Pierson* case, in Chapter 10—the portion where Justice Haight defines "medical attendance." Chapter 5 then offers an explanation, in the light of present-day knowledge, of the true nature of faith healing, together with the legal view: an account of Maine's early *Sandford* trial in which it was held that as a matter of law a jury cannot try the question of whether or not faith healing really works.

Part II does not proceed to the problem but backs off for a wider view of the principles on which the problem is to be worked out. For present-day decisions such as a court's right to order blood transfusions are founded upon previous decisions having nothing to do with medicine—decisions, for example, as to the right of a man to have 17 wives and 47 children. Attempted denial of medical aid is only one small precinct of the large conflict over "freedom versus license." Part II, then, traces the historical working out by legislature and court of the general problem of freedom versus license. How far are acts done under claims of freedom of religion, speech, press and assembly to be tolerated? At what point, when such acts begin to threaten the general welfare, must they be proscribed as license? In the United States, no other landmark is so prominent as the Supreme Court's decision in 1878 in the test case of Brigham Young's polygamous secretary. Chapter 6 traces the Mormon Church's beginnings; its leaders' attempts to establish an absolute church-state in a succession of hostile environments; licentious Prophet Smith's promulgation of polygamous marriage as a religious duty; and the Federal government's determined course in stamping it out again. In this running account of the events leading to Utah's statehood, the *Reynolds* decision is noted only briefly; and the fact is, it was only under the double threats of total disfranchisement posed by the later *Davis v. Beason* decision and of physical destruction of the Mormon Church by the Federal government in accordance with the *Late Corporation* decision, that polygamy finally ended. But these hinged upon *Reynolds,* and so have all later decisions involving the meaning of religious freedom under the First Amendment.

Chapter 7 presents the Reynolds case more fully, then traces the fortunes of the other liberties guaranteed by the First and later amendments against infringement by *Congress;* the originally very limited application of the Fourteenth Amendment; and as late as 1925 the extension of the freedoms of the First, by means of the Fourteenth, against infringement by the *states.* Without this last, the "handbill" cases of Chapter 8, wherein communities attempted to apply handbill ordinances as instruments of oppression against unpopular evangelists, could never have happened. Chapter 8 also describes the Supreme Court's wise holding (finally) that an enforced flag salute is not, after all, a likely way to inculcate American ideals; and its not-so-wise decision in *Prince.* And Chapter 9 calls urgent attention to the area of custody and adoption, wherein today—in Massachusetts at least—an unconstitutional church-state alliance exists in fact.

After this tour of the surrounding territory, we enter in Part III the province where medicine, religion and law collide over denial of medical aid because of religious belief. Chapter 10 begins with faith healing at common law, where though required to provide his child necessary medical care, a parent's resort to prayer instead excused him from any criminal liability for the consequences—a situation underlined by the Wagstaffe trial in 1868, which led to enactment of child protection statutes. Three landmark decisions—England's *Senior* in 1899, *Lewis* in Canada in 1903, and New York's *Pierson* that same year—then established that religious belief was no defense under such a statute. Too, *Lewis* and also Pennsylvania's 1903 *Hoffman* decision established that Christian Science "treatment" was not a legal substitute for required medical attendance. Chapter 11 describes the knock-down, dragout fight to bring faith healers and Christian Science practitioners under the prohibitions of medical practice acts—a fight probably lost for good in 1916 after the five-year battle in New York's *Cole* case. Chapter 12 considers a reverse question, the adult's right to submit to the faith healer; looks briefly at the variety of civil actions involving faith healing; the peculiar problem the Jehovah's Witness presents his prospective physician; then considers the question of accessory liability of the faith healer or Christian Science practitioner who counsels, aids or abets a parent in refusing to provide a child the medical care required by statute—a liability soundly established in Canada but fearfully avoided in the United States. Part III's final chapter recounts the bizarre Ballard case, with its question, *"At what point does disbelief in a religious representation become actionable fraud?"* and gives the Supreme Court's three answers, including Justice Jackson's notable dissent in which he points out the profound psychological and philosophical problems raised by any attempted inquiry into intellectual honesty in religion and why present laws—tolerant to an extent many people think foolhardy—had, after all, best be left alone.

But what did society gain in establishing its right to punish a dead child's parent? If it can punish a crime, can it not also attempt to prevent the crime's happening? Part IV traces the development of this way of thinking, whereby in its role of *parens patriae* the state has come more and more to assert its right to interfere actively with parents' rights where the morals, health or life of a child are threatened; how, in emergency situations, courageous judges have asserted the court's right to step in, over the parents' objections, to save a child's life; and how, where the propriety of such action has been questioned, appellate courts have held the traditional rights of religion and parenthood to come second, after all, to the even more elemental proposition that a child has the right to live.

# 2

# The Faith Healers

*And these signs shall follow them that believe; In my name shall they cast out devils; they shall speak with new tongues; They shall take up serpents; and if they drink any deadly thing, it shall not hurt them; they shall lay hands on the sick, and they shall recover.*

*—Mark 16:17, 18.*

Disease was first believed caused by gods and demons (and still is, by some people).[1] The cure: assault the demons and appeal to the gods. A Cro-Magnon painting *circa* 20,000 B.C. on a cave wall in France shows a medicine-man in animal skins. He doubtless danced, shouted and shook a rattle to drive out his patient's demons, then left him an amulet to maintain confidence in his cure. In Homer, Asklepios was a mortal hero-physician, later the Greek god of healing. The physician-priests of Asklepios, realizing its therapeutic power, based their art on the patient's faith, at the same time using what mechanical means they could. In Epidarus, Argolis, in southern Greece, in the fourth century B.C., they claimed in writing to have so cured blindness, hernia, snake-bite, baldness, boils, consumption, paralysis and gout. They employed hypnotic suggestion and sleep. Under this "temple sleep" they cut open the abdomen and stitched it up again, the patient remembering it as a dream. During Rome's terrible pestilence of 293 B.C., a sacred serpent was brought from Epidarus and the worship of Asklepios introduced.[2] In the second century A.D., Aristeides, a neurasthenic by modern standards, reported his cure in a temple of Asklepios of a 17-year illness. The treatment: a mixture of faith healing, diet, river bathing, bleeding, anointing with mud, walking barefoot, riding, purging and numberless drugs.

In *Marius the Epicurean,* published in 1885, Walter Horatio Pater describes fictional young Marius' visit *circa* 161 A.D. to such a temple in Italy, at a time "when Christianity was being tolerated," the "old religion of Numa still surviving in the rural areas," while Emperor

Marcus Aurelius "carefully practiced" the "fashionable Stoic philosophy."

Marius was taken to a certain temple of Aesculapius, among the hills of Etruria, as was then usual in such cases, for the cure of some boyish sickness. The religion of Aesculapius, though borrowed from Greece, had been naturalized in Rome in the old republican times; but had reached under the Antonines the height of its popularity throughout the Roman world . . .

*Salus,* salvation, for the Romans, had come to mean bodily sanity. The religion of the god of bodily health, *Salvator,* as they called him absolutely, had a chance just then of becoming the one religion . . . The priesthood or "family" of Aesculapius, a vast college, believed to be in possession of certain precious medical secrets, came nearest, perhaps, of all the institutions of the pagan world, to the Christian priesthood; the temples of the god, rich in some instances with the accumulated thank-offerings of centuries of a tasteful devotion, being really also a kind of hospitals for the sick, administered in a full conviction of the religiousness, the refined and sacred happiness, of a life spent in the relieving of pain.

Elements of a really experimental and progressive knowledge there were doubtless amid this devout enthusiasm, bent so faithfully on the reception of health as a direct gift from God; but for the most part his care was held to take effect through a machinery easily capable of misuse for purposes of religious fraud.

After his first night there,

summoned at length by one of the white-robed brethren, he went out to walk in the temple garden. At a distance, on either side, his guide pointed out to him the *Houses of Birth and Death,* erected for the reception respectively of women about to become mothers, and of persons about to die; neither of those incidents being allowed to defile, as was thought, the actual precincts of the shrine . . . But among the official ministers of the place there was one, already as of great celebrity, whom Marius saw often in later days at Rome, the physician Galen, now about thirty years old. He was standing, the hood partly drawn over his face, beside the holy well . . .

In the central space, upon a pillar or pedestal, hung, *ex voto,* with the richest personal ornaments, stood the image of Aesculapius himself, surrounded by choice flowering plants. It presented the type, still with something of the severity of the earlier art of Greece about it, not of an aged and crafty physician, but of a youth, earnest and strong of aspect, carrying an *ampulla* or bottle in one hand, and in the other a traveller's staff, a pilgrim among his pilgrim worshippers; and one of the ministers explained to Marius this pilgrim guise.—One chief source of the master's knowledge of healing had been observation of the remedies resorted to by animals labouring under disease or pain—what leaf or berry the lizard or dormouse lay upon its wounded fellow; to which purpose for long years he had led the life of a wanderer, in wild places.

The Jews believed in demons and possession by devils: at the time of Christ one hardly could have put forth any serious claim to divinity unless prepared to demonstrate it by miracles of healing. From wild "John the babtiser," operating in Judea along the Jordan River, Jesus of Nazareth first heard the words "Repent ye (Mt. 3.2) for the kingdom of heaven is at hand." When John was imprisoned, Jesus fled north to Capernaum, on the north shore of the lake of Galilee, where he began to preach the gospel of the kingdom, recruited his disciples and became famous "healing all manner of sickness (Mt. 4.23) and all manner of disease among the people." To him were brought "all sick people that were taken with divers diseases and torments (Mt. 4.24) and those which were possessed with devils, and those which were lunatick, and those that had the palsy; and he healed them." After the Sermon on the Mount a leper worshipped him, saying that Jesus could cleanse him if he willed. Jesus touched him (Mt. 8.3) and he was healed.

When Jesus offered to go to a Roman captain's home to cure his palsied servant, the captain said Jesus need only speak the word. Jesus did (Mt. 8.13) and the servant was healed in the same hour—the first "absent treatment." Returning to Capernaum (Mt. 9.6) he healed a man of palsy. A woman diseased twelve years with "an issue of blood" came up behind Jesus and touched his garment, believing this would cure her. He turned (Mt. 9.22) saying "Thy faith hath made thee whole," and she was cured. He took the hand of a certain ruler's dead daughter (Mt. 9.25) and she arose. Two blind men came to him, affirming their faith; he touched their eyes (Mt. 9.30) and they were opened. He cast out a devil from a dumb man (Mt. 9.33) and the man spoke. When his disciples failed to cure a "lunatick" boy who often fell into fires or the water, the father brought the boy to Jesus (Mt. 17.18) who cast out the boy's devil and cured him. Aside, Jesus explained to his disciples (Mt. 17.20) that they had failed because of their unbelief. But when he returned to Nazareth to preach, he was belittled as a local carpenter's son and because of their unbelief "could there do no mighty work, save that he laid his hands upon a few sick folk (Mk. 6.5) and healed them."

Feeling the immensity of his task, Jesus now gave his twelve disciples "power against unclean spirits" and sent them off to preach: "And (Mt. 10.7, 8) as ye go, preach, saying, the kingdom of heaven is at hand. Heal the sick, cleanse the lepers, raise the dead, cast out devils." Peter accordingly bade a beggar lame from birth "in the name of Jesus

Christ of Nazareth" to rise up and walk, and lifted him up. The man entered the temple with Peter and John, "walking, and leaping (Acts 3.8) and praising God." At Lydda, Peter in the name of Christ healed Aeneas, who had "kept his bed eight years (Acts 9.34) and was sick of the palsy." At Joppa (Acts 9.40) he raised a woman named Dorcas, who had been "full of good works," from the dead. But he may have used his power (Acts 5.1–10) to cause the death of Ananias and his wife.

At Lystra (Acts 14.10) Paul bade a cripple who from birth had never walked, to stand, "and he leaped and walked." But at Paphos, when sorcerer Elymas tried to turn a local deputy from the faith (Acts 13.11) Paul used his power to blind Elymas for a year. At Phillippi, a soothsayer followed Paul and Silas, crying they were servants of God; annoyed, Paul cast out her spirit. Her power and her master's source of revenue gone, the latter (Acts 16.19) haled Paul and Silas off to court. Handkerchiefs or aprons brought from Paul's body (Acts 19.12) caused diseases and evil spirits to depart from the sick.

The apostles' successors practiced faith healing, but after the third century, with the scriptures' custody and interpretation in the priesthood's hands, faith healing largely gave way to reliance on contact with saints' holy relics—in which a large and dubious traffic arose. St. Augustine (354–430 A.D.) advised: "All diseases of Christians are to be ascribed to demons, chiefly do they torment the fresh baptised, yea, even the guiltless newborn infant."

Edward the Confessor, king of the English from 1042 to 1066, is said to have originated the "royal touch," a faith-healing "specific" for curing the "king's evil" (scrofula, or tuberculosis of the glands of the neck) and epilepsy. With the touch a gold piece—an "amulet"—was hung around the patient's neck. Dr. Samuel Johnson, one of the last so touched—at the age of four, by Queen Anne—afterwards had scrofula all his life. Some kings continued the practice only under pressure and against their better judgment. Said William III (1650–1702) as he touched: "May God give you better health and more sense."

Faith healing revived with the Reformation's popular access to the gospels. Luther performed faith cures. When Cromwell, after driving out King Charles in 1650, refused to be king or to practice the royal touch, Valentine Greatrakes of Cromwell's army was inspired by a dream to become "toucher" in his place. Succeeding dreams inspired him to extend his touch against almost every known disease; even Robert (Boyle's law) Boyle praised him. Giuseppe Balsamo (1743–1795), a Sicilian, assumed the name of Count Alessandro di Cagliostro and became a most successful charlatan of faith healing.

In London in 1838 John Banyard founded the faith-healing sect of the "Peculiar People"—a name (I Pet. 2.9; Tit. 2.14; Deut. 7.6) applied to Israel in the Old Testament—or "Plumstead Peculiars."[3] Their belief centered around *James 5.14, 15*. In cases of sickness they accordingly resorted to oil and prayer, and "trusted to providence." They claimed that medical aid was not expressly forbidden but indicated a lack of faith. In 1899, member *Senior* was convicted of manslaughter (Ch. 10) after eight of his children died without medical attention. But Sir William Osler, the great Canadian physician, had a kindly word for them:

> In England a small sect, the Peculiar People, carry out a consistent gospel system of faith healing. A pious, simple folk, only heard of when in collision with the law of the land, they base their belief on the plain saying of Scripture, "Whatsoever ye shall ask in My name," etc. The prayer of faith is all they need, and in consequence, when one of their number dies, there is an inquest, and someone is sent to prison for criminal negligence. One of the recent cases was very pathetic, as both father and mother expressed the most touching confidence that what God willed was best for their child with scarlet fever, and what they asked in prayer would be granted. This primitive Christian attitude toward disease has never lacked adherents in the Church, and medieval literature is full of illustrations of a practice identical with that of the Peculiar People.[4]

In the 1840's, Andrew Jackson Davis, a Poughkeepsie cobbler, developed a metaphysical theory of life and disease, reported marvelous cures, attracted a large following and made a fortune. In 1854 he appeared before the U.S. Senate to urge federal financing for his method. His book was republished until the Civil War. Around 1850, George O. Barnes, Kentucky's "Mountain Evangelist," attracted a large following. Believing the devil caused disease, he cured by anointing with oil and invocations. In 1893, Francis Schlatter, led by divine inspiration, left Denver to wander barefoot, then returned as a faith healer. Each day, four to five thousand patients from all over the United States filed past his picket fence to be touched. But when he tried Paul's absent treatment — sending "blessed handkerchiefs" in the mail — the government stopped him for fraud.

Frank W. Sandford, born in Bowdoin, Maine in 1862, had careers as an "able ball player" and Free Baptist minister. Around 1893, in Durham, he founded the durable faith-healing "Holy Ghost and Us Society" or "Legion of God"—now "Kingdom, Inc." On a hilltop there he built guilt-domed frame houses, called his $250,000 community "Shiloh," named himself "Elijah," claimed he had the Holy

Ghost's ear and collected money in abundance from five thousand followers. He staged cures and claimed he raised the dead, but at Shiloh at least twenty sick people died without medical care and he was three times tried for manslaughter but never convicted. In 1910, under his command, the 85-foot schooner *Coronet* sailed for Africa with a 15-man crew and 30 evangelists to await the end of the world he had predicted. During the voyage, six followers died of scurvy, exposure or starvation, for which, on his return in 1911, he was tried for manslaughter, convicted and sentenced to ten years in the Atlanta Penitentiary. Released after six, he disappeared from public sight. In 1938, in connection with the much publicized spiritual scrimmage of Dartmouth quarterback Harrington Gates, it was reported on hearsay that Sandford, a bearded prophet of 76, was to be seen of moonlit nights near the cult's farm at Amherst, New Hampshire.[5,6]

A fanatical Scot, John Alexander Dowie (1847–1907), one-time Congregational minister in Australia, opposed anatomical dissection, physicians and all science, taught that the world was flat, and believed that disease was devil-caused and that the only cure was prayer and the laying on of hands. In 1896 he founded the faith-healing Christian Catholic Church at Zion, near Chicago; its members figured in *Brooks* (Ch. 12) and *Chenoweth* (Ch. 10).[7]

It is not within this study's scope to trace the chiropractic school's development from its dubious beginnings to its equally dubious present, or to develop the thesis that any actual benefits from such treatment are brought about through suggestion or faith healing. But one incident of that movement's early days as described by Dr. Victor Heiser warrants retelling here:

> In Denver, Colorado, chiropractors loudly proclaimed the uselessness of vaccination as a protection against smallpox, and for a time succeeded in winning a large section of the public to their point of view. But just as surely as a dry shaving will burn when a match is applied, just so will the unprotected contract smallpox when exposed to the contagion. As time went on, it became increasingly apparent that the unprotected were furnishing all the victims while the properly vaccinated were escaping. Finally the unvaccinated chiropractors began to contract the disease. One of them who fled not only himself died, but started smallpox in faraway Arkansas which had previously been free.[8]

Mark's passage, in addition to its promise to the faith healer, still inspires enthusiasts to "speak with new tongues," to "cast out devils" and to undertake the faith-proving rituals of handling serpents and drinking deadly things. Prophet Smith cast out one devil, and there was speaking in tongues (Ch. 6) at Kirtland. But these were the least of the antics in the orgies of the American frontier's evangelistic camp meetings. Famed Methodist circuit rider Peter Cartwright (1785–1872) stated that an evil man might have anywhere from "one small, sickly devil" to "legions" of devils, and of the wife of a fellow minister: "the devil was in her as large as an alligator."[9]

In the Sacramento *Bee,* Ernest Y. Cox reports how, on the evening of April 16, 1956, in the tent of "Miracle Healer" A. A. Allen, a patient was suffering from nervousness. Healer Allen shouted "Amen, hallelujah," placed one hand on the man's forehead, forced his head far back and struck him in the stomach. "I rebuke you, evil spirit!" Allen screamed. "Free this man. Come out of there. Open your mouth wide now, brother, so the evil spirit can come out." Six associate ministers then gathered around the "demon possessed" man and hid him from view. Allen shouted and prayed for fifteen minutes, then, breathing heavily, said "That demon has left him. I felt it leave."

The man said, "I don't feel much different. I can still feel that demon in there. It's fluttering around in my stomach like a bird in a cage."

Allen insisted, "I felt the evil spirit leave you; he's gone, all right."

"No, Brother Allen," the man said, "he's still there. You'd better pray for me some more."

Allen put his hand on the man's forehead. "I don't feel a thing," he said. "God won't let me pray for you anymore. He has stopped me." The man was then dismissed, and—Cox notes—walked away unaided.[10]

In Summerville, Georgia, one evening in August of 1947, the Rev. Gordon Miller of the "Free Church of God" took a bottle from the church rostrum and called for Ernest Davis, 33: "Brother Davis, if you feel the power of the Lord great enough, you can take what's in this bottle; if you don't feel the power, I wouldn't take it." Davis poured a teaspoonful into a glass of water and took three swallows. Then the Rev. Miller took "a couple of sips." Afterwards, Davis "just sat around playing his guitar and praying," until, several hours later, he became ill. Over his protest that "God's will be done," his father-in-law took him to a hospital, where Davis died. Afterwards, Miller announced that services would be resumed the following Wednesday: "I don't know whether anyone will drink strychnine or not, but if the Lord moves us and it's there, we'll drink it." Arrested by a sheriff at Davis's graveside and charged with his murder, Miller opined: "He must not have had enough faith."[11]

The highest courts of Kentucky, Tennessee and North Carolina[12] have held that the state may prohibit snake handling as part of a religious ceremony, even though the act is part of the religious belief and

practice of the performer. On November 1, 1947, in the Zion Taber-
nacle Church in Durham, North Carolina, C. H. Bunn, standing in the
pulpit before a large gathering, in his bare hands held up a poisonous
copperhead or highland moccasin. No one was harmed. On November 8,
after Benjamin R. Massey did the same thing, police who had witnessed
the performances took the snakes and placed healthy rats with them.
The snakes immediately struck the rats with their fangs, and within
minutes the rats died. The two men were charged with endangering the
public health, safety and welfare by handling poisonous reptiles, in violation of a Durham ordinance. Both conceded that their conduct came
within the ordinance but pled not guilty on the ground that it impinged
upon their freedom of religious worship and therefore was void. Each
was found guilty as charged and fined $50 and costs. On appeal to the
Supreme Court of North Carolina, Chief Justice Walter P. Stacy upheld the verdicts and judgments, saying:

> . . . the ordinance was enacted as a protective measure and its primary
> purpose is not to interfere with any ritual which the defendants may
> wish to observe. They are at liberty to handle reptiles in public, if
> they so desire; provided the reptiles are harmless to human safety,
> health and welfare.
> The defendants say, however, that the handling of poisonous rep-
> tiles without harm to themselves or others is the power which they
> are commanded to show to the people, and to extract the venom of
> the reptiles renders them useless for such purpose. It was suggested
> on the argument by the defendants in person that in all probability
> we would not understand this. Even so, as a matter of law the case
> comes to a very simple question: Which is superior, the public
> safety or the defendants' religious practice? The authorities are at
> one in holding that the safety of the public comes first . . .

Bunn and Massey then brought their cases, on the same ground of
violation of religious freedom, to the United States Supreme Court,
which dismissed the appeals "for want of a substantial federal question"
and afterwards denied a rehearing.

In La Crescenta, California, James Inwood, 87, met two "faith healers" who promised to cure his ills by patting his body. During the
treatment, the pair appropriated his wallet containing $35.[13] I mention
this untypical incident introductory to confessing some personal opinions: 1) If the above operators were proved to be pickpockets, this
would not prove they were not sincere faith healers. 2) A faith healer's
making a fortune does not prove him insincere. 3) A faith healer can
be sincere and at the same time believe God intends him to become rich.
4) With only rare exceptions, faith healers are sincere.

Throughout this study, except for *Ballard* (Ch. 13) and other obvious exceptions, the faith healer is presumed sincere. On the other hand, the patient may be unconsciously insincere. "In my own experience," wrote famous British surgeon Henry Morris in 1910,

> there have been several cases of hysterical or purposive deception, simulating real diseases, which were instantaneously cured, and which in their way are quite as remarkable as those we hear of from Lourdes and other shrines and sanctuaries.
>
> A woman supposed to be hopelessly ill with a communication between her stomach and a dilated renal pelvis was immediately made well by our detecting her spitting finely masticated food into her urine. Another . . . was supposed to be afflicted with cancer of the uterus and vagina . . . but she made a most rapid recovery after I removed a candle extinguisher from the upper part of her vagina. An unmarried woman . . . had been for a long time the subject of a peculiar skin rash . . . She recovered at once after being seen early one morning on a surprise visit from her medical attendant frictionizing her skin with a piece of pumice stone. Another young lady was sent to me with a chronic sore on her thumb . . . One day she was caught hiding away a box containing the sticks of wooden matches sharpened to a fine point. She was charged—and confessed after indignant protestations at being suspected and accused—that she was keeping open this wound by irritating it with the pointed match stems. Her object had been to get away from home for treatment, as she was very unhappy with a newly made stepmother . . .
>
> A . . . girl who craved to go on the operatic stage . . . was very anxious to take lessons at the Conservatoire of Music. Consent not being given to this scheme, she became afflicted with a troublesome and persistent sore throat. This excited sympathy, and she was, after a time, permitted to quit her "damp and relaxing" neighborhood for a residence in Paris. At once, after this "change of air"* she gave up applying carbolic acid to her tonsils and fauces, and her sore throat got rapidly and permanently well.
>
> To these cases of feigned or self-induced diseases I will add the mention of two cases of immediate recovery from real disease.
>
> A woman absolutely at death's door . . . was admitted into my cancer ward . . . I found the cause of her condition was not cancer, but a large polypus [tumor] . . . For a day or two I feared to have her moved on to the operation table. When I did so . . . the polypus fell unassisted bodily to the floor, and from that moment she began to get well.
>
> A man who for a long while had been suffering from chronic intestinal obstruction and haemorrhages . . . had been told by surgeons . . . that he had malignant disease of the rectum, and must be operated upon . . . I found he was suffering from a large polypus . . . and its removal at once completely cured him . . .

---

* The title of the chapter in Pater's **Marius** quoted above.

I could add other cases if it were necessary, but those I have mentioned are sufficient, both in number and in character, I think, to justify my scepticism as to the miracles of Lourdes, and as to the remarkable cures there being due to the immediate and direct interposition of the Divinity.[14]

Heads of two state health departments recently wrote me of their experiences with faith healing. Excerpts from one letter:

There is a comparatively small, fairly scattered group of children for whom immunization is a problem. Their families belong to religious sects who disbelieve in this procedure, and discourage it . . . occasionally there is the failure to obtain serological studies in the pregnant woman [now required by law]. More serious is the rare person who refuses syphilitic treatment after diagnosis in the prenatal period.

From the other:

In most communities those who oppose health services and activities on the basis of religious beliefs constitute a small minority . . . When responsible citizens are helped to understand the scientific and social facts involved in protecting individual and community health, invariably this emphasis on positive programs brings about community action which carries over the opposition of the small faith healing group. On the other hand when attention is given to this small minority by dealing directly with their opposition, it sometimes builds the emphasis on this activity beyond its significance.

Insulin costs money, and daily self-injection is an onerous chore with no hope of eventual release. In Barrie, Ontario, one Sunday in 1952, the Rev. R. W. Holmes told Mary Taylor, 19, a diabetic since the age of four, to "turn to God." After a prayer session with him, she stopped taking injections. The following Wednesday, she died. But there was no reason to suspect that faith healer Holmes was insincere. Also, there are insincere *doctors*.[15]

Around 1936, Drs. Charles and Peter Kaadt founded the Kaadt Diabetic Clinic at South Whitley, Indiana. They offered a "magic" alternate to insulin and diet: three tablespoons a day of the Kaadts' "magic medicine." Patients usually stayed three days, at $10 a day, then left with a jug of the "medicine" at $30 a gallon. In twelve years, the pair took in probably $6,000,000. One child, told he now could eat ice cream, ate heartily and sank into a diabetic coma. A diabetic old man followed their advice until his toes turned black and his leg had to be amputated. One fourteen-year-old girl's eyes, after nine jugs, clouded over with cataracts. After four jugs, one man suffered ulcerous sores, went blind and died. Others developed diabetic gangrene. Charged with mail fraud, the brothers sent their literature by Railway Express. In 1947, Indiana started action to take away their licenses. In 1948, they were brought before a federal court, charged with introducing mislabeled medicine into interstate commerce. Experts testified that the magic medicine was essentially vinegar and saltpeter and could do no possible good, and that there was no effective treatment for diabetes except insulin and diet. The brothers, then 74 and 76, were each found guilty and sentenced to three years in prison and fined $7,000 and costs. Said Judge Patrick T. Stone:

> You have been engaged in a wide-scale, sordid, evil and vicious enterprise without the slightest regard or consideration for the patient that consulted you . . . You were cold, vicious and heartless in your quest for wealth.[16]

In 1946, when Holland's Greet Hofmans was 51, God had a personal talk with her and on her promise to "renounce all worldly claims" gave her miraculous powers. At God's direction, she moved to Baron van Heeckeren's estate in Hatem, where lines of afflicted received three minutes of prayer. In 1947, Queen Juliana's fourth daughter, Maria Christina, nicknamed "Marijke," was born with cataracts on both eyes—apparently because the Queen had had German measles during pregnancy. Doctors could save only part of the vision of one eye. After consulting "every specialist in the world," Prince Bernhard heard how Greet had cured a friend's daughter of tuberculosis and brought her to see their child. "Marijke will see," Greet declared. "God will restore her sight in two years." Greet was installed in the palace. During the next two years, Marijke's condition did not improve, but Greet established a dismaying influence over Queen Juliana. Baron van Heeckeren became the Queen's private secretary, his mother "grand mistress" at court. A Dutch paper protested that the Queen's speeches had taken the strange tone of a pacifist and mystic. Bernhard broke with Greet and put her out; Juliana's mother, ex-Queen Wilhelmina, took her in. Greet's group of religious and peace enthusiasts ("Peace through Christ") met on Wilhelmina's estate. In 1951, Eleanor Roosevelt, taken by Queen Juliana to one meeting, afterwards noted her dismay in *My Day*. Meanwhile, in Amsterdam, Greet practiced faith healing on 600 patients a day. The government investigated, found she was not "practicing medicine." Greet's message was submission to God's will:

A disease is not a thing in itself. Thus cancer in a person is connected with the world spiritual disorder of war . . . therefore I cannot cure cancer until war is eliminated.

Reporter Robert Horiguchi queried 15 of Greet's patients. All "had heard" of spectacular recoveries but none could cite a particular case. One 78-year-old, a Greet patient for three years, said, "My stomach troubles are over now, but I now have rheumatism." In June of 1956, on the eve of the Dutch national elections, the long-suppressed story broke outside the country in Germany's *Der Spiegel,* which suggested that the difficulty between Bernhard and Juliana might lead to the latter's divorce or abdication. People wrote from all parts of the world to offer an eye (which would not help, in the case of Marijke's clouded lens). On August 24, a royal communique announced "the solution of difficulties." There would be no divorce, no abdication. Juliana, 47, and Bernhard 45, would work things out together. For Juliana, there would be no more relations, direct or indirect, with Greet. The private secretary and mother "possibly" would go. But the prime difficulty, little Princess Marijke's near blindness, remained unsolved. Healer Greet's explanation: Bernhard had not had enough faith.[17]

To cure her only son's (incurable) hemophilia, Russia's Empress Alexandria surrounded herself with mystics and magic healers, among them notorious adventurer Gregory Yefimovich Rasputin, the "Mad Monk," who gained disastrous influence over the tzar and tzarina. On December 30, 1916, Rasputin was assassinated, allegedly by Prince Felix Yussupov (or Yousoupoff) and others. In June of 1956, during the airing of the Juliana-Greet affair the Dutch dubbed the latter "Rasputin in petticoats." Yussupov, then 70, was living with his wife in Paris. Each morning he arose before dawn for "prayer visits" to a dozen sick and crippled persons; he had become a faith healer.

The Reverend Jack Coe, a tent-meeting revivalist, was connected with the "Herald of Healing Children's Home" and the "Herald of Healing Corp." of Dallas, Texas. In February of 1956, Religion Editor Adon Taft of the Miami, Florida *Herald* investigated Coe's Miami tent show, which was drawing crowds of 6,000 nightly. He reported that there had been no real changes in those Coe claimed to cure: "A crippled woman who had ostentatiously flung aside a pair of crutches had never ordinarily used them." Three ministers offered to pay Coe $2,500 for his cure of anyone first duly certified as ill by two physicians and afterwards certified as cured. Coe said they were inspired by the Devil and did not accept the challenge. Coe ordered Mr. and Mrs. George Willis Clark to remove the braces and crutches worn by their three-year-old son George, a polio victim, and make him walk without them.

They did; the boy collapsed. Later his legs began to swell and it appeared that he had suffered a serious setback. Mrs. Clark signed a warrant charging Coe with practicing medicine without a license. After a noisy hearing the charges were dismissed. Coe denied that he ever cured or claimed to have cured anyone—he merely called God's attention to the plight of the sick. The Clarks later filed suit in federal district court against Coe and two associates for $225,000 damages, but that December, Coe died of bulbar polio.[18]

Granville Oral Roberts,[19] "King of the Faith Healers," was, according to his autobiography, which sold 100,000 copies at $1.50, the son of a struggling revivalist preacher. At 16, afflicted with tuberculosis and stuttering, his family, despairing of his life took him to a revivalist healer. On the way, God told him: "Son, I am going to heal you, and you are to take My healing power to your generation." Oral revived and became a preacher of the Pentecostal Holiness Church, but his healing power did not come until twelve years later. By 1955, Roberts, then 37, and a minister of the Assemblies of God Church, was conducting regular programs on 223 radio and 98 television stations and publishing two magazines with a total circulation of 5,000,000. His "Healing Waters Inc." (book value: $1,250,000), a "non-profit, religious corporation" paying no taxes, was quartered in a modern, air-conditioned building in Tulsa, Oklahoma, and had a staff of 155. Its cash receipts for 1955: $3,000,000. Oral went "on the road" with a $240,000 outfit, including a tent seating 14,000 persons and a 60,000-watt lighting and public address system. His revival meeting routine: lively hymns to warm the audience, a hell-fire sermon, then an invitation to the unsaved to come forward. The climax was the laying on of hands: "I ask the Lord to deliver our sister here from sugar in her blood . . . Heavenly Lord, take the head noises away from this woman." One skeptic: the Rev. Carroll J. Stegall, Jr. of Atlanta, who watched while, at Roberts' command, the braces of a four-year-old girl, a polio victim, were removed by her parents:

> I was within a few feet of the healing line, and saw the little shriveled leg unchanged. She was not able to walk; but Roberts told her parents not to put the brace back or it would be lack of faith and would ruin the "healing."

When Roberts landed in Sydney in 1956, the Australian newspapers described his arrival as "Salvation circus comes to town"; the national weekly *Truth* called him "at best a big blabbermouth"; and a group of preachers denounced him as a "fraud and imposter." Replied Roberts:

"I am but a child of God." When reporters discovered that he was staying at an expensive hotel under an assumed name, he explained: "Christ has no objection to prosperity." Because of this hostile reception, Roberts abruptly ended his proposed tour of Australia and returned home, from where, during his next program, he spoke of the trip in "most glowing terms of success." The following Sunday, Jack Gould, radio and television critic of *The New York Times,* spoke his mind:

Roberts . . . is understood to spend about $20,000 a week for the purchase of time. He does not directly solicit funds but makes it unmistakably clear that he cannot continue on the air without "generous letters" from his audience . . .

No one will dispute that faith can play an enormously vital role in the heartening recovery from bodily ills. Similarly there need not be questioned the existence of seemingly miraculous recoveries that seemingly cannot be explained by medical science.

But it is quite a different matter to pass miracles on a weekly basis and to claim on the screen, without even the most rudimentary proof, permanent cures of an endless variety of ailments.

Last Sunday evening Brother Roberts called up four persons to be helped. A woman said she had a swollen foot, the result of blood poisoning, and a bone infection. Doctors had been unable to cure it, she explained. Brother Roberts struck her head sharply with the palm of his hand. The woman cried, "Hallelujah!" She said she was recovered and stomped her foot to prove it . . .

The climactic moment of the program was the cure of a small boy who suffered from double club feet.

The youngster was held in the arms of a woman relative and, before Brother Roberts invoked his power of faith, the youngster exclaimed with the help of some coaching, "Boy, am I a lucky duck?" He was going to be made well, he said.

Brother Roberts took the boy in his lap. As he placed his hands vigorously on the boy's feet he stressed that "the ligaments had been cut." Under such circumstances, Brother Roberts added, only a miracle, nothing else, now could enable the boy to walk. "Lord, when I put this child down, he's got to walk," he said. The boy scampered off the stage.

The TV presentation, according to the announcer, was "sponsored by Oral Roberts." In short, here was the case of a man buying time on the air to present his own assured miracles. To have failed, obviously would have made totally incongruous the evangelist's guarded closing appeal for further financial support.

Roberts' magical results, according to viewer Gould, were "unsupported by the slightest shred of rational evidence." Roberts "carefully avoids rigid comparative tests before and after his miracles."

If Brother Roberts wishes to exploit hysteria and ignorance by putting up his hands and yelling "Heal," that is his affair. But it hardly seems within the public interest, convenience, and necessity, for the TV industry to go along with him . . .
To allow the enormously influential medium of television to be used week after week to show undocumented "miracles," with all their implied aspersions on the competency of medicine, seems contrary to the spirit, if not the letter, of the industry's code governing mature and responsible broadcasting.

Roberts promptly counterattacked: out of the machinery at his Tulsa headquarters poured circular letters objecting to the article and calling on followers to register a protest with the *Times*. By the time its next Sunday's TV section went to press, the *Times* had received 1,450 letters, the overwhelming majority supporting Roberts. Commented the Rev. John Ellis Large, New York Episcopal minister:

Perhaps Oral Roberts' most outrageous technique is contained in one of his many injunctions to his unseen audience. He urges his TV viewers all over America to hold up their sick babies in front of their home screens, while he extends his hands to the camera before him—implying that this operation will cure the little ones of all their sicknesses.[20]

Added the Rev. Charles Ives, pastor of the Middlebury, Connecticut, Congregational Church:

I am impressed by the fact that more healings are accomplished each day in any one good hospital on the basis of the research and practice of dedicated men working through the laws of God in the natural order, than have been accomplished by faith healers over a decade on the basis of supernatural miracles. This is not to deny the power of God, but only to say that God has given us minds and expects us to use them for his orderly purposes.[21]

A year later, *The New York Times* for Saturday, February 16, 1957 carried the following advertisement: "See / Oral Roberts / *New* Series / See Faith heal Sickness, / Fear, Alcoholism; bring / a whole new outlook / Sunday - 10:00 AM / WOR—TV—9 / Sunday—8:30 AM / WATV—13."
In November, 1963, Roberts founded a coeducational, liberal arts institution on a campus just outside Tulsa. It opened in September of 1965. As of March, 1968, Oral Roberts University, with Oral Roberts as president, boasted an enrollment of 750 students.

# 3

# The Christian Scientists

*Any person desiring to learn how to heal the sick can receive of the undersigned instruction that will enable them to commence healing on a principle of science with a success far beyond any of the present modes. No medicine, electricity, physiology or hygiene required, for unparalleled success in the most difficult cases. No pay is required unless this skill is obtained. Address, MRS. MARY B. GLOVER, Amesbury, Mass.*

f/—*June 20*
—*Banner of Light, official organ of the New England Spiritualists, 1868*

In 1848, a touring French hypnotist told New England clockmaker Phineas Parkhurst Quimby (1802–1868) he had unusual hypnotic power. Quimby followed him until he learned the art, then used it with success to heal. Observing another hypnotist use a suggestible youth, Lucius Burkmar, to diagnose illnesses and then prescribe high-priced remedies—which the hypnotist then sold the patient—Quimby used Burkmar in the same way except that he persuaded him to prescribe cheaper medicines. To Quimby's surprise, these worked quite as well. His conclusion: the medicine's virtue lay not in the drug but in the patient's faith in it.

Convinced the curative process was wholly mental, Quimby abandoned hypnotism, diagnosis and drugs to concentrate on inducing in the patient an attitude of mind and emotion which would result in a buoyant faith as to his cure. He taught that evil existed not in the world but in the mind. Illness came from evil thoughts: with these expelled, the disease disappeared. To avoid disease, one had only to banish all thought of it. His only physical act: placing his hands on the patient's head to establish confidence. He believed he had rediscovered Jesus's method, that it was not supernatural, and that others with no special hypnotic powers could learn it. Within seven years he treated over 12,000 patients. He wrote down his principles in ten bound volumes of manuscript: "Man is made up of truth and belief, and if he is deceived into the belief that he has or is liable to have, a disease, the belief is catching and the result follows it."

He usually referred to his theory as the "Science of Health and Happiness"; sometimes as the "Science of Christ," and the "Science of Health." In 1863, in his manuscript entitled "Aristocracy and Democracy," he called his healing "Christian Science." One day in October, 1862, George, his son and secretary, introduced him to a prospective patient who was so feeble that George had had to help her up the stairs —a Mrs. Glover, an "authoress."

Mark Baker was hot-tempered, strong-willed and a religious zealot. His sixth and last child, highly imaginative Mary Ann Morse Baker (1821–1910), was sickly, subject to sudden pains in the spine, and determined to have her own way. When thwarted, she would lie on the floor, kick, and often apparently become unconscious. When she was 15, the family moved from Bow, New Hampshire, to larger Tilton, where their neighbors were "Shakers." The Shakers' church was "The Church of Christ"; their main organization the "Mother Church." Their leader, Ann Lee, "Mother Ann," was a "healer"—who could, if necessary, use this power in the opposite direction. The Shakers prayed to "Our Father *and Mother* which art in Heaven," and some held Ann greater than Christ. Tilton eyewitnesses described Mary's attacks, which continued throughout her life, as sometimes convulsions, sometimes screams of apparent agony, sometimes the rigidity of catalepsy. The family physician's diagnosis: hysteria mingled with bad temper.

At 22, Mary married stone mason George Glover, and left with him for Charleston, South Carolina, where he died of yellow fever. Pregnant and broke, Mary returned to Tilton, where George Washington Glover was born in 1844. Her seizures now grew to terrible proportions; when the family no longer could endure her, married sister Abigail Tilton took her in. A neighbor took George. Desperately poor, Mary twice tried and failed at teaching school. She began to write poetry and prose for local newspapers. Highly suggestible, she served as subject and medium in the current crazes of mesmerism and spiritualism.

At 32, she married itinerant dentist Daniel Patterson. In 1861, on a mission to Washington, he became involved in the Battle of Bull Run and was imprisoned by the Confederates for the duration. Back with Abigail, Mary in 1862 read a handbill advertising the remarkable cures of "Dr." Quimby of Portland, Maine, who cured the sick by "correcting their error—*The truth is the cure.*" She hoarded her spending money until she had enough for the trip. And there, in his waiting room, she first saw him: a slight, white-bearded man with the shrewd, kindly look of a philosopher. Quimby was 60, Mary 40.

With him, Mary's health improved at once. Seeing in "the authoress" a chance to publicize his work, he let her stay and watch. She published prose and poetry praising him, copied from his manuscripts and tried to cure others by his method. She had rejoined Patterson in Lynn, when, on January 16, 1866, Quimby died. That February, Mary took the fall which (much later) she claimed was followed by her miraculous recovery and "discovery" of Christian Science. The published account under oath of her attending physician is more prosaic. Actually, her tantrums continued; when Patterson no longer could endure her, he so advised her family and left town, but for a time sent her $200 a year. By now her mother had died, Mark had remarried, and Abigail—after Mary accused her children of stealing—had shut her door against her. Mary became a wandering guest or boarder, each new host soon speeding her on her way. She held seances, attempted cures, and advertised (see chapter head) as a teacher.

There is no evidence other than Mary's own later statements that she herself ever cured anybody of anything; her success finally came through the ability she developed to teach others to become "healers." Her first briefly successful student: shoemaker and host Hiram Crafts. But her personal interest in him was such that his wife prepared to leave him, whereupon Hiram put Mary out instead and gave up healing. But Mary was enthusiastic. She now saw her true role: the teacher-partner of the acutal healer. Rooming with Stoughton's Wentworths, paying her board by teaching them Quimby's system, she completed her first version of *Science & Health*. When Mrs. Wentworth refused to mortgage their farm to publish it, Mary raged, tried to burn the house down, and left. It was the spring of 1870. Mary was 50.

In Lynn, she entered a healer-teacher partnership with young student Richard Kennedy. He at once became a success, and this brought more students to Mary. Some accomplished amazing cures, others asked for their money back. She brought many suits for her fees, and defended many others brought by unhappy students. One challenged her in the Lynn *Transcript* "to walk upon the water without the aid of artificial means as she claims she can." Kennedy, who recognized the treatment's practical limits, broke with her in 1872. In 1875, two students put up $2,200 to publish *Science & Health*. Priced at $2.50, it

received poor reviews and did not sell, though advertised as the "opportunity to acquire a profession by which you can accumulate a fortune."

In 1877, after giving him two days' notice, Mary married surprised
student Gilbert Asa Eddy, 40, a quiet, docile sewing-machine agent.
On the marriage license, Mary, then 55, stated her age as 40. Afterwards, Eddy changed his baptismal name of "Gilbert Asa" to "Asa
Gilbert"—why, history does not record.

In 1878, Mary organized her students into "The Christian Scientists'
Association." That year, the defection of star pupil (and apparently
former suitor) Daniel H. Spofford upset her tremendously. In a paid
newspaper notice she denounced him as a malpractitioner. Her hatred
of him grew until she could not sleep at night. She declared he was
employing "malicious animal magnetism"—a sort of black-magic opposite to the so-called "white magic" of Christian Science treatment—to
pursue and crush her mind. In defense, she had a circle of her students
"treat" him in the same way. And like the hero of a Harold Lloyd movie,
husband Asa, thoroughly alarmed, suddenly stepped out of his meek
character.

Asa and Mary's current star pupil, a young carpenter named Edward
J. Arens, visited a pretentious brothel on Boston's Bowker Street,
where Arens had some acquaintance. Through its madam, Laura Sargent, the pair engaged Laura's brother, saloon-keeper James L.
Sargent, to murder Spofford for $500. Through Laura, they paid Sar-
gent $75 in advance. He at once visited Spofford, advised him of the
arrangement and proposed that Spofford leave town long enough to allow
Sargent to claim success and collect the remainder of his commission.
The startled Spofford first conferred with State Detective Hollis C.
Pinkham, then departed. Sargent now reported his mission accomplished
and Asa and Arens paid him an additional portion of his fee.

In October of 1878, the Boston *Herald* announced Spofford's disappearance, and a few days later reported his body in the morgue. On
October 29, Asa and Arens were arrested. Afterwards, Spofford appeared, alive and well, but the pair were still held for trial, charged
with conspiring to procure murder. On November 7, Judge May
heard the case in Municipal Court. James Sargent, Laura—accompanied by a bevy of her girls—and others testified as to the plot. The
judge held Asa and Arens for the Superior Court, fixing their bail at
$3,000 each, while observing that the case was "rather anomalous."
In Superior Court, they pleaded not guilty, and the indictment was
continued until the January term. Later, the District Attorney refused
to prosecute the case further, and on payment of costs they were discharged.

In 1879, Mary chartered "The First Church of Christ (Scientist),"
and in 1881 her profitable "Massachusetts Metaphysical College." The
next year, she and Eddy moved to Boston, where, in spite of Mary's
efforts, Eddy sickened and died of heart disease. Later, Mary said, "My
husband's death was caused by malicious animal magnetism."

Asa had waited on Mary hand and foot—as secretary, butler, nurse,
messenger and bookkeeper. After his death, sorely missing these services, she sought a more durable replacement. Among her pupils she found
just the man: Calvin Frye, who was subject to catalyptic seizures
similar to Mary's. Frye's mother had suffered from insanity for many
years; under the treatment of Christian Science practitioner Mrs. Choate
she apparently recovered to some extent, then suddenly became violent
and died. Through Mrs. Choate, Calvin Frye became interested in
Christian Science, took lessons under Mary, and had been practicing
a short time when Mary "tapped" him for the job. The consideration:
$12 a week and board. Taciturn, shrewd, peculiarly suggestible, he be-
came entirely devoted to her and served her faithfully and with un-
questioning loyalty until her death. He kept a diary which is invaluable
as an eyewitness account of her personal life.

Acutely aware of the value of publicity, Mary constantly wrote and
submitted press notices. In 1883, she started the *Journal,* which offered
testimonials of cures of every known ailment. Free copies were distributed in far away towns—a most effective missionary tool. In 1884
she spent two months in Chicago, teaching to crowded classes.

In 1885 she secretly hired the Rev. James Henry Wiggin, a capable
scholar, theologian, writer and critic, for a complete rewrite of *Science
& Health.* That August, Calvin Frye first called on Wiggin, introducing himself as the secretary to a lady who had written a book which
needed "revision and an index." A few days later, Mrs. Eddy herself
arrived. By Wiggin's later account:

> She was a person of great, stately mien, perfectly self-possessed
> and disposed to be somewhat overbearing and impressive in manner.
> She had a huge package of manuscript which I learned was designed
> to serve as the material for a forthcoming edition of *Science and
> Health,* with *Key to the Scriptures* . . . Some days later I opened the
> package and began a scrutiny of the manuscript. Well I was staggered!
>
> Of all the dissertations a literary helper ever inspected, I do not
> believe one ever saw a treatise to surpass this. The misspelling,
> capitalization and punctuation were dreadful, but those were not
> things that feazed me. It was the thought and general elemental
> arrangement of the work. There were passages that flatly and ab-
> solutely contradicted things that had preceded, and scattered all
> through were incorrect references to historical and philosophical
> matters . . .

But Mary agreed to his terms, and he accepted the assignment. It took him four years.

Around 1888, Mary added to her college curricula a course in "metaphysical obstetrics": six lessons for $100. In this, Mary personally taught how to cope with malicious animal magnetism—a subject which obsessed her, often abbreviated "M.A.M." in her writings—in connection with childbirth: how, sitting by the bedside, to mentally deny the possibility of premature birth or of pain or suffering during delivery. In 1888, former student Mrs. Abby H. Corner so attended her own daughter. Both daughter and infant died. By now, newspapers were featuring deaths caused by Christian Science practitioners, and this double death caused a furore. Mrs. Corner was prosecuted but acquitted on the ground that the hemorrhage causing her daughter's death might have caused death even with a registered physician in attendance. Mary's out: her "Committee on Publication" denounced Mrs. Corner as a quack—she had not attended the obstetrics class and therefore was not qualified as an accoucheur. Afterwards, however, Mary advised her classes that a surgeon might be called in surgical cases. Asked one student:

"What if I find a breech presentation in childbirth?"

"You will *not*, if you are in Christian Science."

"But what if I *do*?"

"Then," said Mrs. Eddy sagely, "send for the nearest regular practitioner!"[2]

There is abundant evidence that Mary did not practice what she preached. According to Frye's diary she resorted regularly to doctors and to morphine. In 1902 she paid a Boston surgeon to operate on her sister-in-law for cancer of the breast. She ordered her grandchildren vaccinated and gave her son George the money to pay the bill. Around 1903 she was paying a dentist a flat fee of $500 a year to take care of her teeth—by which time she had lost all those in her upper jaw.

By now, the movement was growing in all directions. In 1890 the *Journal* listed 250 healers in the United States, 20 incorporated churches, 90 societies not yet incorporated and 33 academies and institutes. In 1889 she moved to Concord for a three-year "exile" and made secret and careful plans to recapture complete control. The plan: a central "Mother Church," absolutely controlling all "branch" churches, and itself absolutely controlled by a board of directors appointed—and thus absolutely controlled—by Mary. Only "Mother Church" members could become healers, teachers, or branch church "readers" (pastors) and any of these could be excommunicated at any time by Mary. Through "straws" the mortgage on Boston's Falmouth Street property was acquired, forclosed, and conveyed to Mary—for $1. Only after the "Mother Church's" first annual meeting in 1893 did her followers at large realize what had happened. All were "locked out." Only those accepted by the Mother Church—and Mary—could get back in. They were hand-picked.

In the reorganized church, an experienced publicity man, answerable through the "Board" to Mary, constituted the "Committee on Publication." Each state had its branch "Committee," similarly answerable: a carefully chosen publicist, his salary paid by that state's three largest branch churches. These ceaselessly urged good news of Mary and her church upon the press. And when a paper, no matter how small, published a slur, no matter how slight, the city editor at once received a letter from the local Committee, politely but firmly correcting his error. If a retraction did not appear forthwith, the matter passed to the local "Committee on Business"—and the *managing* editor shortly was visited by a valued advertiser who complained that the paper was persecuting his church; and . . . no retraction, no more advertising. The device was, and is, highly effective.

Re the "divine" origin of Mary's works, Dakin, in Appendix B of the 1930 edition of *Mrs. Eddy,* in one column sets down Mary's Annual Message dated September 30, 1895, and opposite this a sermon by Hugh Blair, a Scottish Divine. For her paragraph No. 2, Mary took a 54-word sequence from Blair's paragraph No. 1, changing four words. For her third she took Blair's second, intact, deleting 5 words and changing four. Mary's fourth paragraph of 92 words is made up of Blair's third, intact, plus a sequence of 31 words from Blair's fourth— she added one word of her own. Her first paragraph she presumably made up herself.

One paper was not afraid of its advertisers: the crusading New York *World.* In 1906, when Mary did not appear at the dedication of the great "annex," it determined to investigate rumors that she— who of all people least could afford to be—was an invalid, or dead. The *World's* first discovery: Mary's daily carriage drive, on which local followers based their assertion that she obviously was in good health, was in fact taken by a double. To discredit this, Mary, though then in particularly poor health, forced herself to the ride while reporters looked on. But noting the reek of ammonia, how her retainers practically carried her, and how she scarcely could comprehend the simplest question—they gained new suspicions.

On March 1, 1907, at the *World's* urging, son George and others brought a "next friend's" suit in Concord Superior Court, declaring Mary, 86, mentally irresponsible, incapable of managing her affairs and helpless in the hands of the designing defendants, namely, her personal attendants and officials of the Mother Church (cash assets: $12,000,000). Mary's personal fortune then amounted to $2,000,000. One source: in 1889, when she closed her "College," of which she was the whole faculty, some 4,000 persons had taken the $300 elementary course. From this alone—there also were advanced courses—she thus took in $1,200,000. Another source: her royalties on *Science & Health,* which she continuously revised. With each new issue, she withdrew authorization from the previous edition, thus forcing every healer, student and church member to buy the new one. By 1891, about 150,000 copies of all editions had been sold, at a royalty to Mary of $1 per copy. In addition, every loyal follower was expected to buy all her other writings he could afford.

The plaintiffs contended that Mrs. Eddy was a paranoiac, and listed as proof the insane delusions in *Science & Health* and her other writings, e.g.: that the real world did not exist; that God chose to reveal through her a new and supernatural way of curing disease; that her system alone cured and prevented disease; that her system of philosophy and religion now replaced all others; her delusions of persecution by "malicious animal magnetism," delusions of grandeur, etc. But five days later—when Mary signed a deed of trust giving ownership of her property in trust to her editor, a local banker, and a cousin—the issue changed to the question of whether, on March 6, 1907, Mary was mentally competent to sign this document. The court then ruled that no evidence prior to 1890 would be admitted. Since she had produced practically all of her writings before 1890, this ruled out the heart of the plaintiffs' proof—and saved Christian Science itself from standing trial in a sanity test. Fearing their case lost, the plaintiffs began to consider a new action designed to test Mary's competence over a long period of years; whereupon her attorneys, fearing that any more such publicity would irremediably damage the church, offered a compromise: generous trust funds for all plaintiffs. The suit was withdrawn, and George received $250,000.

That summer of 1907 was enlivened by the jumping—for no apparent reason—of Eddy household attendant Mary Tomlinson to her death from a window of Boston's Parker House. During the trial, to combat adverse publicity, the church induced Arthur Brisbane, then at the start of his career, to interview Mary and write a favorable article. He asked the reason for the suit. "Greed of gold," she replied. Later she advised: "I made my money with my pen, just as you do. And I have a right to it." Brisbane's article was published in *Cosmo-*

*politan Magazine* for August, 1907; he then wrote a book about her which was published the following year.

Mary long had hinted of her extensive charities. Newspapers now reported that no trace of any such was to be found. Boston lawyer Frederick W. Peabody, speaking of Miss Milmine (below) said, "She assured me she had searched the whole of Mrs. Eddy's life for a kindly, a generous, an unselfish, a fine womanly deed, and would have been only too glad to have recorded it, but had not found one." To scotch these reports and at the same time cut off greedy relatives, Mary came up with an idea. She revealed it in the *Sentinel* for December 21, 1907: "I desire to commence immediately to found a Christian Science institution for the special benefit of the poor and general good of all mankind. The founding and endowment of this institution will cost at least one million dollars . . ." But when her advisers prevailed upon her to compromise the Next Friend's Suit, the million-dollar foundation idea was dropped.

Around 1890, Mary had set loyal agents to scouring New England for all her early manuscripts, letters and all else that might discredit her. In the face of this, *McClure's Magazine* in 1906 assigned Georgine Milmine and a staff of investigators the two-year task of combing the same area for the facts of Mary's life. Miss Milmine reported their findings in 14 amazing articles, all in the form of eyewitnesses' sworn affidavits, during 1907–1908. Mary wrote indignant denials to the first installments, then was silent. Dakin's *Mrs. Eddy* is largely based on these; his bibliography indicates the also amazing industry with which the organization has brought up or suppressed source-materials on her life.

Mary had met brilliant Mrs. Augusta Stetson, then about 40, in 1884, when Augusta was studying elocution. She had a dynamic personal appeal; Mary knew she must have her. At first Augusta was not interested, but finally took the $300 course as a gift. After twelve lessons, she started healing and lecturing and was much sought after. One success: "Miss H.E.L. of Skowhegan, Maine, was pronounced incurable, and had been unable to stand or walk for six months, from spinal trouble. After one treatment, she walked several times across the room, and after the third was perfectly well." In 1886, when Mary ordered her to New York to establish a church, she began in a cheap furnished room, healing patients and teaching. Her church, chartered in 1887, consisted of eight students and a few converts. It prospered tremendously; Augusta had a special faculty for gathering wealthy converts. By 1903, a church costing $1,250,000—and paid for—seating

2,200 was completed on Central Park West at 96th Street. It contained 25 luxuriously furnished rooms for the use of its 40 healers and their patients. Augusta daily directed the practice of these healers, consulted with them on difficult cases, taught classes of students and ran the church. In 1908, 3,004 different patients were received, 4,704 diseases treated, and 3,331 diseases reported as healed. Poverty being a shameful error, seedy-looking members were taken to a well-stocked secret room and properly outfitted. In 1905, her students gave Augusta a great marble-staircased mansion adjoining the church. Augusta dressed and conducted herself accordingly. For her, healing was literally a big business, bringing her great fame and thousands of followers. One man donated $400,000; one rich woman her entire fortune. High priestess Augusta regarded Mary as her God: "What she says and does is *always right* . . . I . . . would *instantly accept* and *follow,* wherever she leads." One question: should the stone inscription on Augusta's church read "To the Glory of God," or, "A Tribute to our Leader and Teacher, Mary Baker Eddy"? Mary's answer: the first did not belong in stone—"write it on your hearts." Augusta was widely heralded as Mary's successor, but Mary had determined that she should have no successor: her own church manual would rule her flock forever. In 1909, Augusta was excommunicated.

From Calvin Frye's diary:

*Monday, May 9, 1910*
Mr. Adam H. Dickey last night told Mrs. Eddy, that she shall not have any more morphine! She had for several days been suffering from renal calculi and had voided stones in the urine, but yesterday the water seemed normal and so having had hyperdermic injections twice within a few days he believed she did not need it but that it was the old morphine habit reasserting itself and would not allow her to have it.

Mary continued to force herself to her daily carriage drive, to show the world she still lived. After her drive on Thursday, December 1, she was exhausted; she had a bad cold and developed a racking cough. Saturday, breathing with difficulty, she could not get up. That night, she died. On the death certificate the medical examiner write: "*Natural causes—probably pneumonia.*"

During March of 1956, Texas newspapers carried the Christian Science Committee on Publication's announcement that its second group of television films[3] soon would be released: the initial 13 programs in the series, "How Christian Science Heals," broadcast over 160 TV stations, recorded "real-life incidents" of "permanent healings through prayer of asthma, cancer, broken bones, deafness, goiter, tuberculosis, appendicitis and angina pectoris . . ." During that same March, Pennsylvania newspapers featured a "real-life incident" not included in the above. In December, 1955, seven-year-old David E. Cornelius of Swarthmore became ill. His parents first had him treated by Christian Science practitioners. When he failed to respond, they called in Dr. George P. Heckman, who diagnosed diabetes and placed David in a hospital. There, given insulin, he responded quickly and was released in January in "excellent" condition. But Dr. Heckman advised that David would require insulin regularly, and warned that without it the boy "would not survive." Later, the parents informed the doctor that they would not give David insulin because it was against their faith, and that, instead, they planned to watch the boy's diet carefully. When he began to fail, they turned him over to Christian Science practitioners and he was admitted to a Christian Science nursing home. And there, on February 14, 1956, in a diabetic coma, David died.[4]

Public health expert Dr. Victor Heiser had this to say of clockmaker Quimby's two offspring:

If the tenets of the believers in New Thought and Christian Science were true, this class of people would never have smallpox. For surely no bigotry could be more pronounced than that manifested by the anti-vaccinationists of the Philippines. Fortunately these fanatics, although vociferous, were small in numbers and not influential in the Legislature, and the unvaccinated among them contracted smallpox so regularly that they were no problem . . . [In Australia] cultists of all kinds were also unwelcome, although there was no legal barrier to their entrance. When Christian Scientists began their propaganda, the doctors of Melbourne sent them a public challenge, saying the superiority of mind over matter would be freely admitted if they could refrain from vomiting after being given a certain injection. Since sports overshadowed all else in Australia, the populace was agog to see the ordeal by apomorphine, but the Christian Scientists refused to submit, and when their answer was heralded by the press they were discredited.

While Christian Science was growing into a well-organized church, Quimby's other—his "legitimate"—child remained individualistic; the movement did not even receive a permanent name until the 1890's, when it became known as "New Thought."[5] Later, its societies were federated in the New Thought Alliance. Its members, unlike Christian Scientists, believe in the reality of matter, and take only the Bible as their revelation. In 1938, its best-known preacher was the Rev. Emmet

Fox, a onetime British electrical engineer, who believed in a universal Law to which anyone might tune his mind in "scientific prayer." At that time, he preached every Sunday to some 5,000 people in his Church of the Healing Christ in Manhattan's Hippodrome.

A thumbnail sketch of Christian Science is given in the Appellate opinion in New York's *Cole* case (Ch. 11) with statistics for 1907— the year of enactment of the medical practice statute in question—and for "now" (now meaning 1912, when Cole was tried a second time):

. . . Christian Science is a religion based on the Scriptures, founded by Mary Baker Eddy in 1886 . . . Mrs. Eddy's interpretation of the scriptures, which she named Christian Science, is set forth in a book entitled "Science and Health with Key to the Scriptures," first published in 1875 . . . Mrs. Eddy founded a church to represent the Christian Science denomination at Boston, Mass., in 1879 . . . known as the First Church of Christ, Scientist . . . [I]n May, 1907, there were in the state of New York 72 Christian Science churches, and there are now 80 or more of these churches in this state . . . [T]here were in May, 1907 . . . 1,000 Christian Science churches situated in different cities and towns throughout the United States, and . . . there are now more than 1,200 of these churches, besides 100 or more in foreign countries . . . [T]he number of Christian Scientists in the United States is [1912] about 1,000,000 people . . . [T]he healing of moral, mental, and physical disorders was practiced by Christian Scientists in the state of New York for at least 20 years prior to . . . 1907 . . . and has continuously since that time been so practiced . . . [In 1907] there were more than 300 practitioners in the state of New York, whose cards were published in the "Christian Science Journal" and who made this work their only vocation.

Perusal of the *Journal* for November, 1955 proves of interest: for students who "wish at times to listen to rather than read" *Science & Health* the complete work is available on 45 phonograph records, claimed to be unbreakable, at $2 each. The title of one article probably sums up the religion's basic appeal: "Peace of Mind, the Key to True Happiness." From another page jump Mary's own ghosts, still unlaid: "animal magnetism" and "mental malpractice". An editorial bears the semanticist-maddening title, "Consciousness in Truth is True Consciousness." A section titled "Testimonies of Christian Science Healing" contains accounts readily interchangeable with those in my "news" clippings of Chapter 1, preceded by instructions as to submitting same. These, incidentally, clarify the meaning of the expression "Documented examples." Testimonies are "welcomed," and should be typed triple-spaced and "concise." Testimonies should be verified by three members of the Mother Church who either have witnessed the healing or can vouch for the integrity of the testifier. If the testifier is unacquainted with three members, his affidavit may be sufficient, but in this case he should, if possible, obtain verification from one or two members. One contributor describes how conversion promptly cured her "chronic bowel inactivity," later "influenza, pneumonia, oak poisoning, sprains, bone injuries, and other conditions to which no name was given." And finally came the morning she reported her leaking gas jet to the apartment manager. That same evening, returning late, she went directly to bed:

> In the middle of the night I was awakened by the sound of hammering on the door and anxious voices asking admittance. Other tenants had smelled the gas and suspected that something was wrong. As I awakened I found myself with my head thrust out of an open window. Divine Love had led me there while I was still asleep . . . It developed that my request to have the leaking gas jet fixed had been overlooked.

Success in treating ailing animals was early claimed for Christian Science. Cole (Ch. 11) testified that he had been "particularly successful in the case of dogs." This branch of the sect's healing, though not advertised, continues today. Recently a friend wrote me of a middle-aged Christian Scientist lady who lived next door:

> She acquired a dog which proceeded to get itself run over by a car . . . pretty badly injured. [She] calls the practitioner on the telephone for *absentee* treatment for the dog. What the poor animal gets out of this is beyond my comprehension but [she] pays money to someone for all this monkey business. After a few days the dog gets worse so she finally is forced into taking it to a vet. Dog gets well.

Is an owner legally bound to furnish "proper veterinary care" for his dog in spite of his religious belief in other methods? Would intervention by the S.P.C.A. abridge the owner's freedom of religion?

Oddly, today's Christian Scientist visits his dentist as regularly as the next man. I am unable to diagram the feat of theological gymnastics which this involves, and only state it as a well known fact. But granting that fact, and thus with no revenue for the practitioner at stake in this area, it is not surprising to find the organization offering only token opposition to programs for fluoridation of drinking water. A mimeographed notice dated July 17, 1951 from the "Christian Science Committee on Publication for Indiana" to "all Assistant Committees on Publication in Indiana" advises that the former committee has filed the necessary objection to the state's fluoridation program with the State Board of Health, "so it will not be necessary for you to take any action in case such programs come for consideration in your locality. To any one making inquiry you should state that the necessary objection has been filed . . . and no individual action against such programs is necessary or desirable."

But where there is money to be made, all the pressures possible to a large and aggressive business organization are brought to bear upon the legislature. An example of the results: in 1953, Minnesota enacted a statute allowing employees injured on the job to receive Christian Science treatments instead of medical attention under the workmen's compensation law.[6]

Annually, the Mother Church elects an outstanding Christian Science worker as its president. This position, however, is largely honorary; the policy of the Mother Church and its 3,000-odd branch churches is tightly controlled by its five-member board of directors. These, in turn, control the trustees of the profitable Christian Science Publishing Society, which in 1951 reported that the demand for Mary's writings had doubled in the previous decade.[7] I was once asked as to the possibility of federal prosecution of these directors and trustees for using, and for conspiring to use, the mails to defraud. My answer was to recommend a thoughtful reading and re-reading of Supreme Court Justice Jackson's dissent in *Ballard* (Ch. 13).

Instead of a pastor, each Christian Science Church has two "readers": a "First Reader" for *Science & Health* and a "Second Reader" (apparently in that order of importance) for the Bible. Twenty-six lesson-subjects, as determined by Mary herself, are repeated in the same order every six months. The climax of each service is the First Reader's reading of Mary's *Scientific Statement of Being,* which all good Christian Scientists memorize and repeat in time of trouble:

> There is no life, truth, intelligence, nor substance in matter. All is infinite Mind and its infinite manifestation, for God is All-in-all. Spirit is immortal Truth; matter is mortal error. Spirit is the real and eternal; matter is the unreal and temporal. Spirit is God, and man in his image and likeness. Therefore man is not material; he is spiritual.

The average Christian Scientist has been variously described as happy, sweet-tempered, considerate and tolerant of others' opinions though firm in his own, cooperative, socially conscious, excellent citizen—and humorless. Many are well-to-do; those not often consider poverty a sort of disease which God will help cure. One doctor wrote me: "I have personally, in my private practice . . . had to deal with Christian Scientists, and in every instance that I can recall they finally came around to consenting to the necessary surgery or medical care and strangely enough, during their hospitalization, these people were model patients."

But after all the good has been said, there remains the fact, verified by newspapers and courts today, that in the particular brand of "peace of mind" which Christian Science offers, there lies a grave and continuing threat to the happy convert's health and life—a threat equally against the health and life of his children, and on occasion extended against the general public. An early encounter pressed the danger indelibly on my mind. Just out of college in the Depression's depths, I left for a strange city on the rumor of a job. There, the rumor scotched, standing on a corner contemplating my remaining few dollars and the vagaries of civilization, a friend—I shall call him Steve—hailed me. He listened to my story, then immediately said I should share his boarding-house room. I was overcome. He clapped his hand on my shoulder. "You'll find a job, old man," he said confidently. I had known Steve in grade school as a tough member of a tough gang, rough and strong-languaged; now, he was remarkably toned down. He had never been graduated from high school. Once a drinker, he now abstained. Once, after accepting my cigarette, he said with a peculiar shyness: "You know, old man, I'll probably be cutting these out." His father had left a large family behind to work in a factory here; Steve had joined him. When his father died, various relatives took the others. It soon became clear that Steve, though apparently not at all troubled by it, was in nearly the same straits as myself. He had lost several jobs and now worked on call at odd hours in a shipping room at a salary, if it had been full time, of $15 per week. He walked downtown—two miles—to save carfare. He was hard up and having trouble holding even this part-time job. One reason: he had grown seriously deaf. The second morning, I awoke at dawn to see him sitting bolt upright in bed, intent upon the book against his knees. Then he slowly turned to the window. The view was into one of the smallest light wells the law allowed, but his gaze was that of one entranced. He had taken wholeheartedly to Christian Science; proudly he exhibited the copy of *Science & Health* for which he had paid out a hard-saved $3.50, and only indifferently the Bible he had found readily obtainable from a hotel room. I spent my days applying for jobs and my evenings over street map and phone book charting next day's campaign. The third Saturday, I found a job—as a surveyor in the distant San Bernardino mountains. I was to leave, fare-paid, Monday morning. When Steve returned from work late that night, I told him. And I proposed that, with fare and future assured, we should splurge the last of my funds Sunday on a "double date." He was eager; he knew two girls in church to ask. But Sunday morning his efforts failed, and we spent a let-down afternoon in the park near the ocean, he craning back after passing girls. We walked far down the beach. He said, "You know, old man, I'll miss you." He confessed how he had secreted some "literature" in my half-packed suitcase; he blurted out in a rush how to him I often had seemed unhappy and that sometime I should try reading the literature. "It might help you," he said. Turning back, we saw that up the beach a crowd had gathered and a fire-rescue truck had stopped on the bluff behind: offshore a small cabin cruiser, disabled, was drifting in. As we neared the others, the firemen shot a rope across the boat, the crew made it fast, and a winch on the truck kept the line taut as the cruiser grounded in the heavy surf. The crew came off one by one and waded in, holding by both hands to the rope overhead to brace against the waves. During the rescue of one young woman in this fashion, Steve was seized with the greatest excitement and pulled me forward for a closer look. For the size of her bosom, and its animation as well, were truly fantastic—and we both stood breathless until, safely ashore, she paused to extract from inside of her belted jersey what she had placed there for the passage: two lively kittens. At dusk we caught a streetcar into town, and I treated Steve to a large dinner, throughout which the thought of the kittens kept coming back to him; he would move his hands, shake his head and chuckle helplessly. When we came out, it was dark. We sat for a while on a bench, he now smoking as steadily as I. When I proposed to stand treat to a first-run movie, he first was silent, then bent forward earnestly. There was a house where he had gone before; the girls were young; it was only two dollars; we should go now, together. It was his first mention of this, and I was taken aback. Did he not fear to contract syphilis, I asked, or gonorrhea? He shook his head and smiled reassuringly at me. "You don't have to worry about that, old man," he said. "It's all in the mind."

Two cases will underline the continuing danger which the sect presents to the public health. When Christian Scientist Dayis Holcomb registered for her senior year at the University of Washington, she refused to submit to X-ray examination for possible tubercular infection. The Board of Regents denied her admission, and were upheld by the state supreme court.[8] In 1951, Christian Scientist Cora Louise Sutherland, a teacher of shorthand in Los Angeles' Van Nuys High School, developed a hacking cough and began steadily to lose weight. To avoid

the periodic chest X-rays required of teachers she submitted an affidavit declaring her free of communicable disease. In 1953, she became
too sick to teach and took leave of absence. The Christian Science
practitioner treating her (for $62 per month, which he cut to $25 when
her pay stopped) certified her condition as due to "lung congestion
aggravated by activity." In 1954, her brother finally forced her to a
hospital. Her second day there, she died of tuberculosis. The coroner's
report: she probably had had the disease in contagious form at least two
years. For two years she had exposed her pupils (over 70, each term)
to tuberculosis. Afterwards, the alarmed city health department tried
to locate all exposed recent graduates for chest X-rays.[9]

# 4
# The Jehovah's Witnesses[1]

*As Jehovah's Witnesses our sole and only purpose is
to be entirely obedient to his commandments; to make
known that he is the only true and almighty God; that
his Word is true and that his name is entitled to all
honor and glory; that Christ is God's King, whom he
has placed upon his throne of authority; that his kingdom is now come, and in obedience to the Lord's commandments we must now declare this good news as a
testimony or witness to the nations and to inform the
rulers and the people of and concerning Satan's cruel
and oppressive organization, and particularly with reference to Christendom, which is the most wicked part
of that visible organization; and of and concerning God's
purpose to shortly destroy Satan's organization, which
great act will be quickly followed by Christ the King's
bringing to the obedient peoples of the earth peace and
prosperity, liberty and health, happiness and everlasting life; that God's kingdom is the hope of the world
and there is no other, and that this message must be delivered by those who are identified as Jehovah's Witnesses.*

*—From a resolution adopted in 1931.[2]*

In endeavoring to deliver the above message, Jehovah's Witnesses
have run afoul of many local ordinances and have determinedly appealed their convictions to the Supreme Court of the United States.
In 1953, the 45th such case reached that court and was the 38th to be decided in favor of the Witnesses.[3] On the record day of May 3, 1943, when
the Supreme Court decided thirteen Witness cases—twelve in their
favor—Associate Justice Jackson, dissenting as to three, examined the
Witnesses' beliefs, organization and activities in some detail:

Except the case of Douglas . . . all of these cases are decided upon the record of isolated prosecutions in which information is confined to a particular act of offense and to the behavior of an individual offender. Only the Douglas record gives a comprehensive story of the broad plan of campaign employed by Jehovah's Witnesses and its full impact on a living community . . . This record shows us something of the strings as well as the marionettes. It reveals the problem of those in local authority when the right to proselyte comes in contact with what many people have an idea is their right to be let alone . . .

From the record in Douglas we learn:

In 1939, a "Watchtower Campaign" was instituted by Jehovah's Witnesses in Jeannette, Pennsylvania, an industrial city of some 16,000 inhabitants.* Each home was visited, a bell rung or the door knocked upon, and the householder advised that the Witness had important information. If the householder would listen, a record was played on the phonograph. Its subject was "Snare and Racket." The following words are representative of its contents: "Religion is wrong and a snare because it deceives the pople, but that does not mean that all who follow religion are willingly bad. Religion is a racket because it has long been used and is still used to extract money from the people upon the theory and promise that the paying over of money to a priest will serve to relieve the party paying from punishment after death and further insure his salvation." This line of attack is taken by the Witnesses generally upon all denominations, especially the Roman Catholic . . .

When this campaign began, many complaints from offended householders were received, and three or four of the Witnesses were arrested. Thereafter, the "zone servant" in charge of the campaign conferred with the Mayor. He told the Mayor it was their right to carry on the campaign and showed him a decision of the United States Supreme Court, said to have that effect, as proof of it. The Mayor told him that they were at liberty to distribute their literature in the streets of the city and that he would have no objection if they distributed the literature free of charge at the houses, but that the people objected to their attempt to force these sales, and particularly on Sunday. The Mayor asked whether it would not be possible to come on some other day and to distribute the literature without selling it. The zone servant replied that that was contrary to their method of "doing business" and refused. He also told the Mayor that he would bring enough Witnesses into the City of Jeannette to get the job done whether the Mayor liked it or not. The Mayor urged them to await the outcome of an appeal which was then pending in other cases and let the matter take its course through the courts. This, too, was refused, and the threat to bring more people than the Mayor's police force could cope with was repeated.

On Palm Sunday of 1939, the threat was made good. Over 100 of the Witnesses appeared. They were strangers to the city and arrived in upwards of twenty-five automobiles. The automobiles were parked

* Including 5,520 Roman Catholics.

outside the city limits, and headquarters were set up in a gasoline
station with telephone facilities through which the director of the
campaign could be notified when trouble occurred. He furnished bonds
for the Witnesses as they were arrested. As they began their work,
around 9:00 o'clock in the morning, telephone calls began to come in
to the Police Headquarters, and complaints in large volume were
made all during the day. They exceeded the number that the police
could handle, and the Fire Department was called out to assist. The
Witnesses called at homes singly and in groups, and some of the homes
complained that they were called upon several times. Twenty-one
Witnesses were arrested . . .

The national structure of the Jehovah's Witnesses movement is also
somewhat revealed in this testimony. At the head of the movement
in this country is the Watch Tower Bible & Tract Society, a corporation organized under the laws of Pennsylvania, but having its
principal place of business in Brooklyn, N.Y. It prints all pamphlets,
manufactures all books, supplies all phonographs and records, and
provides other materials for the Witnesses. It "ordains" these Witnesses by furnishing each, on a basis which does not clearly appear,
a certificate that he is a minister of the Gospel . . .

The literature thus distributed is voluminous and repititious.
Characterization is risky, but a few quotations will indicate something
of its temper.

Taking as representative the book "Enemies," of which J. F.
Rutherford, the lawyer who long headed this group, is the author,
we find the following: "The greatest racket ever invented and practiced is that of religion. The most cruel and seductive public enemy
is that which employs religion to carry on the racket, and by which
means the people are deceived and the name of Almighty God is
reproached. There are numerous systems of religion, but the most
subtile, fraudulent and injurious to humankind is that which is generally labeled the 'Christian religion,' because it has the appearance
of a worshipful devotion to the Supreme Being, and thereby easily
misleads many honest and sincere persons." . . . It analyzes the income of the Roman Catholic hierarchy and announces that it is "the
greatest racket, a racket that is greater than all other rackets com-
bined." . . . It also says under the chapter heading "Song of the Harlot," "Referring now to the foregoing Scriptural definition of *harlot*:
What religious system exactly fits the prophecies recorded in God's
Word? There is but one answer, and that is, The Roman Catholic
Church organization . . . Those close or nearby and dependent upon
the main organization, being of the same stripe, picture the Jewish
and Protestant clergy and other allies of the Hierarchy at the present
time to do the bidding of the old 'whore' . . . Says the prophet of
Jehovah: 'It shall come to pass in that day, that Tyre (modern Tyre,
the Roman Catholic Hierarchy organization) shall be forgotten.' Forgotten by whom? By her former illicit paramours who have committed
fornication with her." . . . Throughout the literature statements of this
kind appear amidst scriptural comment and prophecy, denunciation
of demonology, which is used to characterize the Roman Catholic

MARK TWAIN//He found a horse doctor more effective.

FRANCIS SCHLATTER//Denver faith healer//The government said no to his sending "blessed handkerchiefs" by mail.

The Rev. Gordon Miller demonstrates his faith by holding aloft two deadly copperheads. This picture was taken in Summerville, Georgia, just before his arrest in connection with the death of member Ernest Davis, who drank poison to prove his faith. (U.P.I.)

Oral Roberts, "King of the Faith Healers," applies his "Healing Touch." (U.P.I.)

**PHINEAS PARKHURST QUIMBY**//To avoid disease, banish all thought of it.

MARY BAKER GLOVER PATTERSON//Boarder Mary gave this
tintype to Lucy Wentworth in 1870. But when Lucy refused to mortgage her farm to publish Science & Health, Mary tried to burn her
house down.

On June 17, 1940, when Jehovah's Witnesses in Litchfield, Illinois, refused to salute the flag, townspeople overturned their automobiles. Sect members were jailed, and when townspeople threatened further violence were transported by state police to neighboring Hillsboro's jail. (U.P.I.)

DR. BEATRIX COBB//"Why do people detour to quacks?"

The murder of presidential candidate Joseph Smith at Carthage jail.

The Mormons' expulsion from Nauvoo.

MORMON APOSTLE ORSON PRATT//"I think . . . that the constitution gives the privilege to all of the inhabitants of this country, of the free exercise of their religious notions."

"Bringing home a new wife. An incident of everyday life of the Mormon stronghold in Salt Lake City." From a woodcut, 1882. (Bettmann Archive)

STEPHEN ARNOLD DOUGLAS//He changed his mind about the Mormons.

religion, criticism of government and those in authority, advocacy of obedience to the law of God instead of the law of man, and an interpretation of the law of God as they see it.

The spirit and temper of this campaign is most fairly stated perhaps in the words, again of Rutherford, in his book, "Religion," p. 196–198:

"God's faithful servants go from house to house to bring the message of the kingdom to those who reside there, omitting none, not even the houses of the Roman Catholic Hierarchy, and there they give witness to the kingdom because they are commanded by the Most High to do so. 'They shall enter in at the windows like a thief.' They do not loot nor break into the houses, but they set up their phonographs before the doors and windows and send the message of the kingdom right into the houses into the ears of those who might wish to hear; and while those desiring to hear are hearing, some of the 'sour-pusses' are compelled to hear. Locusts invade the homes of the people and even eat the varnish off the wood and eat the wood to some extent. Likewise God's faithful witnesses, likened unto locusts, get the kingdom message right into the house and they take the veneer off the religious things that are in that house, including candles and 'holy water', remove the superstition from the minds of the people, and show them that the doctrines that have been taught to them are wood, hay and stubble, destructible by fire, and they cannot withstand the heat. The people are enabled to learn that 'purgatory' is a bogeyman, set up by the agents of Satan to frighten the people into the religious organizations, where they may be fleeced of their hard-earned money. Thus the kingdom message plagues the religionists, and the clergy find that they are unable to prevent it. Therefore, as described by the prophet, the message comes to them like a thief that enters in at the windows, and this message is a warning to those who are on the inside that Jesus Christ has come, and they remember his warning words, to wit: 'Behold, I come as a thief.' (Revelation 16:15). The day of Armageddon is very close, and that day comes upon the world in general like a thief in the night."

The day of Armageddon, to which all of this is a prelude, is to be a violent and bloody one, for then shall be slain all "demonologists," including most of those who reject the teachings of Jehovah's Witnesses . . .

In the Struthers case . . . we find the Witness knocking on the door of a total stranger at 4:00 on Sunday afternoon, July 7th. The householder's fourteen year old son answered, and, at the Witness's request called his mother from the kitchen. His mother had previously become "very disgusted about going to the door" to receive leaflets, particularly since another person had on a previous occasion called her to the door and told her, as she testified, "that I was doomed to go to hell because I would not let this literature in my home for my children to read." She testified that the Witness "shoved in the door" the circular being distributed, and that she "couldn't do much more than take" it, and she promptly tore it up in the presence of the Witness, for while she believed "in the worship of God," she did not "care to talk to everybody" and did not "believe that anybody needs to be sent from door to door to tell us how to worship." . . .

Such is the activity which it is claimed no public authority can either regulate or tax. This claim is substantially, if not quite, sustained today. I dissent . . .[4]

*Awake* for July 8, 1953 asks: "Are you interested in a new world, completely free from the worry, trouble and anxiety besetting the people of earth today? Would you like to live in a world with no sickness, sorrow or death? Then do not fail to hear "After Armageddon—God's New World," free public address by N. H. Knorr, President of Watchtower Society, Yankee Stadium, Sunday, July 26, 4:00 P.M." The Sunday before, 82,861 members had jammed the stadium for the opening of their eight-day new world society assembly. How is such a movement to be interpreted? Milton Czatt called it

a contemporary manifestation of millenarianism. This type of phenomenon is by no means new among those who fail to be instructed by repeated failures of specific predictions in the history of Christian thought. It is commonly an escape from outward calamity, though in this case other motives also appear to have been present. When conditions of life have been hard, especially in times of great physical disaster or significant human conflict, religious thinkers have turned for consolation to the thought of a golden age in some future period of the world's history when conditions would be made right. Defeated and oppressed peoples have repeatedly in the history of the race sought the refuge of this comforting mood. The Plan of the Ages presented by the International Bible Students is a part of this noble succession.[5]

According to John E. Mulder and Marvin Comisky:

It is interesting to consider what drawing power the cult possesses; what induces the ordinary pople who compose their ranks to become such ambitious workers for the cause. Doubtless they are motivated by the thought that they are being led to an exclusive Heaven-on-earth. A "Shangri-La" has always had appeal. If this is so, then their doctrine of hatred can be explained as a means, all too familiar, of unifying a group by directing their destructive criticism towards some external body. The practice is effective even when used on so small a scale . . .[6]

If I were to attempt to interpret the movement (which I shall not) my first draft probably would follow Hoffer's *The True Believer* ("Thoughts on the Nature of Mass Movements"), thus:

. . . the active, revivalist phase of mass movements . . . is dominated by the true believer—the man of fanatical faith who is ready to sacrifice his life for a holy cause . . . Starting out from the fact that the frustrated predominate among the early adherents of all mass movements and that they usually join of their own accord, it is assumed: 1) that frustration of itself . . . can generate most of the peculiar characteristics of the true believer; 2) that an effective technique of conversion consists basically in the inculcation and fixation of proclivities and responses indigenous to the frustrated mind.[7]

Larrabee sums up Hoffer's "true believer" as "an isolated, frustrated person who is fleeing from his hated self. All he needs in order to become a fanatical follower is a completely self-assured leader who holds out hope and 'freedom from freedom' through ardent, mindless activity in a mass crusade against a 'devil' of preferably foreign origin." Such converts are not "moved primarily by intellectual arguments for their doctrines," nor can they "be cured by direct appeals to reason." Their beliefs have "little to do with reason or the realities of life, but are actually shields against them. 'It is the certitude of his infallible doctrine that renders the true believer impervious to the uncertainties, surprises, and the unpleasant realities of the world around him.' What the mass faith supplies is a temporary cure for his hated self, his otherwise 'meaningless' existence."[8]

But any such attempt is pertinent here only for its hint as to the underlying drives which make Witnesses so remarkably ready—in fact zealously determined—to die, and to force their children to die, rather than accept blood transfusions. Here, we shall be concerned only with the substantial effect of the sect's determined litigation in redefining our constitutional freedoms of speech, press, assembly and religion, described in Part II; and in Part IV its inspiring our juvenile courts to an increased determination that children shall not die for their parents' beliefs. I repeat that Jehovah's Witnesses are *not* faith healers; that only the identical *result* before the law—denial of medical aid in the form of blood transfusions because of religious belief—brings them into this study. Indeed, Jehovah's Witness editors specifically warn against Catholic shrines, Christian Science practitioners, and faith healers in general, pointing out that Elisha refused gifts and that profit was furthest from Jesus's mind; they cite the example of Elisha and his servant Gehazi just as Judge Ryan did in *Buswell* (Ch. 11). "God does not work through selfish men . . . The emphasis on financial remuneration makes suspect the claims of all such to divine power." As to James 5:15, they direct attention to the *following* verse, which indicates the sickness referred to is spiritual, not physical. "For Christians today the wise course is to recognize the laws of cause and effect and be governed accordingly . . . It is neither reasonable nor Scriptural to expect physical health by divine intervention today."[9]

The Witnesses have been called "a challenge to the tolerance of the American citizenry." But *they* are American citizens, entitled to practice their religious beliefs within the same limits as anyone else. A few of the various troubles into which they get themselves:

On June 1, 1940, in Odessa, Texas, 70 Witnesses began to distribute their literature; irate townspeople seized and burned the literature and several fist fights began. Someone asked the Witnesses to salute the flag. They refused. Then the sheriff and deputies marched most of the seventy to the courthouse, where the county judge lectured them on citizenship and called for a flag salute. A Witness spokesman replied that they could salute nothing man-made. Twenty were then jailed and the remaining 50 escorted out of town. These stopped at a ranch house, where, after dark, a menacing crowd gathered. Then an electrical storm caused power failure. During the excitement, the sheriff and deputies brought the 50 to the jail. No formal charges were filed, but the county attorney said that all 70 would be held "until they salute the American flag." The following morning, however, the officers escorted them out of town again.

In Waxahachie, Texas, that same day, some 200 Witnesses appeared, armed with phonographs and literature urging allegiance to no man-made form of government. After several fist fights, about 90 were jailed.[10]

By their own standards, *all* Jehovah's Witnesses are "ordained ministers." Could all Jehovah's Witnesses claim exemption from training and service and classification in Class IV-D under the Selective Training and Service Act of 1940? In 1953, the Supreme Court held (6 to 3) that the fact that Witness George Lewis Dickinson of Coalinga, California, worked five hours a week as a radio repairman did not necessarily deny him IV-D classification. In the majority opinion, Justice Tom C. Clark carefully pointed out that what applied to Dickinson did not necessarily apply to all Witnesses. But neither should "a legitimate minister . . . be, for the purposes of the Act, unfrocked simply because all members of his sect base an exemption claim on the dogma of his faith." Part-time preaching and teaching are not enough: "These services must be regularly performed. They must . . . comprise the registrant's 'vocation.'" But there is no reason why ministers may not have secular jobs on the side, since many preachers, including those in the more traditional and orthodox sects "may not be blessed with congregations or parishes capable of giving them a living wage."

On Sunday, April 20, 1952, Miss Grace Marie Olliff, 20, of Midland, Texas suffered a compound skull fracture, a fractured pelvis, and fractures of both legs in an auto accident. She was taken, unconscious, to the Ector County Medical Center in Odessa, where her physician said she was in critical condition and might die if not given a blood transfusion immediately. But her Witness father, William Olliff, refused to allow it. "You're trying to kill my girl," he said. He and her Witness brothers, John, 27, and Ben, 23, guarded her door to make sure no transfusion was given. The following Wednesday, Clyde Wright, Grace's former husband, in behalf of their 18-months-old daughter, obtained an injunction from Special Judge Charles Butts of Ector County Court to restrain the father and brothers from interfering with the needed blood transfusion. Next Sunday, Grace for the first time briefly opened her eyes. In the presence of the three self-appointed guards, her doctor asked if she was a Jehovah's Witness. "No," she replied. "Do you want a transfusion if necessary?" "Yes." Waiting deputy sheriffs then arrested the three men and the transfusion was administered. The following day she was reported "much improved."[11]

In a two car collision on April 29, 1956, Wallace L. Rogers, 30, of East Camden, South Carolina suffered a ruptured spleen, rib fractures and a contused kidney. An immediate transfusion and operation were advised, the doctors explaining that an operation on a ruptured spleen was never attempted without replacing the blood lost from the circulatory system. But Witness Rogers and wife refused to permit the transfusion, and next morning Rogers died.[12]

In Hamilton, Ontario, on January 22, 1956, schoolgirl Donna Jones, 17, after one of a series of spasms of internal bleeding, was admitted to General Hospital. Doctors advised that she would die if not given blood, but she refused to allow it: she and her parents were Jehovah's Witnesses. A magistrate ruled that giving her a transfusion against her will would constitute assault. She then was given other treatment, and improved. On February 18, a hospital doctor reported that though her blood count was poor, she was continuing to improve: "She survived. Probably if we had given her blood, we would have credited it with bringing her through." A week or two later she apparently (see below) went home well.[13]

In Hamilton, Ontario, in the latter part of that February, nine-months-old Robert Cole pulled a boiling pot of water onto himself, was scalded, suffered deep first-degree burns and for a time was critically ill. The family physician, Dr. F. D. Overend, advised the Witness parents that a blood transfusion would help ease the baby's pain, hasten the healing, and lessen the chances of serious permanent scarring, but they refused to allow it. A week and a half later, advised by Dr. Overend of the child's low blood count, they still refused. Said Mrs. Cole:

I told him that under no circumstances whatsoever, regardless of how near death he may be, were they to give him blood. I'd rather see him die than violate the laws of Jehovah. Doctors make me sick. They told Donna Jones she would die of internal bleeding unless she accepted a transfusion. Three weeks ago she was as near to death's door as anyone can get, but only this week she went home as healthy as anyone I ever saw. If God wishes to take our life, all the transfusions in the world can't save us. My trust and life are in the hands of Jehovah. I will not defy Him and stand to suffer the pangs of eternal damnation by openly breaking his sacred laws. My baby will live as did Donna.

Mrs. Cole charged the medical profession with religious discrimination:

All they look for is a Jehovah's Witness so they can immediately prescribe a blood transfusion. This is nothing more than religious persecution. They know what our feelings are on it and they are looking in vain, too, I might add, for a weakling in our sect so they will have something to laugh and joke about. My doctor has told me that the court has been alerted to step in as soon as they get the nod from hospital higher-ups. If a person can't even practice his own religion any more, then it's about time we had a change of government. After all, this is nothing more than Facism. But they won't get away with it this time. This is the showdown. We will settle the matter for once and for all if they start any trouble. We'll fight it to the bitter end if it should come to that.[14]

Hospital officials expected that young Robert would remain hospitalized for another month to six weeks. Brother James, 14, who aspired to become a Witness missionary, said: "He is better to suffer now than after death. I realize he is my brother and I should do all I can for him. However I feel that my parents' decision is the only one that we can possibly give." Mary Blackwood, supervisor of the children's ward, explained why Robert's wounds had not been bandaged and why he was in a special isolated crib: his burns were a red patch which covered him from chin to waist, and were so painful that a bandage could not be applied. "He's in enough agony now. If he were wearing a bandage I'm afraid the pain would either kill him or drive him insane. His continual crying and occasional agonized screams keep the rest of the children awake so we had to isolate him."

## 5

# The Rooster Who Made the Sun Rise

Comedian Jack Benny on TV was treating his "Beaver" troop to an amusement park carnival. The youngsters first encountered Jack's friend "Kitzel" selling hot dogs, later merrygoround tickets, and, still later, serving as barker for the "Five High Flying Finnigans." Kitzel explained he was the park's "utility man—I do everything." The party watched "Gago, the most ferocious gorilla in captivity" bend a thick iron bar. When the crowd left, Gago laid his hand on Jack's shoulder. Jack stood petrified. Then the gorilla removed its head, and inside was Kitzel: "I *told* you, Mr. Benny, I do *everything!*" Later, Jack and his Beavers stopped at the lion cage, wherein roared a most convincing lion. The spieler offered $50 to anyone who would dare step inside. "How about you?" he challenged Jack. "Are you brave enough?" By now, convinced, Jack laughed and accepted. Inside, he went up to the lion—"Come on, kitty,"—petted it and made it lie down. "Shall I make him roll over," he called back to his admiring troop, "or do a somersault?" Then, from outside the bars, came the voice of admirer Kitzel: "Make him do a somersault."

What countless real lions have been overcome by little men suddenly powered by such convictions! I shall state it as an axiom: *oftentimes, confronted by danger, a man with a strong faith will overcome it, while that same man without that strong faith would not even try.* But there is a sobering corollary: in real life, while some men with Jack's strong but ill-founded conviction would subdue the real lion as he did, others would go in to their deaths.

When the city of Elyria, Ohio, resolved to fluorinate its domestic water supply, it scheduled the process to commence on April 22. During the first few days following that date, the Water Department was flooded with complaints as to the resulting taste. But due to a delay in testing, *the fluorides were not actually put into the water until a week later,* on April 29.[1]

So much, for the moment, as to the very real and powerful effects which can proceed from faith and suggestion.

71

Having had a look at the *dramatis personae* in "denial of medical aid because of religious belief," we are about ready to consider, in Part II, the general problem of religious freedom versus religious license and the meandering boundary line our legislatures and courts have drawn between the two. But we still have made no serious investigation of the performance itself in which two of our three groups specialize. Does faith healing really work? If so, how? As claimed, or in some other way? I shall give the straightest answer I know, but only after considerable beating about the bush—this beating to flush out other preliminary and pertinent considerations such as Jack Benny's lion and Elyria's fluorides; that is to say, as to the real effects of faith and suggestion. Some such: the public health services' tremendous accomplishments against disease; some reasons why people go to faith healers and out-and-out quacks instead of to medical doctors; the concept of "controls" in scientific investigation; "hysteria" or "hysterical symptoms," which, as already noted, are sometimes claimed to be the only symptoms the tent-show healer actually cures; and finally, the attitude one must take toward the unprovable, undisprovable claim of supernatural intervention.

The Christian Scientist who prates of the "unreality of disease" may at the same time well owe his health or indeed his life to his more realistic fellows who daily make safe the foods he eats and the water he drinks, and who by vaccination and sanitation have made unreal in fact the plagues of the past. Yet William Elder, whose efforts resulted in the unattended death of Doreen Watson (Ch. 12), asserted that "much of the credit for the reduction in the mortality from diphtheria in the last twenty years must be given to Christian Science treatment." It is hard for any person at all cognizant of the vast but unpublicized accomplishments in public health to listen with equanimity to such unsupported and irresponsible claims.

The *American Journal of Public Health* in 1944 well stated the case in an editorial titled *Who Killed Cock Robin?* Its theme is that they, the P.H. officers, and not the M.D.s in private practice, killed Cock Robin, i.e., disease; so that one senses a brotherly backstage scuffle, not that it matters for our purpose:

The reduction of the death rate by approximately 40 per cent during the first four decades of the present century is one of the most significant events in human history. In such an achievement, there is glory enough for all. Health officers, public-spirited private practitioners, engineers, nurses, laboratory investigators, social workers, educators have all participated in the task . . . The pertinent points of this record are indicated in the following table:

|  | Death Rate per 100,000 | |
| --- | --- | --- |
|  | 1900 | 1940 |
| Typhoid and paratyphoid fevers | 35.9 | 1.1 |
| Diphtheria | 43.3 | 1.1 |
| Diarrhea and enteritis | 133.2 | 10.3 |
| Measles, scarlet fever and whooping cough | 34.8 | 3.2 |
| Tuberculosis | 201.2 | 45.9 |
| Pneumonia and influenza | 180.5 | 70.3 |
| All other causes | 1126.1 | 944.5 |

In this table are shown the actual results accomplished between 1900 and 1940 in the reduction of mortality from the five causes of death with which the organized health forces of the community have been concerned, and also the corresponding reduction in pneumonia and influenza, where responsibility has been shared [with] the private physician . . . typhoid fever and diphtheria mortality rates have been reduced by 97 per cent. The results accomplished in the case of typhoid fever have been due to the work of the engineer, to purification of the public water supplies, improvement in sanitary conditions, and to epidemiological control and immunization programs, conducted by health officers. In the case of diphtheria, administrative control, and the use of antitoxin and later toxoid, are responsible for the accomplishment . . .

Diarrhea and enteritis of infants has been reduced by 92 per cent through the pasteurization of milk supplies, under the leadership of public health authorities and through the establishment by boards of health and visiting nurse associations of well baby clinics for the instruction of mothers . . .

The group of infectious diseases of childhood, measles, scarlet fever, and whooping cough, have shown a 91 per cent reduction in mortality, due in large part to vigorous and energetic epidemiological control on the part of public health authorities. Tuberculosis, which has been cut down by 77 per cent, represents the result of a program carried on in nearly all its phases through the leadership of public health departments, public health clinics, and publicly maintained sanatoria . . .

In the case of pneumonia and influenza the practising physician deserves a lion's share of the credit. Even here, however, it should be pointed out that the basic discoveries in regard to serum treatment and the use of sulpha drugs were made by salaried physicians in the employ of public health laboratories and foundations and universities, rather than by private practitioners . . .

It is no doubt true that the "Other Causes" . . . are much more difficult to control than those which the public administrator has so successfully attacked; but it may be hoped that a sound system of prepayment which will make good medical care available to the lower economic half of the population, now woefully lacking in such services, would produce notable results in the reduction of many other causes of death than those which have so far been successfully attacked.[2]

Dr Beatrix Cobb, research psychologist at Houston's M. D. Anderson Hospital, asked herself: why do some people in the early stages of cancer detour to nonmedical practitioners, and thereby often change a case that could have been controlled into a fatality? She investigated twenty such cases, found they fell into four groups: 1) The miracle seeker,

the person who is in search of a sure-cure over night. This is the woman who sends for a prayer cloth when she realizes she has cancer of the breast. Just last year one negro woman depended upon her prayer cloth for six months before presenting herself for medical help. She confided that she fully expected each morning to wake to find the fungating mass in her breast gone. In the six months, the disease has progressed to the uncontrollable stage. She now is terminal; she still believes that the failure of the prayer cloth was due to her sins. The prayer cloth was much more intelligible to her than the mysterious x-ray machines to which she was subjected during orthodox treatment. Being left alone in a room, strapped to a table, and prey to the fears aroused by the clicking mechanism was an experience of great trauma to her.

2) The uninformed:

. . . an intelligent man of 42, who had completed high school and a business course, explained his detour as follows: "Well, to tell the truth, I went to a nonmedical practitioner without really knowing what the difference in a M.D. and other people who call themselves doctors is. The only time I remember going to a doctor was when I had my tonsils out. I didn't think too much about doctors. Someone told me this man was good with cancers, and I went."

3) The restless ones:

Another man of 53 became impatient during the two-week diagnostic period required for adequate medical workup and laboratory analysis before initiation of treatment. He withdrew from the clinic and went to a quack, who gave him treatment within the hour. Several months later, he returned somewhat shamefaced to confess: "It just took so long to get anything done here, that I got 'antsy.' You know, when you've got cancer, every minute counts. And when you just sit around waiting for two whole weeks, and all they do is examine you once or twice, and then just stick you every day for a blood test . . . well, us people who don't understand why you don't get something done right now, like your home doctor does when you go to him . . . well, we don't know, and we get impatient, and then just plain mad, and do things we wouldn't do, if we understood."

4) The straw-graspers:

These are the people the doctors have told, "We have done all we can do. There is nothing more medical science can do." Few people can accept such an ultimatum. Many are so constituted that for their own peace of mind, they must continue to try to do something about it . . . The mother of a three-year-old girl in terminal stages took her to a nonmedical practitioner. She explained: "I just couldn't sit down and watch her die. The doctors told me they could do nothing more. I kept hearing about this new shot this man was giving and the success he had with it. I just had to try it. For my own peace of mind, I had to know that I had done everything humanly possible to save her."*3

Dr. Cobb found loyalty to the quack, even in the face of his failure to cure, astonishing. Said one woman:

"They was all so courteous to me, I am going to stay with them no matter what else I do. The last doctor I went to was abrupt to me. He said I was in some stage of cancer and the way he said it scared me to death. Now these———people said, 'Look on the bright side and enjoy life all you can.' This doctor took all the joy out of living because he scared me to death. Now with these———people, I feel safe and happy. I went to the———Clinic because I wasn't getting no satisfaction from my doctors. And well, like I said, I'll stick by them if it is the last thing I do . . ."

The words of the patients in this sample group emphasize the fact that often they were searching for reassurance, for hope, for recovery, for kindness, consideration, and for communication with the doctor so they might understand what was being done for them when they detoured to the quack. The physician, then, must give proper consideration to the panic psychology which drives a person to the quack when the doctor tells him he has done all that is medically possible, and sends him home to die. The physician must understand the impatience engendered through professional reticence to discuss the disease with the patient. The role of the doctor in prevention of detouring behavior, then, seems to be a dual one. The cancer patient seeks not only adequate medical care, but sympathetic emotional support as well.

---

* In February, 1956 an American woman (a Lutheran) flew her seven-year-old son, whom doctors said was dying of acute leukemia, to the shrine in Lourdes, France, hoping for a miraculous cure. A year later, he died. For another example of a "straw-grasper" see the case of the California businessman and Susie Jessel (Ch. 11).4

To Dr. Cobb's account, syndicated columnist Dr. Walter C. Alvarez added a footnote:

Recently I was talking with a patient who, because he wasted hundreds of dollars on stupid treatments by an ignorant quack, has now a very slim chance of being cured of his cancer. When the patient learned that the quack's hocus pocus had probably cost him his life, he was not at all angry. "No," he said. "I still love the fellow. Even though he took all my money and did not cure me, I like him and he likes me a lot. He gave me hope and comfort, and he did something that you doctors never did: Often he would sit down and talk to me for an hour. He would explain things to me so I could understand them. All you M.D.'s did was to examine me again and again. You fellows were never interested in me; you never talked to me and I don't think any of you liked me."[5]

During a drought in Santa Fe, Roman Catholic Archbishop Edwin V. Byrne ordered prayers for rain. A few hours later, it rained. Did the prayers cause the rain? The only way to establish any connection, it seems to me, would be to have archbishops order prayers for rain in a number of drought areas. If, after each such order, it rained a few hours later, we would suspect some causal connection. But even then, the requirements for adequate "controls" would not be met. We should require still other drought areas, where *non*-archbishops would order prayers for rain, and the resulting precipitation, if any, noted. But in all seriousness, the question, did the prayers cause the rain? is not easy to answer.[6]

In medical research, the placebo* is a control. Ten subjects are given capsules of a new drug and ten others are given identical capsules filled with, say, sugar. This is because many people improve when they only *think* (as Phineas Parkhurst Quimby noted) they are getting a new drug. With placebo controls, the actual effect of the drug alone can fairly reasonably be taken as the difference between the changes noted in those who thought they were getting the drug and did, and those who thought they were getting it but didn't. Also, in cases where no other treatment is possible, doctors sometimes deliberately prescribe placebos, aiming thus to reinforce the patient's faith in his recovery— a psychological expedient noted with approval in the British *Lancet*.

In a several-times reprinted essay, Dr. A. J. Carlson answers the question, *What is the Method of Science?*

The principle of the scientific method, in fact, is only a refinement, by analysis and controls, of the universal process of learning by ex-

* Latin for "I shall please"; among doctors, "The humble humbug."

perience. This is usually called common sense. The scientific addition to common sense is merely a more penetrating analysis of the complex factors involved, even in seemingly simple events, and the necessity of numerous repetitions and controls before conclusions are established. Where laymen, as a rule, do not understand or apply the scientific method is in the matter of controls. Thousands of honest errors have been committed and ludicrous conclusions promulgated by failure to understand the necessity of controls. Illustrative instances of this may be cited from the field where I have most experience, namely, physiology and disease. Fortunately, man recovers, as a rule, spontaneously from many diseases, such as colds, pneumonia, typhoid fever, headaches, diarrhea, etc. To be sure, some of these diseases may also lead to death, but if the person having these ailments does not die in the process of the malady, there is more or less complete recovery. Now, if the person not aware of this has the notion handed to him by his father, his priest, or his mythology that holy water, holy oil, an amulet, a prayer, the killing of a goat or the laying on of hands will cure these diseases, experience will teach him that after applying any one or all of these measures to the sick persons many of them do get well. Indeed, applying all these to the sick might be a kind of control because a thinking person might be led to wonder which of these measures was the most potent in reestablishing health, and such questioning might lead him to try whether the person might recover without any of them. But usually this is not done. Those who believe that ill health can be cured by prayer will pray. Those who believe that an amulet is a cure will apply the amulet, and those who have faith in holy oil or laying on of hands will try these methods, and most of the people get well. A true statement of the facts is that sick persons so treated do get well after the treatment. The common error made is that the person recovers because of the treatment. The experience is correct. The conclusion is wrong. There is no control. The obvious control, of course, is a sufficient number of people of the same age with the same malady and none of the above measures applied, and the duration of their illnesses and percentages of recovery contrasted with the treated group. Until consciousness of the necessity of controls in all endeavors to ascertain new truths or in evaluating current theories, dogmas or practices, until this consciousness has become a compelling factor in society, man remains essentially unscientific no matter how much detailed scientific facts he may remember and how much scientific patter he may have absorbed. He is like the rooster who crows every morning before daybreak, notices that a little later the sun rises, and then concludes that it was his crowing which brings the sun above the horizon . . . [7]

According to Dr. Laurance Shaffer,[8] Ronald B. lived in a small town, had a promising voice, and locally was considered to have a great future in opera or on the concert stage. When he was 21, his widowed mother at considerable sacrifice sent him to a large city and an expert teacher. But there, after a slight cold and sore throat, a peculiar soreness and stiffness persisted in his throat muscles, not affecting his speaking voice but definitely spoiling his singing. Two throat specialists failed to find anything physically wrong. When a third diagnosed the disorder as "nervous," Ronald submitted to the counsel of a psychologist. His findings: though Ronald strongly desired to become a great singer and to justify his mother and friends' faith, his voice had been greatly overrated. Under the big-city teacher, who probably recognized Ronald's limitations at once, the quality of his singing had not improved but had deteriorated. He probably sensed he was doomed to failure, but could not face it. Meanwhile, during the actual cold and sore throat, he enjoyed a release from singing for reasons "socially acceptable." Unconsciously, in his blind trial-and-error attempts to solve his problem, he had hit upon retaining the "sore throat"—a particularly easy thing to do, since fear and other emotions commonly tighten the throat muscles. Afterwards, his emotions kept them tight. It was a solution of a sort, one that excused him from admitting failure and that was acceptable to his mother and his friends.

Was Ronald guilty of fraud? Or malingering? No. All he knew was that he had a persisting "sore throat" and could not sing. Only after the psychologist's "detective work" and interpretation could Ronald be "cured." In fact, once he saw the truth, he cured himself. Too, it would not have been enough to convince Ronald that the sore throat was a "tension-reducing defense"; for though his hysterical symptom of a "sore throat" would then likely have disappeared, he likely would have come up with some new symptom for solving his underlying problem. And this—though I am getting ahead of myself—is the objection to the tent-show healer's "quickie" cure of the hysteric. The psychologist's job was to make Ronald face his basic problem: his natural singing talent was limited and he would have to reconsider his vocational aim. This Ronald did. He entered business and found satisfaction there. Later, when he sang as an avocation, there was no trace of the throat contracture.

If the reader still suspects Ronald of conscious malingering, let him consider the young actor who first walks on the stage to speak his lines, but "freezes." His throat muscles are paralyzed. Has he suddenly contracted laryngitis? Of course not; the moment he returns to the wings he will become most vocal in lamenting his failure. Then, is he malingering? No; he wants nothing more than to speak. Nevertheless, he *can't*. That is the hysteric's plight.

Let us go back to the beginning of the psychology book and define "adjustment"—which often is "maladjustment." A man proceeding toward a goal encounters an obstacle; it blocks or "thwarts" him. He accordingly makes a number of intelligent attempts, or blind trial-and-error attempts, or both, to overcome it. The obstacle may be environmental—a locked door, another person contending for the same goal; it may be another conflicting desire within himself; or as in Ronald's case it may be a personal defect. The man may achieve a clean victory or an intelligent abandonment—or, in between, some more or less unsatisfactory pseudo-solution or "maladjustment." Psychologists distinguish five general classes of such maladjustments: 1) adjustments by defense; 2) adjustments by withdrawing; 3) adjustments involving fear and repression; 4) persistent nonadjustive reactions (where attempt and failure continue and the tension is not reduced); and, 5) adjustment by ailments, which include hysteria, and which hysteria, again, includes anaesthesias and motor psychoneuroses (e.g., stammering, writer's cramp, stuttering, and Ronald's throat). Hysterical symptoms are one group of end-results of maladjustment processes.

Given two cases, to all appearances identical, where the symptom is "a paralyzed leg." One may be the result of destruction of nerves by invading germs of syphilis or polio, while the other may represent a hysterical ailment-adjustment like Ronald's throat—a habit formation by which the organism as a whole has "solved" a problem. The first is organic, the second psychological.

Some aches, pains, muscular spasms, weaknesses and paralyses—*some*—result from adjustment to an obstacle by development of a tension-reducing ailment. We cannot say, however, that Ronald's "mind" (today's psychologist will not let you use the word "mind") changed a mental conflict into a physical symptom. It was simply the one "successful" (successful in that it *did* reduce the tension) reaction that his organism as a whole hit upon. It worked, and the organism perpetuated it. Spectacular hysterical seizures resembling epilepsy, where the subject screams, falls and becomes unconscious, are an adjustive ailment: they achieve sympathy or consent from parent or spouse. Unlike true epilepsy, they can be cured by psychological treatment.

When one reads Sidney Bechet's reported statement (Ch. 1) that he was cured of ulcers by a Paris faith healer, there is nothing to do but accept the statement. Bechet ought to know. But does he? Other information may cause us to view the reported event and the principal's psychological makeup in a different light. In this case the information is *Time's* report, a year later, of Bechet's opening at Paris's Olympia music hall:

Backstage on opening night, Sidney's white-thatched head was bent over in pain. "I can't go on," he moaned. "It's my stomach. Get a doctor." "But you're on in ten minutes," pleaded the manager. "I'll never make it," cried Sidney. Then the manager noticed a poster, understood the source of the jazzman's distress: Bechet's name was printed in small type, way down on the list of performers. Quickly he explained that it was all a mistake, and promised to get Sidney better billing. Bechet brightened. "Will I get a private dressing room, too?" "*Absolument!*" agreed the manager hurriedly. "Filled with flowers."

Five minutes later, Sidney Bechet (rhymes with say-hey) was onstage . . . [9]

Superficial treatment, aimed only at rendering the symptom ineffective as a tension-reducer, may quickly eliminate the symptom. But disagreeable confinement for the child who, to avoid school, becomes ill, does not get at the child's basic problem. Superficial treatment of hysterical symptoms by "suggestion" may result in a spectacular cure of the symptom—but not of the underlying problem. As Shaffer says:

A suggestion is a partial or incomplete cue or stimulus which is nevertheless effective in producing a response . . . When receiving advice, the subject weighs or evaluates it and makes a deliberative response of some degree which is in turn the stimulus for action. In suggestion, the subject responds to the stimulation directly, without perceiving the source, significance or value of the action to which it leads . . . Maladjusted persons, especially hysterics, tend to be more suggestible than do those who are well balanced and adjusted . . .

Suggestion is a very inferior therapeutic method. This is certainly true of the practice of removing symptoms by suggestion . . . If the practitioner suggests that the symptoms will disappear at a certain time, or after taking a certain medicine or performing some ritual, the result may be temporarily effective. It is inadequate from a farsighted viewpoint because it leaves the fundamental problem of adjustment untouched. Many techniques employing suggestion may be designated as "repressive therapy," for they prevent the patient from gaining insight into his problem instead of promoting this desirable end. Coué's formula for autosuggestion that "day by day, in every way, I am getting better and better," helped many neurotics for a time, but at the expense of a fundamental understanding of the real bases of the ailments. Christian Science, which denies the reality of illness, is the epitome of a repressive technique. Since expression and insight are the bases of adequate psychotherapy, suggestions that close the way to investigation are worse than merely useless; they are actively antagonistic to the achievment of a real and permanent cure.

But Dr. Shaffer is careful to distinguish one special and significant case. Sometimes, after a person has "solved" a frustrating situation by developing the adjustive ailment of a hysterical symptom, surrounding conditions over which he had no control change in such a favorable way (e.g., a domineering mother-in-law dies) that the frustrating situation itself ceases to exist. Afterwards, the no longer needed symptom persists as a "consistency reaction." To such a person the faith-cure offers an attractive means of getting rid of the useless symptom without loss of self-esteem: in such a case, the faith healer may effect a cure not only spectacular but permanent.

Usually, however, the hysteric is not so lucky. Also, fundamental treatment to get at the underlying cause is not often so easy as in Ronald's case. Likely, the hysteric has had a lifelong favorable experience of solving minor problems in a similar but less obvious way, and the big problem is solved by a spectacular development of the same method. Analysis and treatment are frequently quite prolonged, and success comes only after the patient is brought to see the true situation, and then of his own will readjusts and establishes new habits and goals. Here, Dr. Shaffer notes, religion may play a large and necessary part:

Some groups that combine religious beliefs with the healing of ailments, notably "Christian Science," operate on principles somewhat more fundamental than mere suggestion. There is a great emphasis on a routine of reading and study and on a unified outlook on life. Although differences of opinion may exist as to the value and truth of the doctrines concerned, this is a religious and philosophical problem and not one of science. From the psychological point of view, the individual's integration seems to be improved by the rigorous practice of some faith. He may genuinely effect a readjustment of his personal problems on a religious basis and thereby eliminate the need for the ailment-adjustment.

Granted, then, the faith healer is likely to achieve a superficial cure of the hysteric's paralyzed leg. And granted (more doubtfully) that a strong religious belief may lead to integration and readjustment and thereby eliminate any need for an ailment-adjustment such as a paralyzed leg. But our tolerance suddenly is brought up short when we see our same faith healer confidently proceeding to the *other* leg, the one paralyzed by organic disease. We have Cole's assertion (Ch. 11) that "he could cure locomotor ataxia by Christian Science." And later, on cross-examination, his admission, drawn out only after struggle and evasion, that he would not advise a doctor for a child with pneumonia. As Shaffer puts it:

While various systems of faith-cure are somewhat effective in treating psychological or adjustive disorders, there is no very good evidence that they have an appreciable influence on physical diseases. The great harm done by all faith or religious cures is that they almost universally claim to cure bodily disease. Not understanding the difference between an adjustive pain and one due, say, to cancer, a person may depend futilely on magical methods until it is too late for medical aid.

When Frank Sandford (Ch. 2) was prosecuted for the death of Leander A. Bartlett, 15, the question of the efficacy of healing by faith and prayer—the question of whether or not faith healing works—was put up to the jury to decide. Leander, who lived with his mother in Shiloh's main building, around January 11, 1903 was taken sick, and from day to day grew worse. A week later, he was removed to the community's hospital, where his mother, with the assistance of others, continued to care for him. The hospital was under the superintendence of a woman formerly a physician of the school of osteopathy. On Friday, January 23, she diagnosed diphtheria in an advanced state, but no physician was called, nor were any medical remedies whatever prescribed or used. The reason: the community's belief that the proper treatment of the sick was not by the use of medical remedies but by prayer for recovery after a confession of sin.

All this was under the specific or general direction of Sandford, who absolutely dominated the life of the community and the wills of its members. He was well aware of Leander's precarious condition and apparently held some grudge against him: at a chapel meeting he stated that Leander was "in rebellion," and that he would be glad to see his dead body stretched out before him. (One count, on which Sandford presumably was acquitted, was for death caused by direct assault.) That Friday, a general and absolute fast was ordered, applying to all, sick and well, including Leander. He was denied (though here the testimony was contradictory) food until that Sunday morning, when he died.

Sandford was tried for manslaughter, for criminal negligence. Following the general rule in the absence of a statute, the judge in substance instructed the jury: "When the death of a human being from disease is caused or hastened by reason of the omission to call in a physician, or to provide medicines, when such omission proceeds not from any criminal indifference to the needs of the person, but from a conscientious disbelief as to the efficacy of medicines or medical attendance, it is not criminal negligence, and does not constitute a basis for conviction for manslaughter." Then, doubtless certain that Sandford could not be found guilty under this instruction, yet feeling that *somehow*, Sandford *must* be convicted, he qualified:

That is, it must be conscientious disbelief in medicine—a bona fide disbelief—a real disbelief. And if a person having that disbelief in medicine had some other belief, or some other practice, or some other way to help cure the sick, which he honestly believed, it would then be his duty to apply that other method. And so, if he believed in the prayer of faith, he ought to apply that. But if he failed to use the prayer of faith, unless you believe that the lack of it hastened the death, or caused the death of the patient, the omission to use the prayer of faith would not be criminal negligence, because it did not produce any results. On the other hand, if you believe that the omission to use the prayer of faith did hasten the death of Leander Bartlett, and if that was the honest belief of the defendant and he failed, knowing the circumstances, knowing his duty, why it would constitute a basis for manslaughter, would be evidence of negligence.

The jury rendered a verdict of guilty, but on appeal, Chief Justice Andrew P. Wiswell of the Supreme Judicial Court of Maine reversed Sandford's conviction, holding the instruction as qualified to have been error:

It is undoubtedly true that the question whether or not the respondent resorted to the so called "prayer of faith" for the purpose of effecting the cure of Bartlett, was a proper one for the jury to consider in determining whether or not the failure to resort to medical remedies and to employ the assistance of a physician, was based upon the conscientious disbelief in the efficacy of such remedies. But this instruction, or qualification of the general rule given by the presiding justice, went much further than this. It was in effect, that if the respondent conscientiously believed in the efficacy of prayer for the cure of the sick, rather than in the use of medicines and in the employment of physicians, and failed to resort to this method of cure believed in by him, that this failure would constitute a basis for a conviction of manslaughter, provided the jury believed that it caused or hastened the death of Bartlett.

Thus the conviction or acquittal of the respondent would depend not upon the jury's finding as to the truth of some controverted fact, about which there was evidence for and against, nor even as to the truth of some scientific theory, as to which those specially qualified by study and experience had testified and given their opinion, questions which of course could be submitted to the determination of the jury, but upon the belief of the individual members of a jury upon the efficiency of prayer as a means of cure for the sick, a question about which there is undoubtedly a considerable difference of opinion. Tried by one jury, a respondent would be convicted, while before another, he would be acquitted, upon precisely the same state of facts and the same findings of facts, the result depending entirely upon whether the jury, before which a respondent happened to be tried, entertained one belief or the other upon this question concern-

ing which the testimony of no witness can be offered and the determination of which is outside of the domain of the law.

We do not think the guilt or innocence of any person accused of
crime, whatever his belief may be in this respect, or that the results
of a criminal trial should depend upon the beliefs of the members of
a jury on the question of the efficacy of prayer as a means of cure for
the sick, or upon their religious beliefs in any other respect . . . this
qualification of the rule as given by the court . . . left an opportunity
to the jury to convict the respondent upon their belief as to a matter
which the court cannot determine, and of which it cannot take cognizance . . .

By now, the reader has risen to shout that there has been enough
dancing around the ring and that it is high time for the author to come
to grips with his opponent. But I must beg one last excursion; an inquiry into what may be either the most or least important question of
all—the question which all the laws and courts take excruciating pains
to leave unanswered. Does God actually perform miracles of healing?
Is there really a loving God who on occasion is moved to reach down
and restore the sick to health? Any attempt to investigate the phenomenon of "faith healing" scientifically must start in confusion unless this
question, even if it cannot be answered a flat yes or no, can at least
be properly evaluated—or properly put in its place.

According to Justice Haight, in New York's *Pierson* case (Ch. 10),
some people believe only God's response to prayer heals, others trust
only to doctors, while still others both pray and have doctors. In *Cole*,
Appellate Justice Dowling distinguished a fourth group, the Christian
Scientists, who deny that disease exists; but Justice Clarke made it
clear that no doubts that disease exists were entertained by the State of
New York. I shall waste no words on the question, is disease real?
True, to the theoretical physicist a "solid" brick wall consists largely of
holes; just so, today's researcher in biochemistry and clinical medicine
has a concept of "disease" quite different from the rest of us. But as a
practical matter, when I drive an automobile a "solid" brick wall can
cause my death, and so can the symptoms I have come to identify as
"disease."

Too, as I shall explain in a moment, I do not see that I am forced
to answer any of the questions, 1) Is there a God at all? 2) If there is,
is he a loving God? and 3) if so, is he, on hearing the prayer of faith,
at times moved to reach down and restore the sick to health?

Still, if I were asked the first question above, I would answer, "I
don't know." And to the second, "I see no evidence of a loving God."
Such a god could have prevented war, but has not. Such a god could
have prevented tuberculosis, cancer, infantile paralysis and two-headed

babies, but has not. After a boy's arm was almost burned off, doctors operated twenty-eight times (Ch. 1) and managed to give him "some use from it." This, to me, is a remarkable achievement of *men*—not of God working a miracle, as claimed. Miracle, indeed! A loving God could have fully restored the arm in an instant—or kept it from being burned in the first place! A humble preacher, the Rev. J. J. Ivie (Ch. 12), after faithfully serving his silent God for forty years, finally asked for a sign, a single sign. Finally, when his God did not answer, he vowed to fast until answered. And fifty-one days later, when Ivie died, God still had not answered. How uncomfortably the world watched, how hastily it dismissed from mind this courageous adventurer who gave up his life to establish the answer: "You're on your own."

As to the third, I do not see, for what follows, that I must answer, any more than the courts do, the question, does God actually perform miracles of healing? To explain, I shall draw upon Jack Benny a second time. On the radio, he told how an Oak Ridge workman employed in a top-secret area left each night through "security" trundling a wheelbarrow. This odd exit excited the guards' suspicions, but the man volunteered no explanation. After a few nights of this, they searched the wheelbarrow for secret plans, materials or messages, but found nothing. When the performance continued, the FBI was called in, but its agents could not solve the mystery. Finally, in desperation, the authorities offered the man complete immunity from prosecution if only he would confess what he was up to. He then confessed. He was stealing wheelbarrows.

The story illustrates William of Ockham's "Law of Parsimony," a principle which often has paid off in scientific investigation: *Of two alternate explanations for a given event, choose the simpler.*

I shall, then, explain how "faith healing" is brought about by natural means. Afterwards, to the objection, "But you still haven't proved it is not achieved by supernatural intervention," I shall only answer, "My explanation is simpler." And if the questioner persists, "But do you deny that at times it is supernatural?" I shall only reply, "No—I just don't know."

This attitude should satisfy two of Judge Haight's three groups: those who believe only in doctors and those who believe in both prayer and doctors. To his third and to Dowling's fourth I can only retort: "Show me mortality tables that favor faith healers or Christian Scientists."

Faith healing sometimes appears to work. If so, how? With supernatural intervention, *arguendo,* ruled out, the answer must be: "Through some natural means either set in motion by the healer's and/or patient's faith and prayers, or operating in some other way." In attempting to identify such a process, I first ask generally: What is a "well" man? Then: what things make him sick? And finally: how, afterwards, does he become well again?

The man at the next desk is proceeding ably about some important task. Unlike the smaller and wilder animals, he does not appear preoccupied with personally chasing, capturing and consuming even smaller animals to sustain his life. But in fact he is accomplishing just that, through a complicated arrangement with his fellows whereby each agrees to specialize in some single detail of the total effort, in return for his share of the kill.

Inside, this man is kept going by even more complicated means. A slow-working hormone system, diffusing its chemical messengers into his body fluids, governs and coordinates his long-term processes of growth, nutrition and reproduction; in emergencies it rallies to repair injuries and combat infections. A faster-working autonomous nervous system regulates his circulation, respiration, digestion and temperature. And his central nervous system maintains a keen perception of both the possibilities and the dangers in the outer world, and communicates with the other two at top speed. No one system rules the others, and jurisdiction quickly shifts to cope with circumstances; the three work together under what British surgeon Sir Heneage Ogilvie has termed a "gentlemen's agreement."[10]

This, then, is a "well" man, his internal affairs so efficiently carried on that he scarcely is aware of them, going ably about his task and thereby winning for himself some 68 years of a relatively secure and satisfactory existence. Certain events, however, may "make him sick" and bring his usual activities unwillingly to a halt:

*1) A wound or accident.* His flesh is cut; a dog bites him; he falls and breaks his leg.

*2) Deficient foods; poisons.* Forced to a diet lacking fresh meat and vegetables, he develops scurvy; employed at mixing lead paints, his skin absorbs the poisonous lead, which paralyzes the muscles of his forearms.

*3) A defecting organ or process.* His pancreas fails to secrete the insulin which enables his body to utilize sugar as food, so that he becomes diabetic, emaciated and finally lapses into a coma.

*4) An invasion of small, hostile, living creatures.* Airborne diphtheria bacilli settle in his throat and there produce a poison which, passing into his blood, acts upon his nervous system and heart to produce the symptoms (Ch. 12) exhibited by Doreen Watson.

*5) Stress diseases.* Primitive man's rage on encountering a rival and his fear on encountering a lion both accelerated his secretion of adrenin and inhibited his digestion. This increased his heart action, expanded his peripheral blood vessels, sent blood to his arms and legs, decreased muscular fatigue and promoted blood clotting. All these things readied him for imminent fight or flight. Modern man, encountering problems he can neither physically fight nor flee from, still is triggered to that same making ready; constant worry or unrelieved anxiety often brings on that same, but now less than useless preparation. His hormone system then works overtime to increase this unneeded resistance until, worn out, it begins to malfunction, upsetting his body's chemistry and producing high blood pressure, heart and kidney disease, rheumatoid arthritis, asthma, diabetes or duodenal ulcers.

6) *Hysterical symptoms.* Frustrating adjustment problems may be pseudo-solved by achieving a tension-reducing maladjustment such as Ronald's "sore throat" or a great deal worse: hysterical club foot, paralysis, deafness, lameness or blindness. And finally:

7) *Any one of the above may open the door to another.* The open wound of "1" makes entry easy for the germs of "4." The intake of deficient fuels of "2" may cause the defecting organ or process of "3." And the greatest "door opener" of all may be the stress of "5."

In all these ways, a well man is made sick. How, afterwards, does he become well again?

The cut, bite and broken bone of "1" are healed by the ability of the torn or broken parts, under the direction of the hormone system, and using the ordinary techniques of growth, to grow back together again— *nothing else heals them.* The physician, if called in, does *not* cause the healing—except that he causes the sides of the torn flesh and the ends of the broken bone to be held together so that they have the *chance* to grow back together again. His presence, however, is well justified. He will take pains to forestall the possibility of the infection of "4." If there is any chance that the deadly virus of lockjaw already has entered, he will administer an antidote. Or if there is any suspicion of rabies, he will start the Pasteur treatment. And he sets the patient's mind at rest. It is only this last that the faith healer, if called in instead, accomplishes, but when the hurt heals, as it usually does, he loudly claims credit—or, when an occasional patient dies of lockjaw or hydrophobia, asserts that only the patient was to blame for lacking complete faith.

The condition of scurvy of "2," caused by deficient foods, clearly needs a trained observer, the doctor, able first to recognize the condition for what it is, and afterwards to prescribe the lacking food elements. Confronted with the symptom of "wrist-drop" paralysis, the physician may not at first glance be able to tell whether he has an organic or a psychological case. But when he detects anemia, or sees a blue lead line on the patient's gums, or is told he is a painter, the doctor at once suspects lead poisoning. The faith healer prays . . .

Unable to repair the defecting pancreas of "3," the physician does the next best thing: he teaches the diabetic the chore of daily injection with insulin to make up for his body's lack of it. Here, the diabetic's recourse to one of Cole's colleagues, to whom "all diseases are alike," is nothing short of suicidal.

When the invading diphtheria bacilli of "4" start to send their poison into the bloodstream, the body's hormone system sets desperately about manufacturing an antidote. In about half the unattended cases the hormone system wins; in the other half the bacilli win. Up to 1895, when antitoxin first was produced in quantity (in horses), diphtheria was the greatest killer of children. But here, though the faith healer did no good at all, he still could claim success for *fifty per cent* of his cases!

Against invasion by various other germs—measles, mumps, the common cold—the body, if left alone, will almost always win out. In such cases the faith healer, if in attendance, will claim credit. But when the faith healer undertakes to treat lockjaw, hydrophobia or bubonic plague, death is certain. The pages of this study offer courtroom and newspaper testimony enough that faith healing and Christian Science have failed to cure diphtheria, typhoid fever, pneumonia and tuberculosis.

As to "5" where unrelieved anxiety has overstressed the body's resistance and already produced physical ills, the physician has three points of attack. He may try to relieve the emotions, try to derail the process operating between emotions and resulting physical ailment, or treat the resulting ailment directly. In the case of an inflamed appendix, ready to burst at any moment, he does not pause to inquire how it got that way, but removes it at once. In the case of duodenal ulcer he may concentrate on "derailment," attempting by chemistry to restore the balance of the body's chemical processes, or by surgery to remove an overproducing gland. But when he in his role of psychologist attempts by reason to balance the prime cause of the disturbance—the worry or anxiety—he is likely to run a poor second to Sidney Bechet's "Paris faith healer" and his brethren.

Where the faith healer comes into his own is with the hysterical symptom of "6." In the special case where the symptom is one whose utility is past, suggestion may, as already noted, effect a spectacular and permanent cure. But where the underlying cause continues, the cure will be only temporary, and a new ailment-adjustment will soon be hit upon. Here the only true cure lies in the psychologist's labor of unearthing the cause and the patient's then recognizing and adjusting to it. At the same time, whatever a man's problems, the sudden acquisition of a strong religious faith is likely to effect such a change in his aims and values as at once to establish a new mental equilibrium wherein the former drives and accompanying anxieties no longer exist. But here we have gone beyond the faith healer and are considering the total effect of religious conviction on personality.

In all these ways, then, is a sick man made well: by, first of all, the body's own remarkable ability, without any outside help at all, to heal itself; secondly, by the doctor's measures of hygienic therapy and specifics; and thirdly by psychiatry-achieved or religion-achieved "psychological equanimity." The explanation for the apparent success in some cases of "faith healing" should now be clear: *some such cases are explainable merely as a statistically false conclusion, ignoring all negative instances; while the "legitimate" ones are the result of the psycho-physical process set in motion by the belief.*

But here, as clearly, is the final danger in "faith healing": that one converted to the belief by seeing or experiencing its cures or temporary cures of psychological symptoms, or its apparent cures in what are in fact self-curing ailments, thereby is led to conclude its infallibility on *all* fronts, and thereafter stands ready to pit his belief against the deadly diseases as well—the deadly killers that have little regard for "psychological equanimity"—diphtheria, pneumonia, all the insect-carried plagues, the "Rh" blood condition, rabies, tetanus—where only a fool would reject the swift antidotes of modern medical science, and the faith healer's belief will not protect him at all. Truly, the convert to faith healing lives in a fool's haven from reality.

*Part II*

# THE CONSTITUTION

# 6

# The Peep-Stone Operator
# and the Carpenter[1]

*ARTICLE I.*
*Congress shall make no law respecting an establishment*
*of religion, or prohibiting the free exercise thereof; or*
*abridging the freedom of speech or of the press; or the*
*right of the people peaceably to assemble and to petition*
*the Government for a redress of grievances.*

> —The First Amendment to
> the Constitution of the
> United States of America.
> In force December 15, 1791.

Suppose that in a certain state a new sect arises, one divinely dedicated to hacking off non-members' heads. The state, with no statute against this unlikely practice, hastily enacts one. The sect members, however, continue to hack, and when the state remonstrates, they are indignant: their practice is commanded by God and therefore above earthly laws. They point out, furthermore, that the statute is unconstitutional because it prohibits their free exercise of religion. And they invite their would-be prosecutors to reread the First Amendment to the Constitution of the United States, which plainly states, *"Congress shall make no law respecting an establishment of religion, or prohibiting the free exercise thereof."* If the example appears ridiculous, let us strike out "state" and "head-hacking" and substitute "remote new territory" and "polygamy." The proposition now is hardly hypothetical: our grandfathers faced it, and in their solution the above clause of the First Amendment came in for considerable reassessment.

Sidney Rigdon was born in Pennsylvania in 1793. At 26 he became a Baptist pastor in Pittsburgh, there met evangelist Walter Scott of the Disciples of Christ—the "Campbellites"—and was drawn to their view that no existing church was in accord with the Scriptures. He did re-

93

vival work for them with great success. But in 1828, to Rigdon's Scrip-ture-backed argument for a community of goods, Alexander Campbell countered that the apostles sold their goods. Campbell's argument car-ried, and embittered Rigdon. "I have done as much in this reformation as Campbell or Scott," he told his brother, "and yet they get all the honor of it."

Some years before, in the Pittsburgh printing office of a Mr. Patter-son, Rigdon had become interested in, and had made a copy of a manu-script submitted to Patterson by one Solomon Spaulding for considera-tion for publication. Born in Connecticut in 1761, Spaulding had been a preacher, had conducted an academy, and later had an interest in an iron foundry in Conneaut, Ohio, where in 1812, Spaulding's men had dug into some ancient mounds and exhumed human bones, parts of gigantic skeletons, and relics. These inspired Spaulding to write a fanci-ful history, "Manuscript Found," which his brother later described as

> an historical romance of the first settlers of America, endeavoring to show that the American Indians are the descendants of the Jews, or the lost tribe. It gave a detailed account of their journey from Jerusalem, by land and sea, till they arrived in America, under the command of Nephi and Lehi. They afterwards had quarrels and con-tentions, and separated into two distinct nations, one of which he denominated Nephites, and the other Lamanites . . .

Patterson returned the manuscript to Spaulding, who afterwards moved to Amity, Pennsylvania, where he died in 1816. Sidney Rigdon was acknowledged to be "a thorough biblical scholar, a man of fine education and a powerful orator." He likely was acquainted with the story of the thirteenth-century monk Cyril, who received from an angel a divine revelation engraved on copper plates. This revelation was made known to the Abbot Joachim, who thereon founded his "Ever-lasting Gospel"—an expression often used by Rigdon (Rev. 14:6). Joachim offered it to the church to replace the New Testament, thus causing a serious schism against which Pope Alexander IV took severest measures. Rigdon could have read of Cyril and Joachim in the abridg-ment of Mosheim's *Ecclesiastical History, Ancient and Modern,* pub-lished in Philadelphia in 1812, according to which:

> About the commencement of this [the thirteenth] century there were handed about in Italy several pretended prophesies of the fa-mous Joachim, abbot of Sora in Calabria, whom the multitude revered as a person divinely inspired, and equal to the most illustrious prophets of ancient times. The greatest part of these predictions were contained in a certain book entitled, 'The Everlasting Gospel,' and

which was also commonly called the Book of Joachim. This Joachim, whether a real or fictitious person we shall not pretend to determine, among other future events, foretold the destruction of the Church of Rome, whose corruptions he censured with the greatest severity, and the promulgation of a new and more perfect gospel in the age of the Holy Ghost, by a set of poor and austere ministers, whom God was to raise up and employ for that purpose.

During the winter of 1827–1828, Rigdon in his preaching "contended ably for the restoration of the true, original apostolic order which would restore to the church the ancient gospel as preached by the apostles. The interest became an excitement; . . . the air was thick with rumors of a 'new religion,' a 'new Bible.'" His brother-in-law, Adamson Bentley, wrote: "Sidney Rigdon told me there was a book coming out, the manuscript of which had been found engraved on gold plates, as much as two years before the Mormon book made its appearance." Said Darwin Atwater, a Disciples elder:

For a few months before his professed conversion to Mormonism it was noticed that his wild extravagant propensities had been more marked. That he knew before the coming of the book of Mormon is to me certain from what he said during the first of his visits at my father's, some years before. He gave a wonderful description of the mounds and other antiquities found in some parts of America, and said that they must have been made by the aborigines. He said there was a book to be published containing an account of those things.

According to an Ohio physician, Dr. Storm Rosa: "In the early part of the year 1830 I was in company with Sidney Rigdon, and rode with him on horseback for a few miles . . . He remarked to me that it was time for a new religion to spring up; that mankind was all right and ready for it." By 1827, Rigdon apparently had made the acquaintance of one Joe Smith, a "money-digger" and "peep-stone" operator of considerable but dubious fame.

Joseph Smith, Jr., was born in Sharon, Vermont, in 1805. His family was poor, uneducated, and given to frequent moves. Between farming failures his father dug for Captain Kidd's treasure and others, believed in witchcraft, was a "dowser," and was implicated in a counterfeiting venture from which he escaped penalty by turning state's evidence. In 1816 the family moved to New York State, finally settling on a farm near Palmyra. At fourteen, Joe was proficient with a "peep-stone": for a fee he would put the stone in his hat, put his face against the brim, and either tell fortunes or see in the stone the location of lost or stolen articles or buried treasure. The whole family often set out on

Joe-directed "money-digging" expeditions; on one occasion he directed the digging of fourteen men. One difficulty: sooner or later one of the diggers, tempted by the Devil, would break the rule of absolute silence, causing an "enchantment" which removed the almost-reached treasure to a different spot. Such enchantments could be prevented by sprinkling on the ground the blood of a perfectly white dog, but extensive search failed to locate a perfectly white dog.

The Smiths worked for hire when and where they could, sometimes in Pennsylvania, where Joe enlarged his repertoire to include "praying" frost from cornfields. In Susquehanna County, he met and courted Emma Hale. In 1827, after her father, because of Joe's reputation, refused to consent to the marriage, Emma and Joe eloped. After marriage by a justice of the peace, Joe took Emma to his father's farm. When he returned to the Hales' for Emma's belongings, Mr. Hale in tears begged Joe to give up his deceptions and offered to help start him in business. Joe agreed, but on his return his family opposed the resolution and urged him to continue with his peep-stone. Some days later, Joe came home with a peep-stone-located bundle. The bundle, Joe announced, contained a "Golden Bible," which none but himself could look upon and live.

Local farmer Martin Harris, who by his own account had talked with Jesus and visited the moon, advanced fifty dollars toward translation of the "Bible." With this, Joe and Emma moved to Harmony, Pennsylvania. There, with the help of Harris and a "mysterious visitor," Joe, behind a blanket and using his peep-stone, began dictating the "translation." Later, Emma served as his scribe, as, still later, did blacksmith-teacher Oliver Cowdery. In 1829, before completing the translation, Smith and Cowdery went into the woods, where John the Baptist appeared and conferred upon them the priesthood of Aaron. Smith then baptised Cowdery, after which Cowdery baptised Smith. Smith's resulting status: he was God's Prophet and mouthpiece; to him it had been revealed that all existing churches were in error; he had been chosen to reestablish God's "true church" on earth. Soon the pair converted Smith's brothers, Samuel and Hyrum, and others.

The translation was completed in June of 1829; five thousand copies were printed and bound early in 1830. This was the *"Book of Mormon: An Account Written by the Hand of Mormon, Upon Plates Taken from the Plates of Nephi . . . By Joseph Smith, Junior, Author and Proprietor"*—some 275,000 words in 600-odd pages of fine print. It was, Smith explained, the new expression of the everlasting Gospel. Debunker Mark Twain later called it "chloroform in print." Smith, Sr., at once set out to sell the books. The $3,000 cost was met by Harris, whose wife meanwhile had secured a legal separation with a division of property, and had entered a complaint against Joe charging him with obtaining money from her husband on fraudulent representation. But at the hearing, Harris denied that he ever had contributed a dollar to Joe at the latter's persuasion.

Prophet Smith proceeded to cast out a devil from one Newell Knight. When Knight's young sister-in-law announced her conversion, her Presbyterian pastor tried to prevent her baptism by force, but failed. At Smith's resulting trial for disorderly conduct, testimony showed that he had obtained a horse and yoke of oxen by "revelation" and had "behaved improperly" toward several local girls; but the prosecution failed.

The first church conference, effecting formal organization with Smith as president, was held at Fayette, New York, on April 6,* 1830. That October, Cowdery and others set out as missionaries. Cowdery went directly to Rigdon's house in Kirtland, Ohio, where Rigdon, ostensibly viewing the new "Bible" for the first time, openly expressed his doubts as to its truth, but after so warning his congregation, allowed Cowdery to preach. Two days later, Rigdon announced he had been visited by an angel and converted. This strategy resulted in many local conversions. Cowdery there announced the boundaries of the "Promised Land": Kirtland township on the East; the Pacific Ocean on the West. Cowdery and associates then journeyed through Missouri and into the adjacent Indian country, where, stopped by Federal officers, they returned to Independence, Missouri.

That December, Rigdon first openly visited Smith. Because of the new belief's ready acceptance by Rigdon's Ohio followers, and because of the hostility where Smith was personally known, the conference resulted in Smith's "revealing" that the church's gathering place should be Ohio. At Kirtland, Smith reinstituted "speaking in tongues." The elders began to perform miracles, soon claiming to have made the deaf hear, the blind see, to have put dislocated bones into place, to have cured leprosy and cholera, and to have "rebuked" fevers. But after Rigdon assured a man with consumption that he would recover, the man died. Smith and Rigdon persuaded a sick child's parents to trust in prayer instead of calling a physician; the child died; the pair then promised that it would rise from the dead, but it did not. Later, Smith denied that he ever had performed miracles or had claimed such powers.

That winter, Kirtland experienced extravagant religious exhibitions. By the spring of 1831 there were over a thousand converts. All males became "elders": that February, the Lord, through Smith, commanded

---

* Some sources indicate June.

all elders except Rigdon and Smith to go forth, two by two, into the Western countries, preaching the gospel and building up churches. Thus began a highly successful system of proselyting which soon extended to Canada and Europe. In June, after receiving Cowdery's report, Smith and Rigdon visited Independence, a frontier town with a brick courthouse, two or three stores and fifteen or twenty log houses. There they laid the cornerstones of the "City of Zion" and its "Temple," then returned to Kirtland. But having seen the privations to which Missouri border settlers must submit, they decided to concentrate for the time being on a permanent settlement in Ohio. The church there grew rapidly, but along with its conversions came apostasy and "exposures" of Smith's methods, together with rumors of immoral practices. On the night of March 25, 1832, while Smith and Rigdon were at a farm, a mob tarred and feathered them. Next morning, while the older and less hardy Rigdon lay delirious, Smith, his flesh "all scarified and defaced . . . preached to the congregation as usual."

Smith caused the church to open a general store and establish a steam sawmill and tannery. All lost money. An elaborate street plan for Kirtland was laid out; disastrous land speculation followed. Smith commanded a stone church, 60 by 80 feet in plan. Completed in 1836, it left the church deeply in debt. For funds, Smith commanded his followers: "Thou shalt consecrate all thy properties, that which thou hast, unto me, with a covenant and a deed which cannot be broken."

Meanwhile, missionaries were directing enthusiastic converts to the Missouri Zion. By the summer of 1833, 1,200 Mormons had arrived and settled in and around Independence, making up a third of the population of Jackson County. The new arrivals openly boasted that they soon would possess the land, but "Gentiles" who offered to sell found the Mormons had no money. Worst of all, Independence's Mormon *Star* invited free Negroes and Mulattoes from other states to become Mormons and join them in slaveholding Missouri—an event certain to arouse unrest and rebellion among the Gentiles' slaves. With no recourse to law, the non-Mormon residents organized and announced by manifesto their intent to drive the Mormons out. Soon they resorted to violence, stoning and shooting into Mormon houses at night and burning haystacks. In July of 1833, after Mormon leaders refused to agree to move, a mob razed the *Star* office and tarred and feathered two leaders. The Mormons appealed to the Governor; he advised them to secure a warrant from a justice of the peace. But when Mormons caught a Missourian in the act of destroying their property and took him before a Gentile justice, they were themselves jailed for false imprisonment. They now armed and organized. Numerous small "battles" ensued. But outnumbered and believing they could not long hold out, most of the colony, in November of 1833, fled across the Missouri River to Clay County.

In Kirtland, the following May, Prophet Smith "revealed" that the Zion of Jackson County was to be redeemed; to that end he and Rigdon recruited some 200 men, the "Army of Zion," and marched into Missouri. But that June, cholera broke out among them, Smith's attempts at miraculous cures failed, and thirteen died. Smith accordingly had another revelation: the redemption was to be delayed, and the "army" disbursed.

They had called themselves "Saints" and their church "My Church" and the "Church of Christ." On Rigdon's motion, at a council held in 1834, the official title became *"Church of Jesus Christ of Latter-Day Saints."* In Kirtland, Smith in 1835 caused the church to set up several mercantile establishments, securing goods from eastern firms on six-months' notes. A great part went to pay the workmen on the Temple, and much was sold on credit. Attacks on Smith's character and actions continued: he was charged with directing two followers to kill one Grandison Newell, a seceding Mormon, but on formal hearing was discharged for lack of evidence. Another charge: improper conduct toward an orphan girl whom Mrs. Smith had taken into the family. The *Book of Doctrine and Covenants,* published in Kirtland in 1835, set forth that: "Inasmuch as this Church of Christ has been reproached with the crime of fornication and polygamy, we declare that we believe that one man should have one wife . . ."

Desperate for funds, Smith, Hyrum, Rigdon and Cowdery in July, 1836, journeyed to Salem, Massachusetts, to rent a house where Smith had heard treasure was buried. But the "money-digger" failed to find it. Smith then tried to set up a bank. Cowdery went to Philadelphia and had printed $200,000 in bills of the "Kirtland Safety Society Bank." When the Ohio legislature refused a charter, Smith had the word "Bank" stamped on either side to read "ANTI-BANK-ING CO." Subscribers for stock were allowed to pay in town lots. In 1837, Smith and Rigdon were indicted for violating the banking law. Convicted that October, they appealed on the ground that the institution was an association, not a bank. Pressed by creditors, the bank that November suspended payments and closed its doors. On the evening of January 12, 1838, before the appeal had been argued, hearing a rumor (later proved unfounded) that a warrant had been issued for their arrest on a charge of fraud, Smith and Rigdon fled from Kirtland on horseback.

The aim of the Mormon Church—not an unusual aim for a new sect—was to establish an absolute, priest-ruled church-community which would expand and take over the United States and then the rest of the world. Being the only true religion, this aim was justified and right. It held out an irresistible appeal to the hopelessly "have-nots," justifying immediate action to improve their economic status at the expense of their better-off neighbors, plus eternal salvation afterwards. They were God's chosen people, Prophet Smith their Moses, and the whole country their Canaan.

In Clay County, Missouri, in spite of such tenets, peace prevailed for three years, but by the spring of 1836 the natives had become as hostile as those of Jackson County. In June, at a public meeting in Liberty, they demanded the Mormons leave; on July 1, the Mormons agreed. They moved north to Ray County—from which Caldwell County, an almost unsettled territory, was formed for their use. Around "Far West" (later Kerr), the county seat, a going community of Mormons sprang up. Here, at a conference in 1837, the "First Presidency" was established, consisting of Smith, Hyrum and Rigdon. And here Smith, fleeing from Kirtland, joined them in March of 1838.

At Far West, that May, Smith by revelation instituted tithing—Smith and Rigdon excepted. Here, at about this time, originated the dread secret society of Danites, pledged to any deed of murder or vengeance the Prophet might require. Smith at once pushed for expansion; at his order, towns were started up in adjacent counties. On July 4, the cornerstone of the third "Temple" was laid, and Rigdon preached a sermon that blazed with defiance against all non-Mormons. Published, this fanned anti-Mormon sentiments to an election-day fight in Gallatin, Daviess County, to where Smith and Rigdon promptly marched with 150 volunteers, but arrived too late. For this armed entry, warrants were issued for the leaders' arrest; after their return, a formidable number of Missourians gathered to see that the arrests were carried out. On advice of counsel, Smith and others surrendered and were bound over in $500 bail for a hearing on September 7. By September, Daviess and Caldwell counties were fortified camps of Mormons and Gentiles. Armed bands from both sides began to ride out, looting and burning; a period of absolute lawlessness followed. Smith announced the Mormon purpose: to drive out all non-Mormons from the two counties. Alarmed, Governor Boggs directed General John B. Clark to ride with 400 men to protect the citizens of Daviess County, his order of October 27 instructing: "The Mormons must be treated as enemies, and must be exterminated or driven away from the State if necessary for the public peace—their outrages are beyond all description."

On October 31, with the militia drawn up outside Far West, the terms of surrender were sent in: the Mormons to give up their leaders for trial and punishment; the others to leave the State under protection of the militia. Smith, Rigdon and others surrendered and were taken to Richmond, then to Liberty, where they were held on charges of treason. Rigdon soon was released and went to Quincy, Illinois, where there existed a Mormon colony. To Quincy, most of the others from Far West now migrated. On April 6, 1839, Smith was taken to Daviess County for trial, where he and four others were indicted for murder, treason, burglary, arson, larceny, theft and stealing, but secured a change of venue to Boone County, 120 miles east. On the way, they escaped their captors and arrived at Quincy on April 22.

In Illinois, the Mormons found a surprising welcome: they would be qualified as voters for the coming year's Presidential election. The Quincy Democratic Association issued a report strongly favoring them and condemning their treatment by Missouri. Too, in Hancock County to the north (population 438) there was a great deal of land to be sold. There, under Smith's guidance, the Mormons bought around tiny "Commerce," renamed it Nauvoo, and this by revelation became the third "Zion." In November, Smith journeyed to Washington, where he unsuccessfully sought federal aid from President Van Buren to secure redress from Missouri. In 1840, Smith, intimating a divine revelation, caused the Mormons to vote for Whig Harrison. Hancock County gave him a 752 majority and thus demonstrated the Mormons' political weight. Representatives of both parties now became anxious to show them favor, and this directly caused the granting of the notorious Nauvoo charter—a charter which soon allowed Nauvoo to become in many respects a state within a state. One of the Nauvoo Council's ordinances: no writ issued outside of Nauvoo for the arrest of a person within that city should be executed until approved by the Mayor; violators to be liable to life imprisonment and with no pardon in the Governor without the Nauvoo Mayor's consent.

Nauvoo being a pioneer town, the numerous river pirates, horse thieves, counterfeiters and miscellaneous desperadoes operating along the Mississippi soon found valuable protection in being baptised into the faith and staying there—for Nauvoo defended its flock. The town became receptacle for their stolen goods. Too, the Mormons' religion-fostered disregard for Gentile property rights soon incited hostilities with their Illinois neighbors. Warned Smith in 1840:

> We are no longer at war, and you must stop stealing. When the right time comes, we will go in force and take the whole state of Missouri. It belongs to us as our inheritance; but I want no more petty stealing . . .

No non-Mormon could hope to recover stolen property in Nauvoo. One Gentile traced a stolen horse there and brought 60 witnesses before a Mormon justice to identify the animal; the accused promptly produced *seventy* "Saints" to swear the horse was a Mormon's. When an outsider was discovered looking for stolen property, a Saint would silently follow him, whittling at a stick with a long knife; if the man persisted in his search, he soon would find himself fairly surrounded by silent "whittlers."

On May 6, 1842, a would-be assassin severely wounded Missouri Governor Boggs; a Danite was indicted as agent, and Smith as instigator. Missouri authorities requested extradition and Smith was arrested on the Illinois Governor's warrant, whereupon the Nauvoo Municipal Court released him on its own writ of *habeas corpus*—a gross assumption of power which aroused indignation throughout Illinois. The Governor offered $200 for his arrest, and Smith went into hiding. In December, after Rigdon obtained an opinion, Smith finally surrendered. Taken on a writ of *habeas corpus* before the U.S. District Court at Springfield, he was held not a fugitive from Missouri, and discharged.

On all evidence, the doctrine of plural marriage was the offspring not of Rigdon, who scripted most of Smith's pronouncements, but of Smith himself, its original aim no loftier than the unrestricted indulgence of his passions. Indeed, it was Rigdon's determined resistance to this doctrine that embittered first Smith, then Young ( I am coming to Young) against him. By now, there were rumors enough that the prophet and a few intimates were in the habit of "marrying" the wives of Mormons absent on missions. Two facts: 1) Smith sent Orson Pratt to England, then tried unsuccessfully to seduce his wife; 2) Smith tried to seduce Rigdon's unmarried daughter Nancy; she fled to her father, and Smith, faced with incontrovertible proof, said he only had wished to ascertain whether she was virtuous or not. The "revelation" sanctioning plural marriages is dated July 12, 1843. Smith dared not then proclaim it publicly but taught it in confidence, urging his associates to surrender themselves to God in this matter for their salvation.

On February 15, 1844, Smith announced his candidacy for President of the United States. Three weeks later, he named Rigdon as his running mate for Vice President. Two or three thousand missionaries, including Brigham Young and others of Smith's ablest allies, at once set out for the Eastern and Southern states to campaign. Yet even with this bold move under way, Smith apparently realized how untenable was the Mormon position in Illinois, writing as he did in his diary:

Feb. 20, 1844. I instructed the Twelve Apostles to send out a delegation and investigate the locations of California and Oregon, and hunt out a good location where we can remove to after the [Nauvoo] Temple is completed, and where we can build a city in a day, and have a government of our own . . .

Meanwhile, the rumored "spiritual wife doctrine" and other evils led to serious dissention. Opponents established the Nauvoo *Expositor*. The newspaper's first—and last—issue was published June 7. It set forth Smith's methods to induce women who had come from other countries to become his "spiritual" wives, and opposed his candidacy for President. Smith at once convened the City Council, which promptly found the *Expositor* a "public nuisance" and ordered it destroyed. On June 10, while four thousand Nauvoo Legion troops commanded by "Lieut. General" Smith stood by, the order was carried out. Fleeing to Carthage, the *Expositor's* owners sued out a writ for the removal to there of Smith and his Councillors on a charge of riot. The Nauvoo Municipal Court set the writ aside.

Afterwards, non-Mormons met at Warsaw, Hancock County, and resolved to drive all Mormons from surrounding settlements into Nauvoo, to demand the surrender of Smith and others, and, if not given, to wage on the Mormons "a war of extermination." One hundred and fifty men were mustered for the "war." Urged to call out the militia, Governor Ford on June 17 visited Carthage and sent word to Smith to surrender himself and associates on the riot charge, warning that otherwise he would use the State's entire militia to secure them. On June 24 they surrendered. Three days later, while two militia companies guarded the Carthage jail, a party of men with blackened faces entered and shot Prophet Smith and Hyrum dead.

Brigham Young was born in Vermont in 1801. At sixteen he was working as a carpenter, painter and glazier. He first saw a Mormon Bible in 1830, at a brother's house. Influenced by the Mormon elders' preaching, he was baptised in 1832 and began to preach. That autumn, visiting Kirtland, he first saw the Prophet. From there he went on foot to Canada, where he preached and brought back a company of converts. In 1834 he accompanied Smith's cholera-plagued "Army of Zion" as a "captain of ten," then worked on church buildings in Kirtland. When Smith and Rigdon fled Ohio to Far West, Young followed. In 1840 he sailed for Liverpool for a year's mission. By the time of the Prophet's murder, Young had become head of the Twelve Apostles.

With news of their candidate's death, the campaigners returned to

Nauvoo. Rigdon, now the only surviving member of the church-presidency, at once declared to a meeting of the Twelve that in a vision he had been ordained the Prophet's spokesman. But next day at a special meeting, Young, long determined to drive Rigdon from the Church, argued against his claim and for supreme authority of the Twelve. Young won. In September, he brought Rigdon to "trial" before the High Council, charging that Rigdon believed himself to hold authority above any other man in the Church. Rigdon was cut off. He returned to Pittsburgh, where he attempted to set up a church with himself as "First President, Prophet, Seer, Revelator, and Translator," but failed. During the winter of 1844–1845, charges of stealing became more frequent. Young warned: "Elders who go to borrowing horses or money, and running away with it, will be cut off from the church without any ceremony. They will not have as much lenity as heretofore."

In January of 1845, the Illinois legislature finally repealed Nauvoo's charter. Mormons became more hostile than ever against their neighbors. Daring murders across the river in Iowa were charged to the Danites. On April 8, Governor Ford wrote Young in confidence: "If you can get off by yourselves you may enjoy peace," and suggested California. On September 16, Gentile Phineas Wilcox, in Nauvoo to have his wheat ground, but apparently suspected of being a Gentile spy, simply disappeared. The pattern of shootings and burnings began again. Mormons who had been burnt out assembled in Nauvoo, from where they sallied to ravage the countryside. But again they realized their position was hopeless. In September, they agreed to move the following spring. During that winter, a measure of peace was maintained by the Governor's militia. Early in February, 1846, the Mormons began crossing the Mississippi with their livestock and wagons. There was fighting in July. On September 11, 700 anti-Mormons laid seige to Nauvoo. They entered the city on September 17. By next day, the last Mormon had fled.

On the Iowa side, companies of 50 to 60 wagons were organized. Young and the leading party set off for their first objective, 400-mile-distant Council Bluffs, which they reached in June. Here and at intermediate camps, some 12,000 Mormons endured the winter of 1846–1847. On April 14, 1847, Young's band of 142 men, 3 women and 2 children started on for the Rockies, blazing a trail for the others. They did not know their destination and did not decide until, in July, Orson Pratt and Erastus Snow, scouting ahead, first looked down on the Salt Lake valley.

Here, by themselves, in a region only nominally ruled by Mexico, was the Mormons' big chance to establish their church-state. Under

Young's driving, a city was quickly laid out, the church organization perfected and a scheme of European immigration worked out. But on July 4, 1848, their hope of living in effect under their own government went glimmering, when, with the end of the War (1846–1848) with Mexico, the Treaty of Guadalupe Hidalgo gave the territory to the United States. Young and his community now faced either territorial rule by the federal government as soon as Congress should act, or the possibility, if the Mormons acted quickly enough, of being admitted to the Union as a new state. The latter was infinitely more desirable. They planned accordingly. Recruiting efforts were stepped up to increase the population to that required for statehood. Every possible device was resorted to, to bring more "Saints" to Utah, as well as to drive out non-Mormons. On October 9, 1849, the New York *Tribune* published an account by a correspondent who had passed through Salt Lake City that July on his way to California:

> There are no hotels, because there had been no travel; no barber shops, because every one chose to shave himself and no one had time to shave his neighbor . . . mechanics' shops . . . tailors, etc. . . . needed no sign . . . they were crowded with business. Besides their several trades, all must cultivate the land or die; [there was] no cultivation but their own within 1000 miles. Every one had his lot and built on it; every one cultivated it, and perhaps a small farm in the distance . . . good bridges were erected over the principal streams, and the country settlements extended nearly 100 miles up and down the valley.

On March 4, 1849, Young set up his provisional government, the "State of Deseret" (Mormon for "honeybee"). That December, through Stephen Douglas, "Deseret" applied to Congress for admission to the Union. But Congress, already engaged at legislation to establish a territorial government, ignored the application. One reason: a petition by the citizens of Lee County, Illinois, charging Deseret's organizers with treason, murder, robbery, the levying of duties on goods brought into Salt Lake, the desire for a kingly government, and polygamy.

On September 9, 1850, Congress passed but did not implement the organic act establishing the Territory of Utah. The territorial governor, secretary, chief justice, two associate justices, attorney general and marshal were to be appointed by the President. President Fillmore, with helpful advice from Mormon representatives—he later denied that either he or the Senate knew at the time that polygamy was an accepted Mormon practice—appointed Brigham Young governor. The posts of attorney general, marshal, and one associate justice also went to Mormons. On October 4, the Mormon-dominated new territorial legislature confirmed all existing "laws" of Deseret insofar as they did not conflict with those of the Territory, thus confirming the charter Deseret already had granted to the religious *"Corporation of the Church of Jesus Christ of Latter-Day Saints"*—Brigham Young, president. The three non-Mormon appointees soon learned that no one could oppose Governor and High Priest Young's will without a military force. When they spoke out against polygamy, Young censured and terrorized them. Mormons openly expressed their contempt for the federal government. The three soon returned ("fled" is more correct) East. One judge wrote that the Mormons were "a desperate and murderous sect."

Many Mormon leaders crossed the plains with several wives. When necessary, they had denied the relationship; once in Utah they did not conceal it. In 1852 the official Church doctrine of "plural marriage" as a right and duty was first publicly proclaimed by Orson Pratt. Young added: "Though that doctrine has not yet been preached by the Elders, this people have believed in it for many years." As to the possibility of legal action against them, Pratt advised:

> I believe that they will not, under our present form of government (I mean the government of the United States), try us for treason for believing and practicing our religious notions and ideas. I think, if I am not mistaken, that the constitution gives the privilege to all of the inhabitants of this country, of the free exercise of their religious notions, and the freedom of their faith and the practice of it. Then, if it can be proved to a demonstration that the Latter-Day Saints have actually embraced, as a part and portion of their religion, the doctrine of a plurality of wives, it is constitutional. And should there ever be laws enacted by this government to restrict them from the free exercise of their religion, such laws must be unconstitutional.

Under polygamy, the Mormon was taught that he "married" for time, but was "sealed" for eternity. The "sealing" was therefore the more important ceremony, and was performed in the Endowment House with secret oaths and mystic ceremonies. If a wife disliked her husband and wished to be "sealed" to a man of her choice, the church would marry her to the latter—a marriage made actual in every sense. If the first husband also wanted to be "sealed" to her, the church would perform a mock ceremony to satisfy this husband. "It is impossible," said one writer, "to state all the licentiousness, under the name of religion, that these sealing ordinances have occasioned." Horace Greeley, pro-Mormon before his visit to Salt Lake City in 1859, afterwards branded their polgamy "the degradation (or, if you please, the restriction) of women to the single office of childbearing and its accessories . . ."

Today's otherwise loyal "Baker Street Irregular" is likely to discount, in the novelette which brings Watson and Holmes together for their first adventure, the lurid accounts in its section titled *"The Country of the Saints."* But Doyle's *"Study in Scarlet,"* published in 1892, understates the case, and the attempted flight in 1860 of his fictional Ferriers and Jefferson Hope from the "Avenging Angels" is topped by many factual accounts. Discovery of gold in California brought a first rush of "Forty-niners" through Salt Lake that August, with profitable and sorely needed trade. But when his Saints started to leave for California, Young first rebuked them, "The true use of gold is for paving streets," then warned those who still proposed to leave, "Let such men remember that they are not wanted in our midst. Let such leave their carcasses where they do their work; we want not our burial grounds polluted with such hypocrites." Those who felt such a need of gold would "go down to hell, poverty-stricken and naked." The warning was effective. In 1851, 250 emigrants for California, after passing through Utah, petitioned Congress for abrogation of the territorial government and substitution of a military government. Their charges: that emigrants suspected of having taken part in earlier Mormon persecutions were murdered by Mormons; that dissatisfied Mormons who tried to leave Utah were pursued and killed; that Mormons levied a two per cent tax on the property of emigrants forced to pass the winter there; that it was impossible for emigrants to obtain justice in Mormon courts; that Mormons openly expressed treasonable sentiments against the United States government; and that letters mailed by emigrants at Salt Lake City were opened and many destroyed.

Young was absolute dictator. After the revelation of polygamy, a group led by Gladden Bishop protested; Young thereupon described his dream wherein he had seen two men creeping toward the bed of one of his wives; he had taken a bowie knife and slit one man's throat from ear to ear, saying, "Go to hell across lots." Gladdenism quickly ended.

The Mormon habit of stealing carried with them to Utah, but here, for the most part, they were forced to steal from each other. The resulting insecurity of property brought lectures from Young against stealing and rebranding cattle and the disappearance of his own woodpiles. As to newcomers from Europe, already in debt to the Church for their passage: "And what do they do when they get here? Steal our wagons, and make off with them to Canada . . ." In 1855, Young and his closest associates did not conceal their intention to take the life of anyone they considered an offender: "If a man rebels . . . *he is unwise* . . ." The "Reformation," a system of prying inquisitors rivaling the Spanish Inquisition, and "Blood Atonement" began about 1856. Under the "Reformation," the life of no man who incurred the wrath of the church was of any value: "No household was safe from the lust of any aged elder; no person once in the valley could leave it alive against the church's consent." When Bishop Warren Snow desired to add one already engaged young woman to his collection of wives, and she declined, he commanded her fiance to give her up. He refused. The Bishop then summoned him to a meeting, where he was beaten, tied to a bench and castrated with a bowie knife by Bishop Snow himself. An example of "Blood Atonement": during an elder's absence, one of his wives broke her marriage vows. On his return, she agreed to accept the atonement: "Seating herself, therefore, on her husband's knee, she gave him a last kiss, and he then drew a knife across her throat."

In June, 1856 the Republican National Convention called for prohibition of polygamy. Continuing Mormon demands for statehood were ignored. Stephen Douglas by now had turned against them; aspiring to the Democratic nomination, he called for "a thorough and searching investigation into all the crimes and enormities which are alleged to be perpetrated daily in that territory under the direction of Brigham Young and his confederates; and to use all the military force necessary to protect the [federal] officers in discharge of their duties and to enforce the laws of the land." President Buchanan directed the organization of a body of troops to march into Utah to uphold federal authority, and appointed a new governor, justices, secretary and marshal. In his message to Congress on December 8, 1857, he explained:

The people of Utah almost exclusively belong to this [Mormon] church, and believing with a fanatical spirit that he [Young] is Governor of the Territory by divine appointment, they obey his commands as if these were direct revelations from heaven. If, therefore, he chooses that his government shall come into collision with the government of the United States, the members of the Mormon church will yield implicit obedience to his will. Unfortunately, existing facts leave but little doubt that such is his determination. Without entering upon a minute history of occurrences, it is sufficient to say that all the offices of the United States, judicial and executive, with the single exception of two Indian agents, have found it necessary for their own safety to withdraw from the Territory, and there no longer remained any government in Utah but the despotism of Brigham Young. This being the condition of affairs in the Territory, I could not mistake the path of duty. As chief executive magistrate, I was bound to restore the supremacy of the constitution and laws within its limits. In order to effect this purpose, I appointed a new governor and other federal officers for Utah, and sent with them a military force for their protection, and to aid as a posse comitatus in case of need in the execution of the laws.

With the religious opinions of the Mormons, as long as they remained mere opinions, however deplorable in themselves and revolting to the moral and religious sentiments of all Christendom, I have no right to interfere. Actions alone, when in violation of the constitution and laws of the United States, become the legitimate subjects for the jurisdiction of the civil magistrates. My instructions to Governor Cumming have, therefore, been framed in strict accordance with these principles.

That September 11 had occurred the largest single Mormon outrage, the plunder and slaughter of a party of about 140 California-bound Arkansans—men, women and children—in the "Mountain Meadows Massacre," apparently to avenge the shooting, in Arkansas, of a Mormon by a man whose wife had been induced to elope with the Mormon.

A federal force of about 1,500 men was gotten up, with provisions for six months. Meanwhile, Young enrolled all able-bodied Mormons between eighteen and forty-five in his Nauvoo Legion and sent companies east along the usual route to "aid incoming immigrants." Scouts kept Young informed as to the federal army's advance. Its Captain Van Vliet, sent ahead to confer with Young, was warned that if federal forces entered Salt Lake Valley, they would be sold no supplies; if a larger force was sent the following year, it would find every house and field burned, Utah again a desert, and the Mormons taken to the mountains. In October, after Mormon scouts burned several wagon trains of federal supplies, the federal force took winter quarters near Fort Bridger—which the Mormons also had burned. That December, a territorial United States District Court grand jury indicted Young and others for treason, but no arrests were made.

Congress now authorized enlistment of two regiments of volunteers. Three thousand regular troops and two batteries were to set out in the Spring. In June, 1858, when two peace commissioners arrived, 25,000 Mormons had left Salt Lake City—which they intended to burn upon the advance of federal troops—and were encamped 50 miles south. The commissioners advised Young that they were empowered to offer Presidential pardon on his submission, but declared the government's determination to employ the whole military force of the nation, if necessary, to enforce submission. Young then agreed to entry of the troops, provided they quarter not less than 40 miles from the city, and the Mormons began to return.

The East was more concerned with the Civil War when President Lincoln in 1862 signed the Morrill Bill, "An Act to punish [$500 fine and 5 years' imprisonment] and prevent the Practice of Polygamy in the Territories of the United States . . ." Also provided: that no territorial religious corporation should acquire over $50,000 in real-estate holdings. By 1867, not a single case had been tried under this law. In 1869, President Grant appointed a governor and judges who dared assert federal authority. These judges at once ruled that the United States—not the territorial—marshal should impanel federal juries and that the U.S. attorney-general should prosecute federal indictments. In 1871, under the territorial *adultery* statute, Brigham Young and others were indicted for lewdness and improper cohabitation. But in 1872, the United States Supreme Court reversed the judges' ruling. Young was released, and Utah federal courts were left practically powerless. In 1873, Ann Eliza, "wife No. 19" of Young, sued for divorce, charging neglect, cruel treatment and desertion. A court order for interim payments of $500 a month alimony had the embarrassing result of appearing to give legal sanction to the marriage, but on the trial, the polygamous marriage was decreed void.

In 1874, against desperate Mormon pressure, the Poland Bill was passed, removing civil, chancery and criminal jurisdiction from Utah's probate courts, restoring the U.S. marshal's and attorney's powers, and allowing challenge of a juror for polygamous practice or belief. The stage was set for a test case. Brigham Young's private secretary, George Reynolds, was indicted for bigamy and convicted, but freed on appeal because the grand jury had been illegally drawn. In 1875, Reynolds was again indicted and convicted, and in 1878 the Supreme Court sustained this conviction, holding that religious belief could not justify an act made criminal by law.

During the four-year progress of the Reynolds case, no other attempt was made to enforce the law. Presidents Hayes, Garfield, and Arthur all urged Congress, in the light of the Reynolds decision, effectively to implement enforcement. Passage of the Edmunds Bill, in 1882, sharpened the original definition of bigamy, added mere "cohabiting" with more than one woman, and barred from voting (women had voted since 1869), serving as jurors in such trials, or holding any public office, all who were guilty of, or believed in, such practices. The Act also vacated all existing Utah registration and election offices, and provided that the President, with the advice and consent of the Senate, should appoint a board of five persons to administer the registration of voters and conduct elections.

In September, 1882, registration commenced for the Territory's November election. Refusals by deputies to register certain persons brought five actions for damages against Alexander Ramsey and the four other Board members, and against five of their deputies—the latter including Arthur Pratt, the frustrated subpoena server (Ch. 7) of the

Reynolds case. The cases reached the Supreme Court under the inclusive title, *Murphy v. Ramsey,* where on March 23, 1885, Associate Justice Stanley Matthews gave a resounding denial to the plaintiffs' inference that the act of 1882, if not unconstitutional, at least was unjustifiable:

> . . . certainly no legislation can be supposed more wholesome and necessary in the founding of a free, self-governing commonwealth, fit to take rank as one of the co-ordinate States of the Union, than that which seeks to establish it on the basis of the idea of the family, as consisting in and springing from the union for life of one man and one woman in the holy state of matrimony, the sure foundation of all that is stable and noble in our civilization; the best guaranty of that reverent morality which is the source of all beneficent progress in social and political improvement. And to this end, no means are more directly and immediately suitable than those provided by this act, which endeavors to withdraw all political influence from those who are practically hostile to its attainment.

With passage of the Edmunds act, vigorous crusades against polygamy and the "cohabs" began in Utah, Idaho and Arizona. By 1884, not one of the 1,351 elective public officers was a polygamist, and some 12,000 voters had been disfranchised. There were 3 polygamy convictions in Utah in 1884, and 39 in 1885. But that year, the church's officers openly urged opposition to the new laws, reiterating that "celestial marriage" was divinely revealed and obligatory. Church leaders who accepted imprisonment were honored as heroes; others went into hiding or exile.

In 1886 there were 112 polygamy convictions. By then, about one marriageable Mormon in five was partner to a polygamous marriage, teachers and preachers were continuing to urge the practice, and the Church was doing nothing to stop them. By now, too, the church corporation, in violation of the 1862 act, had acquired some $2,000,000 in real estate. Accordingly, in 1887, Congress enacted the Edmunds-Tucker law, dissolving the church corporation and directing legal proceedings for seizing its property and winding up its affairs. On September 30, 1887 (Brigham Young had died a month earlier, on August 29, leaving 17 widows and 47 children) the U.S. Attorney General filed a bill in the Territorial Supreme Court, in the name of the United States, against "the late corporation known and claiming to exist as the 'Corporation of the Church of Jesus Christ of Latter-Day Saints.'"

This case went to the United States Supreme Court. While it was pending, the Idaho case of *Davis v. Beason* posed a second grave threat to Utah's Mormons. An Idaho statute required of a prospective voter or office holder his oath that he was neither a polygamist nor a *member* of an order which taught, advised, counselled or encouraged the crime. This in effect barred even non-polygamist members of the Church from voting or holding office in Idaho. In 1889, one Davis and others, though Church members, took this oath. They were indicted for conspiracy to pervert administration of the Territory's laws, and convicted. Davis then obtained a writ of *habeas corpus,* contending that the facts in the indictment did not constitute an offense, since the statute was contrary to the First Amendment and therefore void. On appeal, on February 3, 1890, the Supreme Court held the statute constitutional, inspiring the governor of Utah to draft a similar bill. And with this—which would disfranchise and put out of office *all* Utah Mormons—under consideration in Congress, the Supreme Court, that May, affirmed the confiscation of the Church's property.

To church president Wilford Woodruff (himself, in his younger days, an enthusiastic polygamist) the price of polygamous belief finally appeared too high. He issued a manifesto announcing his intention to submit to the laws of the land in regard to plural marriage and advising all other Latter-Day Saints to do the same. A general readjustment followed. On January 4, 1896, Utah was admitted to the Union, its constitution declaring polygamous or plural marriage forever prohibited. Presidential pardon, on condition of future obedience to the law, was proclaimed for all polygamists, and Congress restored the escheated property to the Church.

# Reynolds v. United States

In Short Creek, Utah, in 1956, state welfare officials visited Leonard Black and one of his three wives, Vera, and asked them to give up polygamy and teach their eight children that polygamy is wrong in the eyes of the state. They refused. "Ours is a nation of equal rights before the law," said Vera. "Why should I be required to sign . . . any oath of any kind in order to keep the children I have honorably borne unless all mothers in our state be required to sign an oath?" Later, a Utah court ruled that their home was an immoral environment, and the children were placed in foster homes. The Blacks, like most of the other 400 residents of Short Creek, were "Fundamentalists." They followed Smith's divine revelation of 1843. Mormons do not recognize them. "What they practice openly," said *Time,* "thousands of others throughout the West practice in secret." Said one:

> We believe as a people that polygamy is a divine institution. People live this way in heaven . . . Woodruff's manifesto of 1890 was not a revelation of God. It was a submission to expediency . . . Without plural marriage, men cannot become Gods.
> And it takes a real man to live it. It is not a matter of lust. To take plural wives, a man doubles, triples or quadruples his responsibilities. He has more problems to solve. He must create a home in which harmony and selflessness prevail. He must provide. And it takes a real saint of a woman. She must overcome human weaknesses. In the polygamous home, there can be no jealousy, no selfishness. The whole family must live for the family, not for individuals. The children are finer. They never acquire the pettiness of other children. They live in a home where all are true brothers and sisters and love and serve one another, as God intended it.[1]

In Boston's Public Library, a marble stair leads to lofty Bates Hall. On shelves opposite the entrance stand the fat "U.S. Reports," the decisions of the United States Supreme Court. If one lifts out Volume 98, he will see a strikingly darkened lamina of page edges. Laid on the table, this volume obligingly falls open somewhere between pages 145 and 169 of the lamina. Page 145 has many times been folded over and then uncreased again. Throughout these pages, the text has been underlined and annotated (a misdemeanor) by many hands. "Reynolds v. U.S., (1879) 98 U.S. 145" is required reading for the student of law.

On his second indictment, in 1875, as in his first, George Reynolds was charged with bigamy, in violation of section 5352 (the Poland Bill) of the Revised Statutes:

> Every person having a husband or wife living, who marries another, whether married or single, in a Territory, or other place over which the United States have exclusive jurisdiction, is guilty of bigamy, and shall be punished by a fine of not more than $500, and by imprisonment for a term of not more than five years.

Indicted by a territorial District Court's grand jury of 15 persons, he afterwards pleaded in abatement that this was not legal, since U.S. statutes required 16, but the court held that Utah's territorial enactment, setting the number at 15, governed. Reynolds then pled not guilty.

During the examination of jurors, prospective juror Homer Brown was asked: "Are you living in polygamy?"

"I would rather not answer that," Brown replied.

The district attorney challenged Brown for favor and the court sustained the challenge. He asked the same question of John W. Snell, who replied: "I decline to answer that question."

"On what ground?"

"It might criminate [sic] myself," said Snell," but I am only a fornicator." The challenge of Snell for cause was likewise sustained.

At the trial, the district attorney proved that Reynolds had first married Mary Ann Tuddenham, then offered to prove the defendant's second marriage to Amelia Jane Schofield. Amelia herself was not present. As to this, deputy marshal Arthur Pratt was called on; he gave a detailed account of his attempts to serve a subpoena for witnesses upon, first, "Mary Jane Schobold," as her name had first been put down, and then under her true name. But it was not this mixup that had deterred Pratt: "I know the party, and am well acquainted with her." The real difficulty: during Pratt's visits, both Reynolds and wife No. 1 had given him a determined "run-around"; Amelia just wasn't there. Accordingly, Amelia's testimony on the first trial was read, tending to show her marriage to Reynolds.

The jury found Reynolds guilty as charged, and the Court rendered judgment that he be imprisoned *at hard labor*—an error which afterwards slipped past even the solons of the Supreme Court—for two years, and fined $500. On his writ of error, the case went to the Supreme Court of the Territory of Utah, which affirmed judgment. Reynolds then sued out a writ of error to the Supreme Court of the United States, which, in October of 1878, again affirmed judgment.

After disposing of Reynolds' claims that the jury had been improperly drawn and that Amelia's testimony had been improperly admitted, Chief Justice Morrison R. Waite took up the basic question of religious belief or duty:

> On the trial, [Reynolds] proved that at the time of his alleged second marriage he was, and for many years before had been, a member of the Church of Jesus Christ of Latter-Day Saints, commonly called the Mormon Church, and a believer in its doctrines; that it was an accepted doctrine of that church "that it was the duty of male members of said church, circumstances permitting, to practice polygamy; . . . that this duty was enjoined by different books which the members of said church believed to be of divine origin, and among others the Holy Bible, and also that the members of the church believed that the practice of polygamy was directly enjoined upon the male members thereof by the Almighty God, in a revelation to Joseph Smith, the founder and prophet of said church, that the failing or refusing to practice polygamy by such male members of said church, when circumstances would admit, would be punished, and that the penalty for such failure and refusal would be damnation in the life to come." . . .
>
> Upon this proof he asked the court to instruct the jury that if they found from the evidence that he "was married as charged—if he was married—in pursuance of and in conformity with what he believed at the time to be a religious duty, that the verdict must be 'not guilty.' "
> This request was refused, and the court did charge "that there must have been a criminal intent, but that if the defendant, under the influence of a religious belief that it was right,—under an inspiration, if you please, that it was right,—deliberately married a second time, having a first wife living, the want of consciousness of evil intent—the want of understanding on his part that he was committing a crime—did not excuse him; but the law inexorably in such cases implies the criminal intent."
> Upon this charge and refusal to charge the question is raised, whether religious belief can be accepted as a justification of an overt act made criminal by the law of the land. The inquiry is not as to the power of Congress to prescribe criminal laws for the Territories, but as to the guilt of one who knowingly violates a law which has been properly enacted if he entertains a religious belief that the law is wrong.
> Congress cannot pass a law for the government of the Territories which shall prohibit the free exercise of religion. The first amendment to the Constitution expressly forbids such legislation. Religious

freedom is guaranteed everywhere through the United States, so far as congressional interference is concerned. The question to be determined is, whether the law now under consideration comes within this prohibition.

The word "religion" is not defined in the Constitution. We must go elsewhere, therefore, to ascertain its meaning, and nowhere more appropriately, we think, than to the history of the times in the midst of which the provision was adopted. The precise point of the inquiry is, what is the religious freedom which has been guaranteed.

Before the adoption of the Constitution, attempts were made in some of the colonies and states to legislate not only in respect to the establishment of religion, but in respect to its doctrines and precepts as well. The people were taxed, against their will, for the support of religion, and sometimes for the support of particular sects to whose tenets they could not and did not subscribe. Punishments were prescribed for a failure to attend upon public worship, and sometimes for entertaining heretical opinions. The controversy upon this general subject was animated in many of the States, but seemed at last to culminate in Virginia. In 1784, the House of Delegates of that State having under consideration a "bill establishing provision for teachers of the Christian religion," postponed it until the next session, and directed that the bill should be published and distributed, and that the people be requested "to signify their opinion respecting the adoption of such a bill at the next session of assembly."

This brought out a determined opposition. Amongst others, Mr. Madison prepared a "Memorial and Remonstrance," which was widely circulated and signed, and in which he demonstrated "that religion, or the duty we owe the Creator," was not within the cognizance of civil government . . . At the next session the proposed bill was not only defeated, but another, "for establishing religious freedom," drafted by Mr. Jefferson, was passed . . . In the preamble of this act . . . religious freedom is defined, and after a recital "that to suffer the civil magistrate to intrude his powers into the field of opinion, and to restrain the profession or propagation of principles on supposition of their ill tendency, is a dangerous fallacy which at once destroys all religious liberty," it is declared "that it is time enough for the rightful purposes of civil government for its officers to interfere when principles break out into overt acts against the peace and good order." In these two sentences is found the true distinction between what properly belongs to the church and what to the State.

In a little more than a year after the passage of this statute the convention met which prepared the Constitution of the United States. Of this convention Mr. Jefferson was not a member, he being then absent as minister to France. As soon as he saw the draft of the Constitution proposed for adoption, he, in a letter to a friend, expressed his disappointment at the absence of an express declaration insuring the freedom of religion . . . but was willing to accept it as it was, trusting that the good sense and honest intentions of the people would bring about the necessary alterations . . . Five of the States, while adopting the Constitution, proposed amendments. Three—New

Hampshire, New York, and Virginia, included in one form or another a declaration of religious freedom in the changes they desired to have made, as did also North Carolina, where the convention at first declined to ratify the Constitution until the proposed amendments were acted upon. Accordingly, at the first session of the first Congress the amendment now under consideration was proposed with others by Mr. Madison. It met the views of the advocates of religious freedom, and was adopted. Mr. Jefferson afterwards, in reply to an address to him by a committee of the Danbury Baptist Association . . . took occasion to say: "Believing with you that religion is a matter which lies solely between man and his God; that he owes account to none other for his faith or his worship; that the legislative powers of the government reach actions only, and not opinions,—I contemplate with sovereign reverence that act of the whole American people which declared that their legislature should 'make no law respecting an establishment of religion or prohibiting the free exercise thereof,' thus building a wall of separation between church and State."* . . . Coming as this does from an acknowledged leader of the advocates of the measure, it may be accepted almost as an authoritative declaration of the scope and effect of the amendment thus secured. Congress was deprived of all legislative power over mere opinion, but was left free to reach actions which were in violation of social duties or subversive of good order.

Polygamy has always been odious among the northern and western nations of Europe . . . At common law, the second marriage was always void . . . and from the earliest history of England polygamy has been treated as an offense against society . . .

By the statute of 1 James I. (c. 11), the offense, if committed in England or Wales, was made punishable in the civil courts, and the penalty was death. As this statute was limited in its operation to England and Wales, it was at a very early period re-enacted, generally with some modifications, in all the colonies. In connection with the case we are now considering, it is a significant fact that on the 8th of December, 1788, after the passage of the act establishing religious freedom, and after the convention of Virginia had recommended as an amendment to the Constitution of the United States the declaration in a bill of rights that "all men have an equal, natural, and unalienable right to the free exercise of religion, according to the dictates of conscience," the legislature of that State substantially enacted the statute of James I., death penalty included, because, as recited in the preamble, "it hath been doubted whether bigamy or poligamy be punishable by the laws of this Commonwealth." . . . From that day to this we think it may safely be said there never has been a time in any State of the Union when polygamy has not been an offense against society, cognizable by the civil courts and punishable with more or less severity. In the face of all this evidence, it is impossible to believe that the constitutional guaranty of religious

---

* The author cannot refrain from a footnote to direct the perhaps hasty reader's attention to Jefferson's famous phrase in its original context.

freedom was intended to prohibit legislation in respect to this most important feature of social life . . .

In our opinion the statute immediately under consideration is within the legislative power of Congress. It is constitutional and valid as prescribing a rule of action for all those residing in the Territories, and in places over which the United States have exclusive control. This being so, the only question which remains is, whether those who make polygamy a part of their religion are excepted from the operation of the statute. If they are, then those who do not make polygamy a part of their religious belief may be found guilty and punished, while those who do must be acquitted and go free. This would be introducing a new element into criminal law. Laws are made for the government of actions, and while they cannot interfere with mere religious belief and opinions, they may with practices. Suppose one believed that human sacrifices were a necessary part of religious worship, would it be seriously contended that the civil government under which he lived could not interfere to prevent a sacrifice? Or if a wife religiously believed it was her duty to burn herself upon the funeral pile of her dead husband, would it be beyond the power of the civil government to prevent her carrying her belief into practice?

So here, as a law of the organization of society under the exclusive dominion of the United States, it is provided that plural marriages shall not be allowed. Can a man excuse his practices to the contrary because of his religious belief? To permit this would be to make the professed doctrines of religious belief superior to the law of the land, and in effect permit every citizen to become a law unto himself. Government could exist only in name under such circumstances . . .

Later, a petition for rehearing called attention to the irregularity of the sentence to hard labor. Accordingly, the sentence was set aside and a proper one entered. Reynolds finally was committed to jail[2] in January of 1879.

We may now ask, what of the other freedoms—of speech, press and assembly? Have similar lines been drawn? And how about the other nine amendments of the "Bill of Rights"?

In 1895, dissatisfied merchant seaman Robert Robertson, and others who had signed for the extended voyage, deserted the American barkentine *Arago* at Astoria, Oregon. The master, proceeding under federal statutes, applied to a justice of the peace for a warrant. They were seized, "somewhat as runaway slaves were in the days of slavery," and held in jail 16 days without bail. When the ship was ready to sail, a U.S. marshal forced them aboard, where they defied the master's order to "turn to" and work. For this—a federal crime—they later were arrested in San Francisco and held for trial in the Alameda County jail. They obtained a writ of *habeas corpus,* claiming unlawful restraint of their liberty by Marshal Barry Baldwin, since the statutes under which they were seized and returned to ship at Astoria compelled involuntary servitude, in violation of the Thirteenth Amendment. Thus the statutes were unconstitutional and their subsequent refusal to work could not be held an offense since at that time they were illegally held.

The District Court dismissed their writ, and on appeal to the Supreme Court, Associate Justice Henry Billings Brown on January 25, 1897, affirmed judgment, holding that from ancient times a sailor's contract had always been treated as exceptional and involved to a certain extent the surrender of personal liberty; and that the Thirteenth Amendment, forbidding slavery and involuntary servitude, was never intended to apply to seamen:

> But . . . even if the contract of a seaman could be considered within the letter of the Thirteenth Amendment, it is not, within its spirit, a case of involuntary servitude. The . . . first ten Amendments . . . were not intended to lay down any novel principles of government, but simply to embody certain guaranties and immunities which we had inherited from our English ancestors, and which had from time immemorial been subject to certain well-recognized exceptions arising from the necessities of the case. In incorporating these principles into the fundamental law there was no intention of disregarding the exceptions, which continued to be recognized as if they had been formally expressed. Thus the freedom of speech and of the press (art. 1) does not permit the publication of libels, blasphemous or indecent articles, or other publications injurious to public morals or private reputation; the right of the people to keep and bear arms (art. 2) is not infringed by laws prohibiting the carrying of concealed weapons; the provision that no person shall be twice put in jeopardy (art. 5) does not prevent a second trial, if upon the first trial the jury failed to agree, or if the verdict was set aside upon the defendant's motion . . . nor does the provision of the same article that no one shall be a witness against himself impair his obligation to testify, if a prosecution against him be barred by the lapse of time, a pardon or statutory enactment . . . Nor does the provision that an accused person shall be confronted with the witnesses against him prevent the admission of dying declarations, or the depositions of witnesses who have died since the former trial.

In August, 1917, one Schenck, Socialist Party secretary, and a woman named Baer of the Executive Board, mailed 15,000 leaflets passionately urging that draftees were little better than convicts, that the Conscription Act was in violation of the Thirteenth Amendment, was despotism at its worst, and was in the interest of Wall Street's chosen few: "Do not submit to intimidation against your rights." They were convicted under the Espionage Act, for causing and attempting to cause insubordination in the military forces and obstruct recruiting and enlistment. In 1919, in affirming conviction against the claim of protection of freedom of speech and press by the First Amendment, Supreme Court Justice Oliver Wendell Holmes said:

> We admit that in many places and in ordinary times the defendants in saying all that was said in the circular would have been within their constitutional rights. But the character of every act depends upon the circumstances in which it is done . . . The most stringent protection of free speech would not protect a man in falsely shouting fire in a theatre and causing a panic . . . The question in every case is whether the words used are used in such circumstances and are of such a nature as to create a clear and present danger that they will bring about the substantive evils that Congress has a right to prevent. It is a question of proximity and degree . . .

Holmes' "clear and present danger" rule was applied that year without dissent in *Frowerk* and in *Debs*. But in *Abrams,* involving Russian Communists distributing inflammatory pamphlets, where the claimed attempted damage to the Allies' war efforts was only (—or "only") incidental to the defendants' efforts to further the Russian revolution, Holmes in a strong dissent urged the rule in the defendants' favor:

> Persecution for the expression of opinions seems to me perfectly logical. If you have no doubt of your premises or your power and want a certain result with all your heart you naturally express your wishes in law and sweep away all opposition. To allow opposition by speech seems to indicate that you think the speech impotent, as when a man says that he has squared the circle, or that you do not care wholeheartedly for the result, or that you doubt either your power or your premises. But when men have realized that time has upset many fighting faiths, they may come to believe even more than they believe the very foundations of their own conduct that the ultimate good desired is better reached by free trade in ideas—that the best test of truth is the power of the thought to get itself accepted in the competition of the market, and that truth is the only ground upon which their wishes safely can be carried out. That at any rate is the theory of our Constitution. It is an experiment, as all life is an experiment. Every year if not every day we have to wager our salvation upon some prophecy based upon imperfect knowledge. While that experiment is a part of our system I think that we should be eternally vigilant against attempts to check the expression of opinions that we loathe and believe to be fraught with death, unless they so imminently threaten immediate interference with the lawful and pressing purposes of the law that an immediate check is required to save the country . . .

**In Los Angeles, in 1938, two labor union members were found guilty**

of assaulting non-union truck drivers. About a month before the scheduled date for pronouncing sentence, the Los Angeles *Times,* under the
title *Probation for Gorillas?* editorialized:

> Two members of Dave Beck's wrecking crew, entertainment com-
> mittee, goon squad or gorillas, having been convicted in Superior
> Court of assaulting nonunion truck drivers, have asked for probation.
> Presumably they will say that they are "first offenders," or plead
> that they were merely indulging a playful exuberance when, with
> slingshots, they fired steel missiles at men whose only offense was
> wishing to work for a living without paying tribute to the erstwhile
> boss of Seattle.
> Sluggers for pay, like murderers for profit, are in a slightly different
> category from ordinary criminals . . .
> It will teach no lesson to other thugs to put these men on good
> behavior for a limited time. Their 'duty' would simply be taken over
> by others like them. If Beck's thugs, however, are made to realize
> that they face San Quentin when they are caught, it will tend to make
> their disreputable occupation unpopular. Judge A. A. Scott will make
> a serious mistake if he grants probation to Matthew Shannon and
> Kennan Holmes. This community needs the example of their assign-
> ment to the jute mill.

The *Times* published two other editorials, similar in tone, in the interval between a jury's verdict and the judge's pronouncing sentence:
"Sit-Strikers Convicted," and "The Fall of an Ex-Queen" (Mrs.
Helen Werner). The Times-Mirror Company was cited for contempt,
found guilty and fined. Meantime, while a motion for a new trial was
pending in a dispute between his and another union, Harry R. Bridges
telegraphed the Secretary of Labor:

> This decision is outrageous . . . Attempted enforcement . . . will
> tie-up port of Los Angeles and involve entire Pacific Coast. Inter-
> national Longshoremen-Warehousemen Union . . . does not intend
> to allow state courts to override the majority vote of members in
> choosing its officers and representatives and to override the National
> Labor Relations Board.

Bridges then caused, or acquiesced in, the telegram's publication in
San Francisco and Los Angeles papers. For this, Bridges was cited for
contempt, found guilty and fined. The Bridges and Times-Mirror convictions were carried to the Supreme Court, considered together, and on
December 8, 1941, reversed. As to the editorials, the Court found they
only threatened further adverse criticism in the future, in the event the
cases in question were leniently disposed of. And as to the telegram,

the strike threatened was not prohibited either by the decree or by California law. Said Justice Black:

> The assumption that respect for the judiciary can be won by shielding judges from published criticism wrongly appraises the character of American public opinion. For it is a prized American privilege to speak one's mind, although not always with perfect good taste, on all public institutions. And an enforced silence, however limited, solely in the name of preserving the dignity of the bench, would probably engender resentment, suspicion, and contempt much more than it would enhance respect.

In a footnote he quoted Thomas Jefferson: "I deplore . . . the putrid state into which our newspapers have passed, and the malignity, the vulgarity, and mendacious spirit of those who write them . . . These ordures are rapidly depraving the public taste. It is however an evil for which there is no remedy, our liberty depends on the freedom of the press, and that cannot be limited without being lost." And as to Holmes' "clear and present danger" rule:

> What finally emerges from the "clear and present danger" cases is a working principle that the substantive evil must be extremely serious and the degree of imminence extremely high before utterances can be punished. Those cases do not purport to mark the furthermost constitutional boundaries of protected expression, nor do we here. They do no more than recognize a minimum compulsion of the Bill of Rights. For the First Amendment does not speak equivocally. It prohibits any law "abridging the freedom of speech, or of the press." It must be taken as a command of the broadest scope that explicit language, read in the context of a liberty-loving society, will allow.

I should like, now, to emphasize an important point. In *Reynolds, Murphy, Davis, Late Corporation, Robertson, Schenck, Frowerk, Debs* and *Abrams* the defense contended that a law enacted by *Congress* violated the federal Constitution. But in the Bridges and Times-Mirror cases the federal Constitution's first amendment forced reversal of a *state* court's judgments. This was not always so. The proposition that the Fourteenth Amendment imposed the guarantees of the First upon the states as well as upon Congress was not established until as late as 1925. One early case will emphasize the original limitations of the First Amendment.

On November 9, 1842, in New Orleans, Roman Catholic priest Bernard Permoli caused the corpse of Louis Le Roy to be brought in a coffin into church and exposed while he officiated on it. For so doing, a warrant was issued against him demanding a $50 fine. At that time,

New Orleans was visited annually by yellow fever, and since Catholic practice was to expose their dead in church, while Protestants performed their ceremonies at the cemetery, for fifteen years the Catholics had been required by ordinance—a public health measure aimed at checking the pestilence—to bring all corpses to an isolated obituary chapel (owned by "notorious schismatics") on Rampart Street for funeral rites. Permoli's act apparently was inspired by a new superior more aggressive than the last, and who found it intolerable that concern for mere health of mortals should presume to interfere with sacred rites.

The case eventually reached the United States Supreme Court in 1845, where Permoli's counsel, William G. Reade, argued that the guaranty of religious freedom contained in the ordinance of 1787 as to the northwest territory ("Art. 1st. No person demeaning himself in a peaceable and orderly manner, shall ever be molested on account of his mode of worship or religious sentiments, in the said territory.") and extended to the inhabitants of the Orleans territory by the Act of 1805, afterwards continued to exist:

> This ordinance, so comprehensive, so far-reaching, so simple, and sublime, established a new era for millions who were destined to swarm the sphere of its benevolent operation . . . Till then, the right of the civil power to control the religion of the state had always been practically asserted and recognized . . . Such has been the theory and practice of European governments, from the time when the emperors lighted the streets of Rome with blazing Christians, to the last liturgy forced on his Protestant subjects by the despot of Prussia. Even these American states, planted as they were by refugees from religious persecution, presented for generations any thing but a land of religious liberty. The government of the Puritans was the very opposite of tolerant . . . Even old Maryland, the primal seat of Christian freedom, has enfranchised  the Israelite within our own brief memories. It was but yesterday that the Catholic was made eligible for office in North Carolina; and his continued exclusion from it disgraces New Hampshire today. But the ordinance of 1787 drew a broad line of distinction between the thirteen original states . . . and the new ones to be carved out of the immense regions north-west of the Ohio . . . The United States have guarantied, to their inhabitants, religious liberty; as absolutely as they have republican government to us all . . .

But after a great deal more of this, the Supreme Court dismissed the suit for lack of jurisdiction: the Ordinance and Act had no further force after adoption of the state constitution. Said Associate Justice John Catron:

> The [city] ordinance complained of, must violate the Constitution

or laws of the United States, or some authority exercised under them; if they do not, we have no power . . . to interfere. The Constitution makes no provision for protecting the citizens of the respective states in their religious liberties; that is left to the state constitutions and laws; nor is there any inhibition imposed by the Constitution of the United States in this respect on the States . . .

As of 1845, then, the First Amendment meant just what it said, and no more—that *Congress* should make no law respecting an establishment of religion, and that *Congress* should not prohibit the free exercise thereof.

# 8

# The Fourteenth Amendment

*ARTICLE XIV.*
*1. All persons born or naturalized in the United States,*
*and subject to the jurisdiction thereof, are citizens of*
*the United States and of the State wherein they reside.*
*No State shall make or enforce any law which shall*
*abridge the privileges or immunities of citizens of the*
*United States, nor shall any State deprive any citizen*
*of life, liberty, or property without due process of law,*
*nor deny to any person within its jurisdiction the equal*
*protection of the laws . . .*

*—The Fourteenth Amendment*
*to the Constitution of the*
*United States of America.*
*In force July 28, 1868.*

The year following enactment of the Fourteenth Amendment, the state legislature of Louisiana passed "An act to protect the health of the city of New Orleans, to locate the stock-landings and slaughter-houses, and to incorporate the Crescent City Live Stock Landing and Slaughter-House Company." This granted an exclusive right to one company: afterwards, animals could not be landed or slaughtered anywhere else. The act forced out of business—it was claimed—a multitude of small and large establishments. Actually, it did not "deprive butchers of the right to exercise their trade," for the one large concern was required to provide under its roof, at specified rates, ample conveniences for all who asked for them. The need to concentrate such activities in one place could hardly be argued against as to public health and safety, or indeed, by any resident possessing eyes, ears or nose. But it sharply affected the habits of about 1,000 butchers and others. The cry of "Monopoly!" was raised and hundreds of suits were brought. All that reached the Supreme Court of Louisiana were decided in favor of the Crescent City company. At least five were brought on writ of error to the United States Supreme Court, where dismissal of some was achieved by questionable means. The three remaining, *The Butchers' Benevolent Association of New Orleans v. The Crescent City Live-Stock Landing and Slaughter-House Company* and two others, were given the more workable title, *Slaughter-House Cases.*

On April 14, 1873, Associate Justice Miller delivered the opinion of the Court, denying that any rights under the Constitution had been abridged by the act, as claimed. He first asked, in effect: "Would the act have been constitutional *before* adoption of the Thirteenth and Fourteenth amendments?" His answer: it would have, for our state legislatures, like the Parliament of Great Britain, had always exercised the power of granting exclusive rights when such were necessary and proper to effectuate a purpose which had in view the public good. And the power exercised here clearly was of that class. He then undertook to define the scope of the Thirteenth Amendment and first section of the Fourteenth: the main purpose of the Thirteenth, Fourteenth and Fifteenth Amendments was to secure the freedom of the African race. The Thirteenth intended primarily to abolish slavery; its notion of "involuntary servitude" hardly could be stretched to fit the situation of a butcher forced, as a public health and safety measure, to do his slaughtering in a prescribed area if he did it at all. The first sentence of the Fourteenth primarily was intended to confer citizenship on the Negro race, and secondly to define "Citizenship in the United States" and "Citizenship in the states," and to recognize the difference. The second sentence was to protect from hostile state legislatures the privileges and immunities of *Citizens of the United States* as distinguished from the privileges and immunities of citizens of the States.* Furthermore, there were *two* kinds of "privileges and immunities": first, the privileges and immunities of *Citizens of the United States,* those arising out of the nature and essential character of the National government, the provisions of its Constitution, and its laws and treaties—and these privileges and immunities were placed under the protection of Congress by this clause (a view which still prevails). The second kind of "privileges and immunities," those of citizens of the States, embraced generally fundamental civil rights, and these were *not* protected by Congress, but were under the care of the State governments. And since the claimed privileges and immunities set up by the plaintiffs were of this class, they were not protected by this clause. And finally, the words, "equal protection of the

---

* Example: a person with established residence in the District of Columbia is a "Citizen of the United States" but not a "citizen of a state." A person with established residence in, say, Ohio, is both a "citizen of Ohio" and a "citizen of the United States."

laws," was to prevent discrimination against Negroes, and had nothing to do with butchers.

As to such "fundamental civil rights," not protected by Congress but under the care of State governments, we may examine two early cases in which a state asserted its police powers, as against claimed infringement of religious freedom guaranteed under its state constitution, and cited *Reynolds* as authority. In Arkansas, in 1885, one Scales was convicted for "Sabbath breaking." On appeal to the Supreme Court of Arkansas, Chief Justice Cockrill, after discussing the proposition of religious belief as a defense to the violation of the provisions of the Sunday law, affirmed judgment:

> The proof showed that the appellant was found painting a church on Sunday. He offered to prove that he was a member of . . . the Seventh Day Baptists, one of the tenets of which is the observance of Saturday as the Sabbath, instead of Sunday, and that he had regularly refrained from all secular work and labor on Saturday agreeably to his religious faith and that of his church . . . It is said that every day in the week is observed by some one of the religious sects of the world as a day of rest, and, if the power is denied to fix by law Sunday as such a day, the same reason would prevent the selection of any day; but the power of the Legislature to select a day as a holiday is everywhere conceded. This state, from the beginning has appropriated Sunday as such. On that day the business of our courts and public offices has always been suspended; the issuance and service of legal process prohibited; presentment and notice of dishonor of commercial paper not allowed; and the performance of an act in execution of a contract which matures on Sunday postponed to the next day. This observance of Sunday as a day of refrainment from secular business has always been required of the people generally, without reference to creed, and they continue to so observe it without complaint that, as a municipal institution, it violates any of their constitutional or religious rights . . . The law which imposes the penalty operates upon all alike, and interferes with no man's religious belief, for in limiting the prohibition to secular pursuits it leaves religious profession and worship free . . . The Appellant's argument, then, is reduced to this: That, because he conscientiously believes that he is permitted by the law of God to labor on Sunday, he may violate with impunity a statute declaring it illegal to do so . . .

On Boston's Washington Street, in 1887, George Plaisted, taking part in a Salvation Army parade, performed on "a certain musical instrument, to-wit, a cornet; he, the said Plaisted, not being licensed by the board of police of said city so then and there to do." On appeal to the Supreme Judicial Court of Massachusetts, Plaisted's conviction was affirmed. Said Chief Justice Morton:

It is . . . also objected that the defendant's act of playing the cornet in the parade in the street was done as a matter of religious worship only. But this defense cannot avail to protect him from the consequences of an act which is made subject to a penalty under the law . . . The provisions of the [Massachusetts] constitution which are relied on, securing freedom of religious worship, were not designed to prevent the adoption of reasonable rules and regulations for the use of the streets . . .

And in 1897, the United States Supreme Court upheld the conviction of one Davis, who had spoken on Boston Common without having first secured the permit required by ordinance—against Davis's claim that the ordinance abridged his privileges and immunities as a citizen of the United States and denied him due process of law because it was arbitrary and unreasonable.

In February, 1902, in accordance with a statute authorizing compulsory vaccination by local boards of health when deemed necessary for the public health or safety, the city of Cambridge, Massachusetts adopted the following regulation:

Whereas, smallpox has been prevalent to some extent in the city of Cambridge, and still continues to increase; and whereas, it is necessary for the speedy extermination of the disease that all persons not protected by vaccination should be vaccinated; and whereas, in the opinion of the board, the public health and safety require the vaccination of all the inhabitants of Cambridge; be it ordered, that all the inhabitants of the city who have not been successfully vaccinated since March 1st, 1897, be vaccinated or revaccinated.

That July, Henning Jacobson refused to be so vaccinated, was arraigned, found guilty, and sentenced to pay a fine of $5. The case reached the United States Supreme Court, which upheld the validity of the statute. Said Justice Harlan:

We pass without extended discussion the suggestion that the . . . statute of Massachusetts . . . is in derogation of rights secured by the preamble of the Constitution of the United States. Although that preamble indicates the general purpose for which the people ordained and established the constitution, it has never been regarded as the source of any substantive power conferred on the government of the United States . . .

We also pass without discussion the suggestion that the . . . statute is opposed to the spirit of the Constitution . . . We have no need in this case to go beyond the plain, obvious meaning of the words in those provisions of the Constitution which, it is contended, must control our decision . . .

PRESIDENT JAMES BUCHANAN//"The people of Utah . . . obey {Young's} commands as if these were direct revelations from heaven."

SUPREME COURT JUSTICE STANLEY MATTHEWS//One man and one woman.

JAMES MADISON//"Religion, or the duty we owe the Creator, is not within the cognizance of civil government."

THOMAS JEFFERSON//"A wall of separation between church and state."

SUPREME COURT CHIEF JUSTICE MORRISON REMICK WAITE
//"Laws are made for the government of actions, and while they cannot interfere with mere religious belief and opinions, they may with practices."

SUPREME COURT JUSTICE OLIVER WENDELL HOLMES//"The ultimate good is better reached by free trade in ideas."

SUPREME COURT JUSTICE SAMUEL FREEMAN MILLER//Denied in 1873 that the Fourteenth Amendment extended the First to the states.

SUPREME COURT JUSTICE JOHN MARSHALL HARLAN// Argued in 1907 that the Fourteenth Amendment did extend the First to the states.

SUPREME COURT JUSTICE FRANK MURPHY//"No chapter in human history has been so largely written in terms of persecution and intolerance as the one dealing with religious freedom." (Harris & Ewing)

Melvin B. and Frances V. Ellis with Hildy in Brookline before their flight from Massachusetts. (U.P.I.)

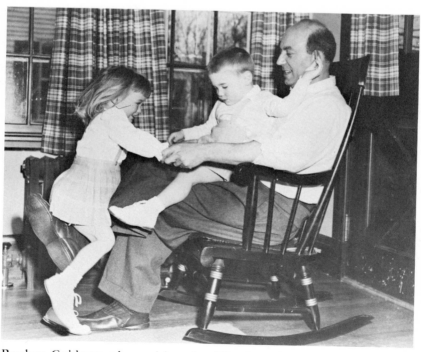

Rouben Goldman plays with twins Wanda and Bruce in Marblehead before their flight from Massachusetts. (U.P.I.)

MASSACHUSETTS SUPREME JUDICIAL COURT CHIEF JUSTICE
MARCUS PERRIN KNOWLTON//In *Purinton v. Jamrock:* "The
law assumes that the child will be as well taught in one church as in
the other, and that her future happiness is as likely to be promoted
in one as in the other."

We come, then, to inquire whether any right given or secured by the Constitution is invaded by the statute as interpreted by the state court. The defendant insists that his liberty is invaded when the state subjects him to fine or imprisonment for neglecting or refusing to submit to vaccination; that a compulsory vaccination law is unreasonable, arbitrary, and oppressive, and . . . is nothing short of an assault upon his person. But the liberty secured by the Constitution of the United States to every person within its jurisdiction does not import an absolute right in each person to be, at all times and in all circumstances, wholly freed from restraint . . . Society based on the rule that each one is a law unto himself would soon be confronted with disorder and anarchy . . . it is to be observed that the legislature of Massachusetts required the inhabitants of a city or town to be vaccinated only when, in the opinion of the board of health, that was necessary for the public health or the public safety . . . To invest such a body with authority over such matters was not an unusual, not an unreasonable or arbitrary requirement. Upon the principle of self-defense, of paramount necessity, a community has the right to protect itself against an epidemic of disease which threatens the safety of its members.

. . . An American citizen arriving at an American port on a vessel in which, during the voyage, there had been cases of yellow fever or Asiatic cholera, he, although apparently free from disease himself, may yet, in some circumstances, be held in quarantine against his will on board of such vessel or in a quarantine station, until it be ascertained by inspection, conducted with due diligence, that the danger of the spread of the disease among the community at large has disappeared. The liberty secured by the 14th Amendment, this court has said, consists, in part, in the right of a person "to live and work where he will" . . . and yet he may be compelled, by force if need be, against his will and without regard to his personal wishes or his pecuniary interests, or even his religious or political convictions, to take his place in the ranks of the army of his country, and risk the chance of being shot down in its defense . . .

. . . the propositions embodied in the defendant's rejected offers of proof . . . are more formidable by their number than by their inherent value. Those offered in the main seem to have had no purpose except to state the general theory of those of the medical profession who attach little or no value to vaccination as a means of preventing the spread of smallpox, or who think that vaccination causes other diseases of the body . . . the legislature of Massachusetts was not unaware of these opposing theories, and was compelled, of necessity, to choose between them. It was not compelled to commit a matter involving the public health and safety to the final decision of a court or jury . . . That was for the legislative department to determine in the light of all the information it had or could obtain . . .

The defendant offered to prove that vaccination "quite often" caused serious and permanent injury to the health of the person vaccinated, that the operation "occasionally" resulted in death; that it was "impossible" to tell "in any particular case" what the results of vaccination would be, or whether it would injure the health or result in death; . . . that the defendant refused to submit to vaccination for the reason that he had, "when a child," been caused great and extreme suffering for a long period by a disease produced by vaccination; and that he had witnessed a similar result of vaccination, not only in the case of his son, but in the cases of others.

These offers, in effect, invited the court and jury to go over the whole ground gone over by the legislature when it enacted the statute in question. The legislature assumed that some children, by reason of their condition at the time, might not be fit subjects of vaccination; and it is suggested —and we will not say without reason—that such is the case with some adults. But the defendant did not offer to prove that, by reason of his then condition, he was in fact not a fit subject of vaccination at the time he was informed of the requirement of the regulation adopted by the board of health . . .

We are not prepared to hold that a minority, residing or remaining in any city or town where smallpox is prevalent, and enjoying the general protection afforded by an organized local government, may thus defy the will of its constituted authorities, acting in good faith for all, under the legislative sanction of the state. If such be the privilege of a minority, then a like privilege would belong to each individual of the community, and the spectacle would be presented of the welfare and safety of an entire population being subordinated to the notions of a single individual who chooses to remain a part of that population . . . The safety and health of the people of Massachusetts are, in the first instance, for that commonwealth to guard and protect. They are matters that do not ordinarily concern the national government. So far as they can be reached by any government, they depend, primarily, upon such action as the state, in its wisdom, may take; and we do not perceive that this legislation has invaded any right secured by the Federal Constitution.

. . . Until otherwise informed by the highest court of Massachusetts, we are not inclined to hold that the statute establishes the absolute rule that an adult must be vaccinated if it be apparent or can be shown with reasonable certainty that he is not at the time a fit subject of vaccination, or that vaccination, by reason of his then condition, would seriously impair his health, or probably cause his death. No such case is here presented. It is the cause of an adult who, for aught that appears, was himself in perfect health and a fit subject of vaccination, and yet, while remaining in the community, refused to obey the statute and the regulation adopted in execution of its provisions for the protection of the public health and the public safety, confessedly endangered by the presence of a dangerous disease.

The case of *Patterson v. Colorado,* decided in 1907, was brought to the United States Supreme Court on a writ of error to review judgment upon an information for contempt. Patterson had published articles and a cartoon alleging unconstitutional conduct by the Colorado Supreme Court in aiding a scheme to seat various Republican candidates, including the Governor, in place of Democrats who had been elected. Patterson claimed that two judges had gotten seats as a part of the scheme. The court charged that Patterson's publications reflected upon the motives and conduct of the court in cases still pending and were intended to embarrass the court in the impartial administration of justice. Patterson claimed the right to prove the truth of his assertions, that the articles and cartoon were privileged criticisms, and that in being fined he had been deprived of his property without due process of law. But the U.S. Supreme Court upheld the Colorado court. Said Justice Holmes in the majority opinion:

We leave undecided the question whether there is to be found in the 14th Amendment a prohibition similar to that in the 1st. But even if we were to assume that freedom of speech and freedom of the press were protected from abridgements not only on the part of the United States but also of the states, still we should be far from the conclusion that the plaintiff in error would have us reach. In the first place, the main purpose of such constitutional provisions is "to prevent all such *previous restraints* upon such publications as had been practiced by other governments," and they do not prevent the subsequent punishment of such as may be deemed contrary to the public welfare.

Justice Harlan vigorously dissented, arguing for the view of the "privileges and immunities" clause rejected in the *Slaughter-House Cases:*

. . . the court announces that it leaves undecided the specific question whether there is to be found in the 14th Amendment a prohibition as to the rights of free speech and a free press similar to that in the 1st. It yet proceeds to say that the main purpose of such constitutional provisions was to prevent all such "previous restraints" upon publications as had been practiced by other governments, but not to prevent the subsequent punishment of such as may be deemed contrary to the public welfare. I cannot assent to that view, if it be meant that the legislature may impair or abridge the rights of a free press and free speech whenever it thinks that the public welfare requires that it be done. The public welfare cannot override constitutional privileges, and if the rights of free speech and of a free press are, in their essence, attributes of national citizenship, as I think they are, then neither Congress nor any state, since the adoption of the 14th Amendment, can by legislative enactments or judicial action impair or abridge them.

The privileges and immunities clause, said Justice Harlan, "necessarily prohibited the States from impairing or abridging the constitutional rights of such citizens to free speech and a free press." Furthermore, "the privileges of free speech and a free press, belonging to every citizen of the United States, constitute essential parts of every man's liberty, and are protected against violation by that clause of the 14th Amendment forbidding a state to deprive any person of his liberty without due process of law."

In the New York case of *Gitlow,* decided in 1925, Gitlow was convicted under a statute against advocacy of criminal anarchy. He claimed the protection of the "due process" clause of the Fourteenth Amendment, but the court held that this had not been violated by the application of the statute in his case. At the same time, in the majority opinion, Justice Sanford first recognized what Justice Harlan had argued for in 1907 in *Patterson:*

> For present purposes we may and do assume that freedom of speech and of the press—which are protected by the 1st Amendment from abridgement by Congress—are among the fundamental rights and liberties protected by the due process clause of the 14th Amendment from impairment by the states.

This view has since become settled law. Thus, in *Grossjean v. American Press Co.,* decided in 1936, the United States Supreme Court held that a Louisiana statute taxing the publication of advertisements in newspapers of over a certain circulation was an unconstitutional infringement of freedom of the press. In *DeJonge v. Oregon,* the Court held Oregon's criminal syndicalism statute, as applied to the defendant, to be repugnant to the due process clause of the 14th Amendment because it interfered with the rights of free speech and assembly. And in *Hague v. Committee for Industrial Organization,* it held that a municipal ordinance under which a city official was empowered to refuse a permit for political meetings in public streets or parks if in his mere opinion such refusal would prevent riots or disturbances, violated the freedom of speech and assembly protected by the Fourteenth Amendment's due process clause. Such decisions set the stage for the "handbill" cases.[1]

The first to reach the United States Supreme Court was *Lovell,* decided in 1938. The city of Griffin, Georgia, had an ordinance which forbade as a public nuisance "the practice of distribution, either by hand or otherwise, circulars, advertising, or literature of any kind, whether said articles are being delivered free, or whether same are being sold, within the limits of the City of Griffin, without first obtaining written permission from the City Manager . . ." The defendants, who had not applied for such a permit, claimed that they were doing Jehovah's work and that to so apply would have been an act of disobedience to Jehovah's commandment. The Court held unanimously that, as against the Fourteenth Amendment, the ordinance (municipal ordinances are adopted under state authority) was invalid on its face:

> The liberty of the press became initially a right to publish *"without"* a license what formerly could be published only *with* one. While this freedom from previous restraint upon publication cannot be regarded as exhausting the guaranty of liberty, the prevention of that restraint was a leading purpose in the adoption of the Constitutional provision . . . Legislation of the type of the ordinance in question would restore the system of license and censorship in its baldest form.

On November 22, 1939, the U.S. Supreme Court decided four more "handbill" cases under the title, *Schneider v. State of New Jersey*. The four convictions (only one involved Witness activities) had been affirmed by the state courts, which had in each case distinguished the case from *Griffin*. But the Supreme Court reversed all four judgments. Witness Clara Schneider had been convicted of canvassing without the permit required by Irvington, New Jersey; Kim Young of distributing "Friends of Lincoln Brigade" (*re* the Spanish Civil War) handbills in violation of a Los Angeles ordinance; Harold F. Snyder of distributing handbills to passersby asking them not to patronize the meat market he was picketing, in violation of a Milwaukee ordinance; and Elmira Nichols and Pauline Thompson of passing out leaflets announcing a meeting to protest against the administration of State unemployment insurance, in violation of a Worcester, Massachusetts, ordinance. Said Justice Roberts:

> The freedom of speech and of the press secured by the First Amendment . . . against abridgement by the United States is similarly secured to all persons by the Fourteenth against abridgement by a state.
> Although a municipality may enact regulations in the interest of the public safety, health, welfare or convenience, these may not abridge the individual liberties secured by the Constitution to those who wish to speak, write, print or circulate information or opinion . . . This constitutional protection does not deprive a city of all power to prevent street littering. There are obvious methods of preventing littering. Amongst these is the punishment of those who actually throw papers on the streets . . .
> It is suggested that the Los Angeles and Worcester ordinances are valid because their operation is limited to streets and alleys and leaves persons free to distribute printed matter in other public places. But . . . the streets are natural and proper places for the dissemination of information and opinion; and one is not to have the

exercise of his liberty of expression in appropriate places abridged on
the plea that it may be exercised in some other place . . . the Irvington
ordinance . . . permits canvassing only subject to the power of a
police officer to determine, as a censor, what literature may be distributed from house to house and who may distribute it. The applicant
must submit to that officer's judgment evidence as to his good character and as to the absence of fraud in the "project" he proposes to
promote or the literature he intends to distribute, and must undergo
a burdensome and inquisitorial examination, including photographing
and fingerprinting. In the end, his liberty to communicate with the
residents of the town at their homes depends upon the exercise of
the officer's discretion . . .

We are not to be taken as holding that commercial soliciting and
canvassing may not be subjected to such regulation as the ordinance
requires . . . We do hold, however, that the ordinance in question,
as applied to the petitioner's conduct, is void, and she cannot be
punished for acting without a permit.

Witness Newton Cantwell and sons Jesse and Russell were convicted in New Haven of the statutory offense of soliciting money for
alleged religious, charitable, or philanthropic causes without approval
of the Secretary of Public Welfare. In addition, Jesse was convicted
of the common law offense of inciting a breach of the peace. On appeal,
the U.S. Supreme Court on May 20, 1940 reversed judgments, holding
the statute, as construed and applied, to deprive the three of their liberty
without due process of law. As to Jesse's alleged common-law offense:

Jesse Cantwell . . . was upon a public street [in a neighborhood
ninety per cent Roman Catholic], where he had a right to be, and
where he had a right peacefully to impart his views to others. There
is no showing that his deportment was noisy, truculent, overbearing
or offensive. He requested of two pedestrians permission to play to
them a phonograph record. The permission was granted. It is not
claimed that he intended to insult or affront the hearers by playing
the record. It is plain that he wished only to interest them in his propaganda . . .

The record played by Cantwell embodies a general attack on all
organized religious systems as instruments of Satan and injurious to
man; it then singles out the Roman Catholic Church for strictures
couched in terms which naturally would offend not only persons of
that persuasion, but all others who respect the honestly held religious
faith of their fellows. The hearers were in fact highly offended. One
of them said he felt like hitting Cantwell and the other that he was
tempted to throw Cantwell off the street. The one who testified he
felt like hitting Cantwell said, in answer to the question "Did you do
anything else or have any other reaction?" "No, sir, because he said
he would take the victrola and he went." The other witness testified
that he told Cantwell he had better get off the street before something

happened to him and that was the end of the matter as Cantwell picked up his books and walked up the street . . .

We find in the instant case no assault or threatening of bodily harm, no truculent bearing, no intentional discourtesy, no personal abuse. On the contrary, we find only an effort to persuade a willing listener to buy a book or to contribute money in the interest of what Cantwell, however misguided others may think him, conceived to be true religion.

In the realm of religious faith, and in that of political belief, sharp differences arise. In both fields the tenets of one man may seem the rankest error to his neighbor. To persuade others to his own point of view, the pleader, as we know, at times, resorts to exaggeration, to vilification of men who have been, or are, prominent in church or state, and even to false statement. But the people of this nation have ordained in the light of history, that, in spite of the probability of excesses and abuses, these liberties are, in the long view, essential to enlightened opinion and right conduct on the part of the citizens of a democracy . . .

But that same year, in *Cox v. New Hampshire,* where a group of Jehovah's Witnesses had paraded on the sidewalks of a business street on a busy Saturday evening, without first even attempting to obtain the license required by statute, the Supreme Court upheld their convictions, saying that a state has the right to control the use of its public streets for parades. And in 1942, in *Chaplinsky,* the Supreme Court denied the claimed immunity under freedom of speech to a Witness who, while distributing literature on a public street, called another a "damned Fascist" and a "damned racketeer."

In 1942, in three cases titled *Jones v. Opelika,* the city of Opelika, Alabama, required an annual license fee of $5 from transient distributors of books, which Witness Roscoe Jones had failed to obtain; Fort Smith, Arkansas, similarly required $25 per month, $10 per week, or $2.50 per day, and had convicted Lois Bowden and Zada Sanders for noncompliance; and Charles Jobin had been convicted under a Casa Grande, Arizona, ordinance requiring $25 quarterly. In all three, the Supreme Court affirmed conviction, holding that a non-discriminatory license fee, presumably appropriate in amount, could be imposed upon such activities. But the following year, it had a change of heart as to these three decisions, as we shall see presently.

The *Martin* case, which the Supreme Court previously had refused to consider but later changed its mind, was decided during its eventful day of May 3, 1943. A Struthers, Ohio, ordinance made it unlawful "for any person distributing handbills, circulars or other advertisements to ring the door bell, sound the door knocker, or otherwise summon the inmate or inmates of any residence to the door for the purpose of receiving such handbills, circulars or other advertisements they or any person with them may be distributing." Witness Thelma Martin nevertheless rang Struthers doorbells and was fined $10 in the Mayor's Court. In reversing judgment, Justice Black said:

> For centuries it has been a common practice in this and other countries for persons not specifically invited to go from home to home and knock on doors or ring doorbells to communicate ideas to the occupants or to invite them to political, religious, or other kinds of public meetings. Whether such visiting shall be permitted has in general been deemed to depend upon the will of the individual master of each household, and not upon the determination of the community. In the instant case, the City of Struthers, Ohio, has attempted to make this decision for all its inhabitants . . .

In *Murdock,* seven Witnesses had been convicted of violating a Jeannette, Pennsylvania, ordinance similar to that of Opelika, Alabama, and the convictions brought on *certiorari* to the U.S. Supreme Court. Having determined to reverse them, but faced with the opposing precedent of *Jones v. Opelika,* the court accordingly first vacated and reversed its judgments in *Jones.* In reversing the judgments of conviction in *Murdock,* Justice Douglas said:

> The First Amendment, which the Fourteenth makes applicable to the states, declares that "Congress shall make no law respecting an establishment of religion, or prohibiting the free exercise thereof; or abridging the freedom of speech, or of the press . . ." It could hardly be denied that a tax laid specifically on the exercise of those freedoms would be unconstitutional. Yet the license tax imposed by this ordinance is in substance just that.
>
> Petitioners . . . claim to follow the example of Paul, teaching "publickly, and from house to house." Acts 20:20. They take literally the mandate of the Scriptures, "Go ye into all the world, and preach the gospel to every creature." Mark 16:15. In doing so they believe that they are obeying a commandment of God . . .
>
> The way of the religious dissenter has long been hard. But if the formula of this type of ordinance is approved, a new device for the suppression of religious minorities will have been found. This method of disseminating religious beliefs can be crushed and closed out by the sheer weight of the toll of tribute which is exacted town by town . . .
>
> Considerable emphasis is placed on the kind of literature which petitioners were distributing—its provocative, abusive, and ill-mannered character and the assault which it makes on our established churches and the cherished faiths of many of us . . . But those considerations are no justification for the license tax which the ordinance imposes. Plainly a community may not suppress, or the state tax, the dissemination of views because they are unpopular, annoying or

distasteful. If that device were ever sanctioned, there would have been forged a ready instrument for the suppression of the faith which any minority cherishes but which does not happen to be in favor. That would be a complete repudiation of the philosophy of the Bill of Rights . . .

The judgment in Jones v. Opelika has this day been vacated. Freed from that controlling precedent, we can restore to their high, constitutional position the liberties of itinerant evangelists who disseminate their religious beliefs and the tenets of their faith through distribution of literature.

Jehovah's Witnesses base their refusal to salute the flag on Exodus 20 :3-5 : "Thou shalt have no other gods before me. Thou shalt not make unto thee any graven image, or any likeness of any thing that is in heaven above, or that is in the earth beneath, or that is in the water under the earth. Thou shalt not bow down thyself to them, nor serve them . . ."

When the Board of Education of Minersville, Pennsylvania, in 1935 adopted a regulation requiring that, each school day, all its pupils and teachers should take part in the ceremony of saluting the national flag, Lillian Gobitis, twelve, and her brother William, ten, refused, and instead stood in respectful silence. Their reason: though they respected the flag, as Jehovah's Witnesses they considered it a manmade "image." A few days later, they were expelled. With school attendance compulsory, the parents were forced to send them to a private school. In March of 1937, the father brought suit in Federal District Court to enjoin the School Board (a state authority) from continuing to exact participation in the flag salute as a condition of attendance, and for $3,000 damages.[2]

In Philadelphia, on December 1, 1937, after trial, Judge Albert B. Maris, a Quaker, so enjoined the School District, and on appeal, the Circuit Court of Appeals sustained this decree. But on June 3, 1940 the Supreme Court, 8 to 1, reversed the affirmance, holding that the regulation requiring the salute was within the scope of state legislative powers and consistent with the Fourteenth Amendment.

By that time, the Supreme Court already had dismissed four other flag salute appeals.[3] The retreat from Dunkirk by the British Expeditionary Force had occurred between May 26 and June 4, and national feeling as to the flag salute is indicated by the mob incidents in Odessa and Waxahachie on June 1–2 (Ch. 4). But two years later, in *Jones v. Opelika,* Justices Black, Douglas and Murphy appended a memorandum stating their belief that when they concurred in the *Gobitis* decision they had, after all, sanctioned a device which suppressed or tended to suppress the free exercise of a religion practiced by a minority group;

and that they now believed the *Gobitis* case had been wrongly decided.

The following year, on June 14, 1943, in the similar case of *West Virginia State Board of Education v. Barnette,* the Supreme Court, with only Justice Frankfurter dissenting, held that no state could force any one to salute the flag or could punish him for not doing so, and overruled its own decision in *Gobitis* and the others. Said Justice Jackson:

> . . . the validity of the asserted power to force an American citizen publicly to profess any statement of belief or to engage in any ceremony of assent to one, presents questions of power that must be considered independently of any idea we may have as to the utility of the ceremony in question . . .
>
> The Gobitis decision, however, *assumed* . . . that power exists in the state to impose the flag salute discipline upon school children in general. The Court only examined and rejected a claim based on religious beliefs of immunity from an unquestioned general rule . . .
>
> If there is any fixed star in our constitutional constellation, it is that no official, high or petty, can prescribe what shall be orthodox in politics, nationalism, religion, or other matters of opinion or force citizens to confess by word or act their faith therein . . .
>
> We think the action of the local authorities in compelling the flag salute and pledge transcends constitutional limitations on their power and invades the sphere of intellect and spirit which it is the purpose of the First Amendment . . . to reserve from all official control . . .

Said Justices Black and Douglas, in concurring:

> Neither our domestic tranquility in peace nor our martial effort in war depend on compelling little children to participate in a ceremony which ends in nothing for them but a fear of spiritual condemnation. If, as we think, their fears are groundless, time and reason are the proper antidotes for their errors. The ceremonial, when enforced against conscientious objectors, more likely to defeat than to serve its high purpose, is a handy implement for disguised religious persecution. As such, it is inconsistent with our Constitution's plan and purpose.

And finally, we come to the questionable *Prince* decision, where a woman alone on a public sidewalk holding up "Watchtower" was within her rights, but who, when her small niece accompanied her, became a criminal.

In downtown Brockton, at 8:45 P.M. on the evening of December 18, 1941, Mrs. Sarah Prince, her two young sons and her niece Betty M. Simmons, nine, of whom Mrs. Prince had legal custody, stood holding up copies of "Watchtower" and "Consolation" for passersby to see.

All were Jehovah's Witnesses. Mrs. Prince previously had permitted the children to help, but George S. Perkins, school attendance supervisor, had warned her not to, and she usually had not taken them with her at night. But that evening the children resorted to tears, and finally she yielded. Mr. Perkins approached and asked for Betty's name. Mrs. Prince refused to give it. Perkins said he would allow five minutes for them to get off the street. They left. He made three complaints against Mrs. Prince, based on Massachusetts' child labor laws: "No . . . girl under eighteen shall sell, expose or offer for sale any . . . periodicals . . . in any street or public place." She was fined on each in Brockton's District Court; then, on her pleas of not guilty, Judge Hayes heard the cases in Plymouth County Superior Court and found her guilty on all three. On appeal to the Supreme Judicial Court of Massachusetts, Justice Qua reversed judgment on the first complaint on technical grounds, but sustained judgment on the second and third. These convictions were appealed to the U.S. Supreme Court on the ground that the statute as applied denied or abridged Mrs. Prince's freedom of religion and denied her equal protection of the laws. In Washington, on January 31, 1944, in a 5 to 4 decision, the convictions were affirmed. Justice Wiley B. Rutledge delivered the opinion:

. . . The rights of children to exercise their religion, and of parents to give them religious training and to encourage them in the practice of religious belief . . . have had recognition here . . .

But the family itself is not beyond regulation in the public interest, as against a claim of religious liberty . . . And neither rights of religion nor rights of parenthood are beyond limitation . . . the state as parens patriae may restrict the parent's control by requiring school attendance, regulating or prohibiting the child's labor, and in many other ways. Its authority is not nullified merely because the parent grounds his claim to control the child's course of conduct on religion or conscience . . .

The state's authority over children's activities is broader than over like actions of adults. This is peculiarly true of public activities and in matters of employment. A democratic society rests, for its continuance, upon the healthy, well-rounded growth of young people into full maturity as citizens, with all that implies. It may secure this against impeding restraints and dangers, within a broad range of selection. Among evils most appropriate for such action are the crippling effects of child employment, more especially in public places, and the possible harms arising from other activities subject to all the diverse influences of the street . . .

Street preaching, whether oral or by handing out literature, is not the primary use of the highway, even for adults. While for them it cannot be wholly prohibited, it can be regulated within reasonable limits in accommodation to the primary and other incidental uses.

But, for obvious reasons, nothwithstanding appellant's contrary view, the validity of such a prohibition applied to children not accompanied by an older person hardly would seem open to question. The case reduces itself therefore to the question whether the presence of the child's guardian puts a limit to the state's power. That fact may lessen the likelihood that some evils the legislation seeks to avert will occur. But it cannot forestall all of them. The zealous though lawful exercise of the right to engage in propagandizing the community, whether in religious, political or other matters, may and at times does create situations difficult enough for adults to cope with and wholly inappropriate for children, especially of tender years, to face. Other harmful possibilities could be stated, of emotional excitement and psychological or physical injury. Parents may be free to become martyrs themselves. But it does not follow they are free, in identical circumstances, to make martyrs of their children before they have reached the age of full and legal discretion when they can make that choice for themselves . . .

Justice Robert H. Jackson (an Episcopalian), in a separate opinion in which Justices Owen J. Roberts and Felix Frankfurter joined, dissented as to the majority's reasoning but arrived at the same result:

. . . the mere fact that the religious literature is "sold" by itinerant preachers rather than "donated" does not transform evangelism into a commercial enterprise. If it did, then the passing of the collection plate in church would make the church service a commercial project . . .

It is difficult for me to believe that going upon the streets to accost the public is the same thing for application of public law as withdrawing to a private structure for religious worship. But if worship in the churches and the activity of Jehovah's Witnesses on the street "occupy the same high estate" and have the "same claim to protection" it would seem that child labor laws may be applied to both if to either . . .

Religious activities which concern only members of the faith are and ought to be free—as nearly absolutely free as anything can be. But beyond these, many religious denominations or sects engage in collateral and secular activities intended to obtain means from unbelievers to sustain the worshippers and their leaders . . . All such money-raising activities on a public scale are, I think, Caesar's affairs and may be regulated by the state so long as it does not discriminate against one because he is doing them for a religious purpose, and the regulation is not arbitrary and capricious, in violation of other provisions of the Constitution . . .

Associate Justice Frank Murphy (a Roman Catholic) presented a separate dissent:

The record makes clear the basic fact that Betty Simmons . . . was engaged in a genuine religious, rather than commercial, activity . . . She was occupied . . . in "an age-old form of missionary evangelism" with a purpose "as evangelical as the revival meeting."

Religious training and activity, whether performed by adult or child, are protected by the Fourteenth Amendment against interference by state action, except insofar as they violate reasonable regulations adopted for the protection of the public health, morals and welfare. Our problem here is whether a state, under the guise of enforcing its child labor laws, can lawfully prohibit girls under the age of eighteen . . . from practicing their religious faith insofar as it involves the distribution or sale of religious tracts on the public streets . . . A square conflict between the constitutional guarantee of religious freedom and the state's legitimate interest in protecting the welfare of its children is thus presented . . .

In dealing with the validity of statutes which directly or indirectly infringe religious freedom . . . we are not aided by any strong presumption of the constitutionality of such legislation . . . The burden was . . . on the state of Massachusetts to prove the reasonableness and necessity of prohibiting children from engaging in religious activity of the type involved in this case . . .

The state, in my opinion, has completely failed to sustain its burden of proving the existence of any grave or immediate danger to any interest which it may lawfully protect. There is no proof that Betty Simmons' mode of worship constituted a serious menace to the public. It was carried on in an orderly, lawful manner at a public street corner . . .

It is claimed, however, that such activity was likely to affect adversely the health, morals and welfare of the child. Reference is made in the majority opinion to "the crippling effects of child employment, more especially in public places, and the possible harms arising from other activities subject to all the diverse influences of the street" . . . Yet there is not the slightest indication in this record . . . that children engaged in distributing literature pursuant to their religious beliefs have been or are likely to be subject to any of the harmful "diverse influences of the street." Indeed, if probabilities are to be indulged in, the likelihood is that children engaged in serious endeavor are immune from such influences . . .

No chapter in human history has been so largely written in terms of persecution and intolerance as the one dealing with religious freedom. From ancient times to the present day, the ingenuity of man has known no limits in its ability to forge weapons of oppression for use against those who dare to express or practice unorthodox religious beliefs. And the Jehovah's Witnesses are living proof . . . To them, along with other present-day religious minorities, befalls the burden of testing our devotion to the ideals and constitutional guarantees of religious freedom. We should therefore hesitate before approving the application of a statute that might be used as another instrument of oppression. Religious freedom is too sacred a right to be restricted or prohibited in any degree without convincing proof that a legitimate interest of the state is in grave danger.

# 9

# Roman Catholic By Law?

In Bologna, Italy, at ten o'clock on the night of June 23, 1858, a Swiss officer led a force of papal soldiers to the house of the Jewish Mortara family and presented an order by the Congregation of the Inquisition for the arrest of their six-year-old son Edgar.

To the Mortaras' protests that there must be some mistake, the officer shook his head. One Anna Morisi, he explained, formerly the Mortaras' servant-girl, had just made a confession to her priest. Four years before, when the infant Edgar was ill, she secretly had baptised him in order to save his soul if he should die. The priest had reported her confession to Rome, and the Holy Office had ordered that, since Edgar had been properly baptised, he must be raised a Roman Catholic. Thereupon, the papal guards took Edgar from his parents by force.

Afterwards, Pope Pius IX remained deaf to the flood of pleas for Edgar's return. These included personal letters from Catholic sovereigns Francis Joseph of Austria and Napoleon III of France. Edgar Mortara was educated in a convent and entered the Augustine order.[1]

It is almost unthinkable, under our constitutional guarantees of freedom of religion and separation of church and state, that such an event could occur in the United States today. In 1952, Supreme Court Justice William O. Douglas thus described in part the First Amendment's restraints upon federal and state government:

> Government may not . . . use secular institutions to force one or some religion on any person . . . The government must be neutral when it comes to competition between sects. It may not thrust any sect on any person . . . It may not coerce anyone to attend church . . . or to take religious instruction.[2]

But Justice Douglas might well have added: "—that is, except in Massachusetts."

On October 2, 1950, Roman Catholic Mrs. Shirley Pereira[3] of New Bedford left her husband Antonio and their two-year-old daughter

142

Linda Marie, and filed for divorce. In granting it the following April, the Bristol county court gave the father custody of Linda. (Prior to the divorce, Mrs. Pereira had agreed in writing that custody be given to the husband. A probate court, however, in considering what is best for a child, is not bound by such an agreement.) Antonio Pereira's parents belonged to the Church of the Nazarene, but Antonio at the time of his marriage was a convert to Catholicism. Upon his wife's desertion he returned to the Church of the Nazarene in New Bedford, where he and his daughter afterwards attended regularly. In December of 1952 he remarried.

The following June, his former wife Shirley petitioned the Bristol court to give Linda to her. Among her claims: that with Antonio and his family, Linda was not receiving "proper care."

The court appointed Franklin T. Waite, local representative of the Massachusetts Society for the Prevention of Cruelty to Children, as guardian *ad litem* to investigate. On May 20, 1954, Probate Judge Walter L. Considine heard Waite's report: as to Linda and Antonio, "everything there suggests the health and happiness of the child in the household of the father." Of former wife Shirley, on the other hand, Waite had found little good to be said. The worst: on July 14, 1951, at the Booth Memorial Hospital in Brookline, under the assumed name of "Agnes Cabral," Shirley had been delivered of an illegitimate child.

But to Judge Considine, a Roman Catholic, it was crystal-clear that Linda was not receiving "proper care." Accordingly, on June 14, 1954, when Linda was five years eight months old, he ordered her removed from her father's home and placed in a Roman Catholic institution, Saint Mary's Home. There, he noted, she would receive "excellent physical and spiritual care." And he gave "limited" custody to Shirley, subject to the home's regulation. Explained Judge Considine:

> I find that, although some of the needs of this child might be pro-
> vided by the father, it is apparent that the spiritual requirement of
> Linda while she was in custody of her father, was not only neglected,
> but also denied her, in that Linda is a Roman Catholic, and the
> father required that she attend the Church of the Nazarene, which is
> not Catholic. She therefore has been denied the privilege of being
> reared in her Catholic faith.
> I find that no one, not even the parents, have the right to deny an
> immature child who has been baptised a Roman Catholic, the priv-
> ilege of being reared in Catholicity. Only this child, when she reaches
> the age of reason, can change her religious faith.[4]

Antonio Pereira appealed, contending that he had been deprived of custody without any finding that he was unfit, that on all the evidence his former wife was not a fit custodian, that he had the right to determine the religion of his own infant daughter, and that it was plain cruelty to take Linda from the only home and family she had known from birth and commit her to an institution. Depriving him of Linda, Antonio's attorney argued in his brief,

> for the religious reasons advanced by the court is a direct violation of his constitutional rights, both federal and state. It imposed on his child a religion not desired by him, and constituted a forbidden state and judicial aid to religion. It violated the guaranty of the free exercise of religion, and punished the child because of the religious affiliation and parental guidance of the father in that regard.[5]

But meantime, Shirley had filed a new petition below for full custody. Acting upon this while Antonio's appeal still was pending, Justice Considine on October 21, 1955, found her "upon all the evidence" a fit person and granted her full custody without restraint. This accomplished, Shirley promptly entered a motion that Antonio's appeal be dismissed for reason that the issue was now moot, and that November 1, the Supreme Judicial Court of Massachusetts did so.[6]

In theory, Antonio Pereira might have brought a second appeal, all the way to the United States Supreme Court—provided he had perhaps $25,000 to spend.[7] His actual circumstances, however, may be inferred from the fact that in the final decree he was not required to contribute to Linda's support. His opponent and her attorneys had behind them all the resources of the powerful Roman Catholic Church. Where, then, was the backer for American citizen Antonio Pereira— and for the American principles of religious freedom and separation of church and state?

According to Leo Pfeffer:

> Probably no problem in the area of the relationship of religion and state is more difficult of equitable solution than that arising out of the desire of a couple of one religious faith to adopt a child born into another faith.[8]

These words find ample illustration in Massachusetts, where, as notoriously in adoption as in custody, hierarchy pressure has transformed the role of Massachusetts courts into nothing short of that of papal guards.

There, in August of 1950, Marjorie J. McCoy, 21, single and Roman Catholic, discovered she was pregnant. Both she and her mother wished to avoid any publicity. To this end the latter consulted a Dr. Sands.

Mother and daughter alike were pleased when he arranged for the coming child's adoption by a Jewish Brookline couple, Melvin B. and Frances V. Ellis. Hildy,[9] as she was named, was born in Boston's Kenmore hospital on February 23, 1951. The Ellises paid all confinement expenses. When Hildy was ten days old they took her home. That April, Marjorie, under extreme pressure from Roman Catholic social workers from the Department of Public Welfare, from Roman Catholic priests and from Roman Catholic relatives, claimed (in the face of extensive testimony to the contrary) that she at first had not known the adopters to be Jewish, and demanded the child back—not for herself, but to place in a Roman Catholic orphanage for later adoption by Catholics. The Ellises refused to give her up.

In June of 1953, Probate Judge James F. Reynolds heard together 1) the Ellises' petition to adopt Hildy, 2) Marjorie's motion that the court allow her to withdraw her consent, and 3) Marjorie's petition that she or some other suitable person be appointed guardian of Hildy with custody. From the printed transcript, it is clear that the hierarchy continued to exert extreme pressure on Marjorie even during her testimony in the supposedly closed hearing. On page 10, the Court is seen excluding "all immaterial witnesses. The general public is excluded. The press is excluded . . . no person is to consult with or give information to the press." But on pages 245–246:

Q. [to Mrs. McMahon] Can you tell me who is the clergyman who has been sitting in the Courtroom during this trial up to now? . . .
Mr. McAULIFFE. His name is Reverend Cornelius Kelley [or Kelly, on page 343] . . . The Roman Catholic Church, Franciscan Order.

And on page 97:

Q. [to Marjorie] You have discussed it with your clergyman?
A. Naturally.
Q. And in fact you have been urged to seek to revoke your consent because of the fact that these people are Jewish?
Mr. McAULIFFE. I pray your Honor's judgment.
The COURT. It is a proper question today.
Q. Isn't it a fact? A. I wouldn't say I have been urged.
Q. You were strongly advised? A. I said that I would not say I was urged but that I was applauded for what I was doing as a Catholic. I was doing what I, as a good Catholic, have to do and should do.
Mr. ZISMAN. The word "applaud"——
The COURT. Strike the word "applaud" out or any sentence connected with the word "applaud."

Judge Reynolds found that the Ellises were suitable persons to adopt Hildy, that they loved her, and that Hildy (by then over two years old) was happy with them. The first concern of Marjorie's mother, he found, had been prevention of notoriety, and Marjorie originally had consented to the proposed adoption under strong pressure by Dr. Sands and her mother. Even so, her consent appeared to be voluntary and made with full knowledge of its legal consequences. Her prime objection was to Hildy's being brought up in the Jewish faith: "Marjorie wants her brought up a Catholic, and the issue has now become a matter of conscience with her."

Judge Reynolds (a Roman Catholic) decreed that Marjorie be allowed to withdraw her consent, and decreed dismissal of the Ellises' petition to adopt Hildy. On the third matter, Marjorie's petition for guardianship, he stayed decision until appeals as to his decrees on the first two should be disposed of. Meanwhile the Ellises kept Hildy.

On February 14, 1955 (in a few days Hildy would be four) the Supreme Judicial Court of Massachusetts affirmed both decrees. Withdrawal of Marjorie's consent, Justice Williams held, was justified by the 1950 "5B" statute[10] under which Massachusetts courts, in passing upon petitions for adoption, are "bound to give controlling effect to identity of religious faith 'when practicable.'" He noted that the year before, the present court had held the "5B" statute constitutional in the case of the Goldman twins (below) and that it was "unfortunate that [Marjorie's] previous consent has resulted in hardship to the petitioners." As to the injury to be inflicted on a four-year-old by tearing her away from the parents she loved and the home she had always known, the judge said nothing.

In September of 1951, illegitimate twins Wanda and Bruce were born to Pearl L. Dome, a divorced Roman Catholic. The "natural father" also was Catholic. Two weeks after the birth of the children, Rouben and Sylvia Goldman[11] of Marblehead took them for adoption. Pearl Dome consented in writing and was agreeable to their being raised in the Jewish faith of the Goldmans. At no time afterwards did she withdraw her consent. But at the adoption hearing, Judge John V. Phelan found that, though the Goldmans otherwise were suitable adopters, many near-by Catholic couples had applications for similar children on file with the Catholic Charities Bureau. It thus appeared "practicable" to give custody of the twins to Catholics instead: therefore, under "5B," the Goldmans' petitions must be denied. On September 27, 1954, after the Goldmans for three years had loved and raised Wanda and Bruce as their own, Chief Justice Qua of the Massachusetts Supreme Judicial Court affirmed the decree. In so doing, he held the natural mother's continuing consent to be of no avail against "5B." He noted that the principle had "received widespread approval" and cited *Purinton v. Jamrock,* the leading U.S. case on adoption across religious lines, *as in accord.* Actually, no other U.S. decision had so held a "where practicable" statute to bar such adoption when the natural mother's expressed wish coincided with her child's welfare.[12] And as will be seen below, the wise principle laid down long before by that same Massachusetts court in *Purinton* was in fact diametrically opposed to the Goldman and Ellis decisions.

In 1955, when the department of public welfare started proceedings to take the twins from the Goldmans and place them in a Catholic institution, "the Goldmans abandoned their home, business (a clothing store in Boston) and other nonmobile assets in Massachusetts and fled with the twins to establish a new home in another state."

To return to the Ellises: after the Supreme Judicial Court's ruling against them in February of 1955, they asked to be allowed to keep Hildy on condition that they raise her as a Catholic. The probate court rejected this plea and ordered them to surrender Hildy to her natural mother by June 30. Marjorie—by then married and Mrs. Doherty, of Hingham— said she probably would turn Hildy over to the Catholic Charitable Bureau for placement in a Catholic home. Thereupon the Ellises, following the course of the Goldmans, fled with Hildy to parts unknown. Afterwards, their attorney, James Zisman, serving without pay and without knowing their whereabouts, continued to press a series of appeals. These were based in part on new evidence that at Hildy's birth Marjorie knew the Ellises to be Jewish. In July of 1956, the court conditioned any further consideration of the case upon Hildy's surrender, and finally, on September 28, dismissed all appeals. Marjorie's attorney, John J. Sullivan, in appearing to oppose Zisman's petitions, noted with approval one justice's label of "kidnappers" for the Ellises and called them "outlaws before the court."

After dodging process servers in six states, the Ellises in May, 1956 settled in Miami, where Massachusetts authorities finally discovered them in March of 1957. Arrested there on Massachusetts Governor Foster Furcolo's warrant requesting extradition to Boston to face kidnapping charges, they were freed in their attorney's care. In Tallahassee, on May 23, Florida Governor Leroy Collins personally conducted their hearing. "Surprise witness" Sullivan asked that the mother's "right" be protected to keep her child in the Catholic Church "in the interest of freedom of religion." When Collins, Protestant father of four, termed the kidnapping charge a "ruse" and denied the request, the crowded hearing room broke into applause. Said Governor Collins:

"The great and good God of all of us, regardless of faith, grants to every child to be born first the right to be wanted and secondly the right to be loved. Hildy's mother denied both of these rights to her." On July 11, Miami Circuit Court Judge John W. Prunty, acting on their petition for adoption, decreed Hildy to be the legal child and heir of the Ellises.

Massachusetts's "5B" statute of 1950, thus interpreted as an absolute prohibition against adoption across religious lines, is a shameful anticlimax for the commonwealth which authored both the first adoption statute and the humane early decision as to religion which is followed— and whether or not they have "where practicable" statutes—in most other jurisdictions today. Up to 1851, adoption in the United States was generally a private matter of contract or indenture. In such transactions the welfare of the child, the least articulate of the three parties, might well be the last consideration. In 1851,[13] under the state's right and duty in its role of *parens patriae* to care for infants within its jurisdiction and to protect them from neglect, abuse and fraud, Massachusetts enacted the first statute requiring court approval of adoptions. This called for a petition by prospective parents to their county judge of probate. The judge, *holding the child's welfare paramount,* was required to satisfy himself that the proposed adoption was fitting and proper and that the petitioners had the means and ability properly to raise and educate the child.

Later, under similar statutes in other states as to custody and adoption, courts usually gave reasonable weight to the religion of the child or of its natural parents. Sometimes, however, that factor was disregarded, and this led to church-sponsored statutes requiring that the child's religious background be continued "where reasonably practicable." Massachusetts enacted such a statute in 1905, and this figured in *Purinton v. Jamrock* in 1907.[14]

The case originated around the turn of the century in Franklin county, Massachusetts, where Mary Jamrock, single and Roman Catholic, supported her illegitimate daughter Kate and herself by working in a cotton mill. Then, on a complaint as to Mary's "neglect, crime, drunkenness, or other vice," the state board of charity took Kate from her. Two years later, when Kate was four or five, Baptists Jesse M. Purinton and his wife took her into their home. After she had lived with them for four years the Purintons petitioned to adopt her. The probate judge found the Purintons to be of good character and education and able properly to support and educate the child. He also found that a strong affection had grown up between Kate and the Purintons, and that her interest would be greatly promoted by the adoption. The probate judge so decreed.

But Mary Jamrock, who in the meantime had never sought to regain custody of, or shown any concern for her daughter, now came forward to appeal from the decree. Her ground: that it was unlawful or improper for her daughter to be brought up in a faith other than her own.

From the language of Chief Justice Knowlton of the Massachusetts Supreme Judicial Court in rejecting her appeal, it is clear that a church battle raged over the issue:

> The Roman Catholic church and the Baptist church are both alike before the law. The court does not hold that the interests of a child will be promoted by education in either of these churches in preference to the other. The parent of the child and the friends of the child, in her interest, may naturally have their preferences, according to their respective beliefs. But if the members of either church have taken an interest in this case as sectarians and promoters of the interests of their church, they have no proper place before the court, and will receive no recognition there. The law assumes that the child will be as well taught in one church as in the other, and that her future happiness is as likely to be promoted in one as in the other. The court, in looking to the interests of the child, will treat the churches as of equal merit, and will be governed by other than sectarian considerations. In a case of this kind, where the mother has lost her right under the statute to prevent adoption by refusing her consent, her wish in regard to the religious education of her child will not be treated as controlling.

Mary Jamrock's attorneys then brought exceptions which, on April 2, 1907, the Massachusetts Court overruled. In his opinion, Justice Sheldon set out the court's guiding principles as to welfare and religion:

> It is undoubtedly the general policy of the commonwealth to secure to those of its wards who are children of tender years the right to be brought up, where this is reasonably practicable, in the religion of their parents . . . But it is the right of the children that is protected by this [the 1905] statute. The rights of the parents are still regulated by the same principles as before. The mother of an illegitimate child has doubtless all the rights of other parents . . . But in such a case as this it is not the rights of the parent that are chiefly to be considered. The first and paramount duty is to consult the welfare of the child. The wishes of the parent as to the religious education and surroundings of the child are entitled to weight; if there is nothing to put in the balance against them, ordinarily they will be decisive. If, however, those wishes cannot be carried into effect without sacrificing what the court sees to be for the welfare of the child, they must so far be disregarded. The court will not itself prefer one church to another, but will act without bias for the welfare of the child under the circumstances of each case.

A fair sample of contested U.S. cases in custody and adoption across religious lines might be expected to reveal a representative cross section of our many sects paired off in conflict. In fact, however, such a sample almost exclusively yields cases of fiercest opposition to custody or adoption of the child of a Roman Catholic mother, no matter how un-Catholic and immoral her conduct, by a family, no matter how exemplary, of a different faith. And yet, at the height of public notice of the Ellis case, when I asked a number of Roman Catholic mothers and fathers as to their feelings, all expressed shock by and opposition to the attempted separation of Hildy from her Jewish foster parents. It is therefore hard to believe that Mary Jamrock, Marjorie McCoy-Doherty or any of the others deliberately and on her own initiative came forward to try to destroy her child's chance for normal family love and security. It seems much more likely that they were pushed. And in at least one recent case—a case in which the pushing backfired—we have the facts.

In 1952, a Rhode Island Jewish couple petitioned to adopt the child of a Catholic mother.[15] Only the local Roman Catholic diocese was opposed. Its representatives prepared a letter for the mother, addressed to the court and stating that she would not consent to her child's adoption by any but Roman Catholics. This spirited woman refused to sign the letter. Instead, she signed an affidavit stating that she *would* consent to the adoption by the Jewish couple and by no one else. Thus the court, though under the most absolute 5B-type statute in the United States,[16] was forced to approve.

But this recounting of the facts is not sufficient to make clear the inhumanity of the Ellis case decision. At no time, even after her marriage, did Hildy's natural mother want the child back for herself. The immediate prospect for Hildy, as for Wanda and Bruce, was to be torn from a warm home and thrust into a Roman Catholic orphanage, there to undergo a merciless attack on her religious beliefs and as merciless an indoctrination in opposing beliefs. Who could ever explain to her such treatment, or her separation from the only human beings who loved her?

It is no accident that Rhode Island, with the highest concentration of Roman Catholics in the country, has also the statute which on its face is the most absolute against adoption across religious lines. It is no coincidence that a court in Boston—the "Irish Catholic capital of the United States,"[17] as Paul Blanshard calls it—should approve and reapprove this inhumane principle of law which the Roman Catholic hierarchy alone seeks to establish everywhere. Working with one mind on all fronts to destroy American traditions of religious freedom and separation of church and state, that hierarchy has thus, in this area, finally achieved that destruction.

It is too late, in over 50 per cent Catholic Massachusetts, to expect any voluntary amelioration of the "5B" statute by its hierarchy-controlled legislature. In July of 1955, a bill was introduced, not to abolish the statute but only to exempt children placed before 1954—and thus allow the Ellises to keep Hildy. The bill was defeated. Now, the only remedy lies with the Supreme Court of the United States.[18]

Of all the recent cases of this kind, the Goldman decision presents the most crystal-clear violation of the First Amendment. Here the children's best interests, the rights and wishes of the adoptive parents and the wishes of the natural mother all concurred. Yet the highest court of Massachusetts ignored all this to affirm a decision which served only the interests of the Roman hierarchy—a clear establishment of religion. On this ground the case was appealed to the United States Supreme Court, which refused to consider it.

Such a refusal—i.e., denying a writ of *certiorari*—by no means implies that the Supreme Court approved the decision. It means only that more and more cases of this nature must be urged upon that court until it becomes concerned enough to review such a case on its merits. The flag-salute cases illustrate how much determination will be required. The Supreme Court dismissed the first three flag salute appeals as "clearly without merit," then summarily affirmed a fourth on the basis of the first three. In 1940, the Gobitis case, though considered, met the same fate. But finally, in 1943, in *Barnette,* the court came around to a resounding approval of the principle that an enforced flag salute was not a constitutional or even a likely way to inculcate loyalty and patriotism. A fight of no smaller proportions will have to be waged to overthrow the "5B" statutes as an unconstitutional establishment of religion.

In 1948, Roman Catholic bishops openly denounced the principle of church-state separation as "the shibboleth of doctrinaire secularism," and summoned Catholics to work "patiently, persistently and perseveringly" for its destruction. Today, "religious protection" statutes like those which forced the Goldman and Ellis decisions are pressed for in all states by the hierarchy. Their ultimate goal, now achieved in Massachusetts, is clear: to make and keep Roman Catholic by law all children born to Catholics and all other children who at any time were baptised as Catholics. (Neither Wanda, Bruce nor Hildy was so baptised.) Thus the hierarchy seeks to destroy the American meaning of welfare and equality of religions, and to write into American law its own presumptive dogma: *Eternal salvation cannot be had outside of the true Roman Catholic Church; therefore, restoration to Catholic custody is all-im-*

*portant to a child's welfare, regardless of any mere temporal harm to
the child.*

To any such exclusive proposition, Americans give short shrift. In
our country, as of 1968, there flourish on equal terms some 241 religious
bodies. Each is free to, though most are more humble than to, file so
extravagant a claim. But none, nevertheless, is free to win or to hold
its adherents by other than ecclesiastical means. None, to say it plainly,
may enlist the law of the land either to regiment its members or to
gain for itself a place of privilege above the others.

*Part III*

# CRIME AND PUNISHMENT

# 10

# Parent Liability

> ... *the law deliberately leaves his idiosyncrasies out of*
> *account and peremptorily assumes that he has as much*
> *capacity to judge and to foresee consequences as a man*
> *of ordinary prudence would have in the same situation*
> ... *the criminal law, which has for its immediate object*
> *and task to establish a general standard, or at least gen-*
> *eral negative limits, of conduct for the community, in the*
> *interest of the safety of all.*
>
> —*Holmes, J., in Com. v. Pierce.*

Two weeks after Bertha Bradley's burning (Ch. 1), Sanchez instituted a proceeding against Bradley in a justice of the peace court, and
then: "I went to him, and told him: 'Now, Jim, now here; I didn't
want to do this, but my sister and her little children must have some
protection, and if you will just agree to have a doctor, or give that child
medical aid, I will drop it, and I will pay for it, if it takes the best
horse I have on my place to do it. If you will just agree to it, I will send
the doctor myself and pay him.' He said: 'Glory to God, I am able to pay
a doctor.' He said: 'It is doing fine, Glory to God; I am in Daniel's
path.' "

T. L. Dorsett, justice of the peace, testified:

I spoke to Bradley about the matter, and told him that it had created
a great deal of talk, and he said that he knew that Frank had sworn
out the papers, and I told him that I wanted to talk to him as a friend,
and not as an officer, and if he would agree to have a doctor that I
would send one out there, and assist him in any way that I could, and
also the Red Cross ladies had offered their services to help him with
the nursing, and that I wanted him to have the doctor, and keep down
the talk anyway, and the trouble, and he told me: "Tom, when I
became converted, I laid all that I possess on earth on God's altar,
and the greatest physician is God; and I am praying over the child,
and no physician on earth could save her if God saw fit to take her;
and if it is His will that she gets well, she will get well, but if not, of

155

course He will take her." I saw that it was no use to argue with them; that was his religion, and I didn't say any more to him about it . . . He said that he didn't want any doctor; that the greatest physician was God himself.

At the trial, the physicians who had treated her testified that her death resulted from the burn, and that, in their opinion, if she had received medical attention promptly after being burned she would have recovered. James Bradley was convicted of manslaughter, but on appeal, the Florida Supreme Court, on April 26, 1920, reversed judgment. Justice Whitfield delivered the opinion:

> This is not a charge that the father did "wilfully deprive his child of necessary medical attention under [the child protection statutes] . . . "
> There is no statute in this state specifically making the failure or refusal of a father to provide medical attention for his child a felony, and the general definition of "manslaughter" contained in the statute does not appear to cover a case of this nature. Neither the allegations of the indictment nor the evidence adduced at the trial show "the killing of" the child "by the act, procurement, or culpable negligence of" the father . . . Manifestly, the death of the child was caused by the accidental burning in which the father had no part. The attentions of a physician may or may not have prevented the burning from causing the death of the child; but the absence of medical attention did not cause "the killing of the child," even if the failure or refusal of the father to provide medical attention was "culpable negligence," within the intent of the statute . . .

Chief Justice Browne and Justices Taylor and Ellis concurred. Added Browne:

> I fully concur . . . The question of the father's religious belief is in no wise involved. The all-important question is: Must a parent call a physician every time his child is sick, or risk being adjudged guilty of manslaughter if the child should die? If not, who is to decide when the child is sick enough to place upon the father the obligation to call a physician? Is it the father, or the neighbors, or must the father call a physician to ascertain if the child needs a physician? . . .
> The reasoning upon which the state's case rests is this: The child was badly injured; it did not have medical attention for three weeks; after that, it was in the care of a physician for two weeks before it died; if the father had called a physician it would have recovered; therefore, the refusal of the father to call a physician caused the child's death. The fallacy of this is that it was not proven, and was not capable of being proven, that if the child had had medical attention it would have recovered.

Justice West strongly dissented:

All the essential elements of the offense charged . . . were proved
. . . The question . . . is whether the facts make a case of manslaughter
within the terms of the statute, and, if so, is the belief of defendant in
"divine healing," as he expressed it, a sufficient justification or excuse for his failure to secure any medical treatment . . .
    The indictment is based upon . . . the general manslaughter
statute . . . Whether defendant's conduct amounts to culpable negligence depends largely upon the answer to the question: What was
his legal duty under the circumstances . . . ? That it is the legal
duty of a father, who is able to do so, to furnish necessary medical
attention for his child, seems to be well settled. Failure to do so is
made a misdemeanor . . . "Necessaries" for which an infant may
legally bind himself are said in Coke on Littleton . . . to be "his
necessary meat, drink, apparel, necessary physic and such other
necessaries." . . .
    Having concluded that the allegations of the indictment are sufficient
under the statute to charge the offense of manslaughter, I pass to the
next inquiry, namely, was the defendant's belief in "divine healing,"
as stated by him, any sufficient warrant in law for his failure and refusal to secure medical treatment for his injured child, and does such
belief justify and excuse him from the performance of a legal duty
when it is proved to the satisfaction of the jury, as it evidently was
in this case, that his failure and refusal to secure such medical attention resulted in the death of the child?

In answer, Justice West quoted from *Reynolds, Rex v. Lewis, Reg. v.
Senior* and *People v. Pierson,* in all of which the defendant's belief was
held not sufficient justification or excuse to exonerate him.

I have never heard the *Bradley* decision seriously defended. Indeed,
it is remarkable to find, as late as 1920, a state supreme court still in a
"pre-Wagstaffe" state of mind—an expression that will be defined
shortly. The Florida court's three opinions, however, offer a representative preview of the different frames of the judicial mind and of the
arguments, pro and con, which have accompanied the historical establishment of criminal liability for religion-motivated denial of medical
aid. Too, the recorded testimony takes us close to the homely events
and persons and to their convictions and emotions that resulted in a
representative "faith death." We hear the earnest professions of a
religion-obsessed father, determined against all pleas and arguments of
reason to lay down his daughter's life—not *his* life—to prove his faith.
And can we ever afterwards lose our suspicion that, somewhere back
in the shadows of his mind, there may have lurked the notion that the
epileptic girl would, after all, be as well off dead? We see Sanchez
making a futile attempt to institute a legal proceeding—the machinery

for which had yet to be invented. And finally, too late, the State obtaining custody on the ground of insanity!

What makes a man's act a crime? In answer, an able judge once offered me the following criterion to be applied to any set of facts: "The only rules of law that make a person liable for a criminal act are 1) the Common Law which makes the act criminal, or 2) the statute which declares the act to be a crime." I should like to note that James Bradley *could* have been prosecuted for *misdemeanor,* for wilfully depriving his child of necessary medical attention as required by the child protection statute; and, for that matter, *before* Bertha's death. In such prosecution, the defense undoubtedly would be raised that Bradley's religious belief exempted him from the duty imposed by the statute, since not to exempt him would be an unconstitutional abridgment of his right to freedom of religion. Of this, more later. But such a pre-death prosecution still would have not aimed at saving the child's life, but only at punishing the parent.

James Bradley was indicted under the manslaughter statute, on the theory that his culpable negligence caused Bertha's death. At the trial, the jury so found. Afterwards, on appeal, Justice Whitfield held that, as a matter of law, the proofs did not show that any "culpable negligence" of the father caused "the killing of" the child. No, manifestly the *burning* caused her death.

Culpable—criminal—negligence is tied to the notion of "a positive duty to act." I may stand on the shore and watch while a stranger struggling in the water and calling for help finally drowns; and though I make no effort to aid or summon help, I remain innocent of any crime—a hard fact of law. But suppose I am the captain of a ship at sea; I am told a railing has given way and caused a crew member to fall overboard; yet afterwards I do not order the ship stopped and a rescueboat lowered. Here, the law holds me guilty of manslaughter at least, and probably of murder. Where is the difference? As to the struggling stranger, the law has imposed no positive duty to act. But as to the captain, the law imposes definite duties of concern for his crew's welfare and safety, duties similar to those of a parent owed his child, and spelled out in considerably more detail.[1] Yet Justice Whitfield presumably would find the captain not guilty even of manslaughter, holding that "manifestly" it was not his culpable negligence that caused the seaman to drown, but the faulty railing.

Chief Justice Browne, in concurring, asks the difficult questions which of course must be answered if such a prosecution is to succeed. Who is to decide when a child is sick enough to make criminal the neglect to call a physician? And how, after an unattended child is dead, can a physician testify that, with competent medical attention, the child assuredly would not have died? But such questions have been carefully and ably answered, as we shall see. We shall see, too, how the reasoning of Justice West, in his dissent, had come to be generally accepted long before the time of *Bradley v. State.*

In England, at common law, it was a misdemeanor for a parent to neglect to furnish his child necessary meat, drink, lodging, clothing or physic—"physic" meaning such available medical attendance or remedies as common sense would dictate, if within the parent's means. And if the parent's neglect caused his child's death, the parent was liable for involuntary manslaughter—under the common-law formula that misdemeanor plus homicide equals manslaughter. Let us examine some early English decisions concerned with the boundaries of such liability, considering first only cases where the neglect was *not* motivated by religious belief.

In *Regina v. Smith,* in 1837, the court declared that a master was bound, in case of the illness of his apprentice, to provide him with proper medicines, and that if the apprentice died as the result of failure so to provide, the master was guilty of manslaughter. In *Regina v. Knights,* in 1860, a woman who knew she was about to be delivered wilfully abstained from taking the precautions necessary to preserve the life of her child after its birth, in consequence of which neglect the child died. She was held not guilty of manslaughter: the common-law duty of proper care presumably being held to begin at birth and not before. And in 1905, in the similar case of *Rex v. Izod,* where a woman was charged with manslaughter after her newly born child died from neglect of proper care, the court held that it was not sufficient to show that she purposely planned to be unattended at the time of its birth, but that evidence must be given of neglect toward the child *after* its birth. In *Regina v. Shepherd,* in 1862, an unmarried girl of eighteen, who had been out to service, returned to her mother's home before confinement, and by reason of the mother's failure to procure a midwife, died. The court held that the mother could not be convicted of manslaughter for her neglect, both because she had been shown to be without the necessary means and because the girl was beyond the age at which the parent was under a duty to maintain and support her.

In 1893, in the Canadian case of *Regina v. Brown,* a lad of fifteen worked for Brown, a farmer. In return, Brown gave the boy a home— of a sort. He required the boy to sleep in the stable, even during intensely cold winter weather. When the boy's hands became frostbitten, Brown asked a neighbor for a remedy for frostbite, but continued to force the boy to sleep in the stable. The boy's feet then became badly frozen, prompting the frugal farmer to drive into town and ask a doctor what to do for frostbite—without disclosing the boy's condition. Gangrene then set in, the boy died, and Brown was indicted for manslaughter. The court held that the evidence warranted a finding at common law that he was bound to supply care and attention reasonably suited to the lad's condition, that he failed to do so, and that thereby the boy's death was accelerated, therefore he was properly convicted.

But where a parent, acting in good faith and believing religiously that it was the only right thing to do, resorted to faith and prayer instead of to medicine or a medical practitioner to heal his sick child, his so omitting to provide "physic" could hardly be held to contain a criminal intent, and neither was his omission considered negligence so gross and wanton as to be criminal. Thus it was that,

> Under the common law no conviction of manslaughter predicated upon an omission to provide medical attendance upon conscientious motives has been reported, and none can probably be had or sustained. Opinions have widely differed in all ages as to the proper mode of ministering to the sick, and, in the absence of a statute declaring it a positive duty upon a parent to call in a medical practitioner, the omission to do so can scarcely be considered negligence so gross and wanton as to be criminal, when the fact is admitted that the defendant acted in all good faith, doing the best he could according to his lights.[2]

This was the status of English law at the time of the Wagstaffe trial.

Thomas and Mary Ann Wagstaffe had three children aged—as of January, 1868—five years, three years, and fourteen months. The two older children were "healthy and well nourished." Lois, the youngest, "had always been delicate, especially in the regions of the lungs." She "coughed a good deal." That January or before, Lois became ill. The parents anointed her two or three times with oil and prayed to the Lord. When the child grew worse, they called in the elders on a Sunday, and these "anointed the child's breast with oil, where the pain was, and offered up prayers to the Lord . . . The child became a little better after that." During the final fortnight, the mother devoted most of her time to Lois. The father worked during the day, but attended the child in his spare time. He was very kind and affectionate toward her. They gave her "barley water, new milk, corn flour, port wine, and gruel, and occasionally a little weak brandy and water." Then the child grew worse again, and "four elders were called in, two of whom came from the branch church in Essex. They again anointed it." The last nourishment:

"a little weak brandy and water. It did not take much, and it seemed to revive a little." But on January 22, Lois died.

Thomas and Mary Wagstaffe were indicted for the manslaughter of their child by neglecting to provide proper medical attendance. The trial was held in Central Criminal Court on January 29, 1868—only seven days after the death—before Justice Willes. One Metcalfe was prosecutor; "the prisoners were undefended."

These were times of toleration, Metcalfe stated,* and any one was entitled to entertain any opinions he chose on the subject of religion; but they should be confined to matters of religious faith, and not go to the extent, for instance, of starving a child . . . In this case no doctor was called in, and the child having eventually died, the question for the jury would be whether the defendants contributed to the death or to the acceleration of the death.

As to the circumstances leading to the indictments: Thomas Cook, the summoning officer to the coroner, went on the day of the death and saw the child. Fanny Hadley, Mrs. Wagstaffe and two men were there. Cook asked what medical man had been employed. The reply was that no medical man had seen the child. Cook,

expressed his surprise, and said had it been otherwise, he should probably not have had occasion to be there. The mother said she trusted in the Lord. He asked what they called themselves. They said, "Peculiar People." He replied that he thought they were peculiar indeed.

Cook reported the case to the coroner, and the latter "gave an order to have the body opened."

Mr. Thomas Malcolmson Donaghue, surgeon, in Westminsterbridge-road, testified that he went to see the child, and found it dead. He found no marks of violence upon it. A *post mortem* examination disclosed that the child had suffered from acute inflammation of the lungs on both sides. On one side the inflammation had been going on eight or ten days, and on the other about five days. The child in other respects had been quite healthy.

According to Donoghue:

In all probability the child's life would have been saved if medical advice had been early obtained. The symptoms must have been very urgent, as any ordinary person must have seen.

---

* The present writer cannot avoid the second-hand sense of these quotations without taking liberties with the past-tense paraphrasing of the original report as set down by Sergeant-at-Law Edward W. Cox in the year 1868.

What the surgeon would have done:

It ought to have been leeched in the first instance, and small doses of antimonial wine administered. Weak brandy and water [as given by the mother] would not do much harm—certainly no good. Port wine would not be proper. To a child with a chest in such a state he [Donoghue] should not have administered any stimulants. The oil would do neither good nor harm.

Witness Fanny Hadley had known the child from its birth. As to the oil, she "thought the brethren prayed over the oil before it was used," and from experience in her own case she "believed the anointing did good."

"Not since we have been living to the Lord," said Fanny Hadley, "have we called in a doctor in case of illness, but before that we did. We are not pressed by the Church not to call in a doctor, but we are taught to have faith in God . . . I have been afflicted severely at times with smallpox and other diseases, and have not had medical assistance. I have always called in the elders."

"Why don't you call in a doctor?" asked Judge Willes.

Fanny: "Because we believe so much in the healing power of God, and have confidence that He will raise us up again. We have many living witnesses."

Willes: "Would it be a sin to call in a doctor?"

Fanny: "I cannot say that, but still we have confidence in God that He will restore us according to His word."

Willes: "You think it a superfluity, but not a sin?"

Fanny: "Yes."

Willes: "You believe that God will answer your prayer, and that He is able to heal without the assistance of any mortal?"

Fanny: "Yes, we have proved it for ourselves many times."

Willes: "I am not at all suggesting a doubt of your perfect honesty, but I want to know what you really do think on the subject. Is the oil used because you think it does any good?"

Fanny: "We read about it in Mark and James, and we go according to the word of God."

Willes: "You go, I suppose, upon the text in St. James's Epistle?"

Fanny: "Yes. We don't say any thing against calling in a doctor, my lord. A doctor is very well for those who do not put their trust in the Lord . . . "

Fanny Hadley went on to say that Lois had not seemed to suffer a great deal and that they (Fanny and the parents) had not known the disease was inflammation but had thought the child's death was due to teething.

Before presenting the judge's summing up, I would like to submit a conjecture as to one part of prosecutor Metcalfe's argument which is not recorded and must be inferred from the judge's remarks: 1) reasonable people do not pray (or merely pray) for food, they go out and get it themselves; 2) reasonable people do not pray (or merely pray) for the setting of a broken leg, they get a bone-setter to do it; 3) in the same way, reasonable people do not pray (or merely pray) for the healing of disease, they get a doctor to do it. With some such statement as 1, above, the judge agreed; as to 2, not entirely; and as to 3, not at all.

Judge Willes,* in summing up to the jury, said, that in order to make out the offence of manslaughter in a case of this description, the proposition to be established was that the prisoners had the charge of the child in question, who would from its tender age not be able to take care of itself; that they had the means of providing things reasonably fit for it, and that they were guilty of gross and culpable negligence in not resorting to those means for its benefit by lack of which its death was occasioned.

The question was whether the jury were satisfied on the evidence that the child came by its death by the gross and culpable negligence of its parents—and that was a very wide question.

If a parent had the means of supplying his child with food and were to keep it starving, even under a notion that he had some religious duty imposed upon him to starve it, and if it could be made out that that was an insane and morbid belief, everybody would come to the conclusion that there must be a conviction, for all the reasoning in the world would not justify a man in starving a child to death.

But, said Judge Willes, when a jury had to consider what was the precise medical treatment to be applied in a particular case, then they got into a much higher latitude indeed.

At different times, people had come to different conclusions as to what might be done with a sick person. Two hundred years (from 1868) ago, if a child was afflicted with the king's evil, the popular feeling was, regardless of medical science, to have it touched with the Royal hand, because that might result in effecting a cure. Again, in some Catholic countries, a custom obtained of taking a child, labouring under a disease, to a particular shrine, under a belief that that was the best course to adopt with a view to effect a cure.

In such cases, a man might be convicted of manslaughter because he lived in a place where all the community was of a contrary opinion, and in another he might be acquitted because they were all of his opinion.

---

* This, again, is Cox reporting.

There was a very great difference, Judge Willes pointed out, between neglecting a child in respect to food, with regard to which there could be but one opinion, and neglect of medical treatment, as to which there might be many opinions.

If a man did his best, according to his knowledge, with respect to food, it might be for a jury to consider whether they would stamp his conduct with the imputation of gross and culpable negligence. An opinion might be so absurd in itself that it could not have been honestly obtained, and when that was the case, of course all pretense of having acted for the best, because that was considered to be a matter of faith, would be removed from the case. But in the case of an opinion merely put forward as a blind or screen for misconduct, of course the good sense of a jury would treat it as if no such belief was suggested.

Judge Willes thought it might be proper to remind the jury of the text of the last chapter of the General Epistle of St. James, on which the views of persons like the defendants were founded: "Is any sick among you? let him call for the elders of the church; and let them pray over him, anointing him with oil in the name of the Lord: and the prayer of faith shall save the sick, and the Lord shall raise him up; and if he have committed sins, they shall be forgiven him."

And he thought he might go so far as to say the construction put upon that verse by the prisoners ("and he spoke with profound respect for any belief honestly entertained in religious matters") was as sensible and reasonable as supposing a man broke his leg it would be absurd to call in the elders of the church and anoint with oil.

Was it intended by God Almighty that persons should content themselves by praying for His assistance, without helping themselves, or resorting to such means as were within their reach for that purpose?

He stated the case of a man breaking his leg. He did not believe the prisoners held dishonestly the belief they professed. The jury had evidence on that subject, and he thought they would be of opinion that they did not act with any dishonesty in the matter.

He thought, on the contrary, this was a case where affectionate parents had done what they thought the best for a child, and had given it the best of food.

The jury's verdict: not guilty.

Reporter Cox headed his report with the following brief of the common law principle which Judge Willes had affirmed: *Where from conscientious religious conviction that God would heal the sick, and not from any intention to avoid the performance of their duty, the parents of a sick child refuse to call in medical assistance, though well able to do so, and the child consequently dies, it is not culpable homicide.*

The Wagstaffe trial apparently publicized the plight of children in such circumstances and the need for a statute declaring the positive duty to furnish them medical aid. On July 31 of that same year the Poor Law Amendment Act was passed, providing that

> When any parent shall wilfully neglect to provide adequate food, clothing, medical aid, or lodging for his child, being in his custody, under the age of fourteen years, whereby the health of such child shall have been, or shall be likely to be, seriously injured, he shall be guilty of an offense punishable on summary conviction.

Afterwards, in 1872, in *Regina v. Hurry,* a father, although he acted from religious motives, was found guilty of unlawfully neglecting to provide medical aid for his minor daughter, whereby her life was endangered. But two years later, in *Regina v. Hines,* an indictment for unlawfully endangering the life of a child by omitting to provide proper and sufficient medicine, the judge held conscientious religious belief to be a defense, saying that if the legislature were minded to pass a law on this subject, that was a different matter: he apparently was unaware of the Poor Law Amendment Act, as was observed, a year later, by one of the justices in the case which follows.

In 1875, in *Regina v. Downes,* a child had "inflammation of the lungs." The father neglected to provide medical aid, but called in an engine driver named Hurvey, a member of the "Peculiar People," who prayed over the child and anointed it with oil. After the child died, Downes was convicted of manslaughter under the 1868 statute, the court holding that his conscientious or superstitious opinion that it was wrong and irreligious to provide medical aid for his infant child was no excuse.

But for such a conviction, it had to be proved that death was imputable to the failure to provide medical aid, or at least that life might have been prolonged by proper medical attention. In *Regina v. Morby,* decided in 1882, a child had smallpox, but the father, because of his religious views, refused to provide medical aid. The child died, and Morby was tried for manslaughter. At the trial, a medical witness testified that, in his opinion, the child's chances of life would have been increased if it had had medical attendance, that its life might possibility have been prolonged thereby, or indeed might probably have been, but he could not say that it would, or would probably, have been prolonged thereby. Morby was freed on appeal, the court holding that the evidence failed to show that the child's death was caused by, or accelerated by, the parent's neglect.

In 1889, and again in 1894, the Act of 1868 was revised. The 1894

Prevention of Cruelty to Children Act provided that if any person over the age of sixteen years, who had the custody or care of any child under the age of sixteen, wilfully neglected such child in a manner likely to cause it unnecessary suffering, or injury to its health, such person should be guilty of a misdemeanor. Here, the words "medical aid" did not appear. Were they to be implied? And if so, could a parent's religious belief justify his refusal to provide such medical aid? Four years later, in 1898, two such cases were decided. In one, *Regina v. Cook,* the answer was "yes"; in the other, *Regina v. Felton,* the answer was "no."

The following year, in 1899, Lord Russell gave a hard-thought-out answer to the whole problem in the case of *Regina v. Senior.* It remains today the leading English decision on this point. Senior was a member of the "Peculiar People." When his nine months old infant contracted diarrhea and pneumonia, Senior called in the elders to pray and anoint the child with oil. And, even though seven of his twelve children already had died under similar circumstances, he refused to call in medical aid. The child died, and Senior was indicted for manslaughter under the 1894 Act. At the trial, it was shown that Senior knew the gravity of the illness, had the means to provide medical attendance, was reported to be a good and kind father in all other respects, and that medical aid would have prolonged and probably would have saved the child's life.

The trial judge directed the jury that 1) they must, first of all, be satisfied that the death of the child had been caused or accelerated by the want of medical assistance; 2) that medical aid and medicine were such essential things for the child, and that reasonable care from the parents in general would have provided them; 3) that the prisoner's means would have enabled him to do so without expenditure such as could not be reasonably expected from him; and, 4) if he had done anything which was expressly forbidden by statute, and by so doing had caused or accelerated the child's death, he would be guilty of manslaughter, no matter what his motive or state of mind. On this instruction, the jury convicted Senior.

On appeal, Chief Justice Lord Russell held that the trial judge's instruction had been substantially correct, that medical aid was a necessity, and that a religious belief to the contrary constituted no defense:

> In the act now in force the expression "medical aid" does not occur, and it becomes necessary to consider whether the omission of those words makes any difference with regard to the present case. It would be an odd result if we were obliged to come to the conclusion that, in dealing with such a subject as the protection of children, the legislature had meant to take what may be described as a retrograde

step: for the course of legislation, and the provisions of the Act of 1894, show an increased anxiety on the part of the legislature for the protection of infants.

Whether the words in the statute, "wilfully neglects," are taken together, or, as the learned judge did in directing the jury, are taken separately, the meaning is very clear. "Wilfully" means that the act is done deliberately and intentionally, not by accident or inadvertence, but so that the mind of the person who does the act goes with it. "Neglect" is the want of reasonable care; that is, the omission of such steps as a reasonable parent would take, such as are usually taken in the ordinary experience of mankind, that is, in such a case as the present, provided the parent had such means as would enable him to take the necessary steps. I agree with the statement in the summing up that the standard of neglect varied as time went on, and that many things might be legitimately looked upon as evidence of neglect in one generation, which would not have been thought so in a preceding generation, and that regard must be had to the habits and thoughts of the time.

At the present day, when medical aid is within the reach of the humblest and poorest members of the community, it cannot reasonably be suggested that the omission to provide medical aid for a dying child does not amount to neglect. Mr. Sutton contended that because the prisoner was proved to be an affectionate parent, and was willing to do all things for the benefit of his child except the one thing which was necessary in the present case,* he ought not to be found guilty of the offense of manslaughter, on the ground that he abstained from providing medical aid for his child in consequence of his peculiar views in the matter; but we cannot shut our eyes to the danger which might arise if we were to accede to that argument, for where is the line to be drawn? In the present case the prisoner is shown to have had an objection to the use of medicine; but other cases might arise, for instance, as the case of a child with a broken thigh, where surgical operation was necessary, which had to be performed with the aid of an anesthetic; could the father refuse to allow the anesthetic to be administered? . . .

That Christian Science treatment is not a legal substitute for the medical attendance required by statute for a child was established in Canada in 1903 in the case of *Rex v. Lewis.* Lewis's six-year-old son, treated only by a Christian Science "demonstrator," died of diphtheria. Lewis accordingly was indicted for manslaughter, under the *Criminal Code,* which enacts that everyone who has charge of any other person, unable by reason of detention, age, sickness, insanity, or any other cause, to withdraw himself from such charge, is under the legal duty to supply such person with the necessaries of life. The court held that the

---

* Sixty-odd years later, we hear this same argument by the defense in **Labrenz** (Ch. 15).

word "necessaries" included medical aid, assistance, care, and treatment, in cases where ordinarily prudent persons would obtain them, and that the conscientious scruples of a parent who is a Christian Scientist, against obtaining medical aid, are no defense:

> . . . while the merits or demerits of the Christian Science or faith are things with which we have nothing to do as long as it does not transgress or lead to a transgression of the law, the law of the land is paramount, and it is not for people to set themselves up in opposition to it . . .

Child protection statutes comparable to those in England and Canada have been enacted in all U.S. jurisdictions and religious belief uniformly denied as a defense. The leading U.S. case on parent liability in a child's "faith death" is New York's *People v. Pierson,* decided in 1903, where the court gave sound answers to three basic questions: 1) Under a statute requiring a parent to furnish medical attendance to a minor, just how sick must a child become, for the parent to come under the statutory duty to call in a physician? A: At the time when an ordinarily prudent person, solicitous for the welfare of the child, would deem it necessary. 2) Just what—or who—will satisfy the requirement of "medical attendance"? A: Attendance by a physician regularly licensed under the laws of the State. Attendance by the father or by any other person who, because of his religious belief, relies on prayer for Divine aid, will *not* satisfy the requirement. And 3) In the case of a parent with a religious belief to the contrary, does not a statute requiring him to furnish medical attendance to a minor violate New York's constitutional guarantee of full and free enjoyment of religious profession and worship? A: No, since such practices are inconsistent with the peace and safety of the state, which involve the protection of the lives and health of its children, as well as obedience to the laws.

The question has been asked, "Since all the elements necessary for manslaughter appear present, why was the prosecution only for misdemeanor? My guess: the state did not want to risk failure; it was anxious, primarily, to establish the certainty of liability under the statute; to have set down, once and for all, the concept of an "ordinarily prudent person" and the definition of "medical attendance"; and to affirm, beyond the possibility of a doubt, the constitutionality of the statute against its claimed abridgment of freedom of religion.

But let us detour, now, as was done on English cases, for a brief look at some early U.S. decisions where the neglect was *not* occasioned by religious belief.

We have noted the harsh fact that one may watch a stranger drown, yet be under no legal duty to try to rescue him or even to summon aid. In 1907, in *People v. Beardsley,* the Michigan court similarly held no such duty to exist in a case where the principals were hardly strangers. Beardsley took to his rooms for a "carousal" a woman with whom he was acquainted, and who was accustomed to debauchery and assignations. After the lapse of a couple of days, during which they had consumed much intoxicating liquor, it became necessary, because of the impending return of Beardsley's wife, for the woman to depart. Instead, she swallowed a drug with suicidal intent. Beardsley then took her to an adjacent room, and, though she already was in a stupor, did not summon medical aid. She died, and Beardsley was indicted for manslaughter for alleged criminal neglect, but the court held he was under no legal duty to summon such aid.

In a Nebraska case decided in 1913, one Stehr's four-year-old stepson, during a very cold night, had his feet frozen. This was discovered about five days later, by the defendant's wife, when the boy's feet began to show signs of discoloration. Stehr then applied hot water and dressed the boy's feet with cloths saturated with vaseline, but did not call or consult a physician until ten days later—by which time the child's feet were so badly decomposed that the stench from them was unbearable. The boy's feet were then amputated, but blood poisoning had already developed and the child died. Stehr was indicted for murder, but convicted only of manslaughter.

In Minnesota, in 1914, one Staples, who by culpable negligence failed to provide care, nurture, sustenance and medical assistance to his child, and so caused its death, was convicted of manslaughter under a statute defining manslaughter in the second degree, "sometimes called involuntary manslaughter," as the killing of a human being when done "without a design to effect such death by any act, procurement or culpable negligence." And in Tennessee's *State v. Barnes,* in 1919, the court held that a father may be found guilty of homicide, when his infant child dies from his neglect to provide it with proper medical attention: "If the neglect be wilful or malicious, it is probably a case of murder. If the omission is not malicious, and is a mere case of negligence, the parent is perhaps guilty of manslaughter only."

J. Luther Pierson belonged to the faith-healing Christian Catholic Church (Ch. 2). He and his wife lived at Valhalla, near White Plains, New York, with their adopted baby girl. In January of 1901, the sixteen-month-old child contracted whooping cough. The condition continued until about February 20, when "catarrhal pneumonia" developed. She died on February 23. As Pierson afterwards testified, he had observed, for about 48 hours previous to her death, that her symptoms were of a dangerous character. Yet he did not send for or call a physician to treat her, although financially able; and he refused to allow others to do so. His reason: he believed in Divine healing, which could be accomplished by prayer; this religious faith had led him to believe that the child would get well by prayer. He believed in disease, but believed that religion was a cure for disease.

The trial judge charged that, before the jurors could convict the defendant, 1) they must find he knew the child was ill, and deliberately and intentionally failed or refused to call a physician, or to give the child such medicines as the science of the age would say would be proper that a child in its condition should have; and 2) that if at the time he refused to call a physician, he knew the child to be dangerously ill, his belief constituted no defense.

On appeal, the Appellate Division ordered conviction reversed on a claimed error of law: the indictment failed to charge a criminal offense, since it did not allege that the case was one in which a regularly licensed and practicing physician ought to have been called. The state then appealed to the Court of Appeals of New York, where Justice Haight reversed the order and affirmed conviction:

. . . We quite agree that the Code does not contemplate the necessity of calling a physician for every trifling complaint with which the child may be afflicted, which in most instances may be overcome by the ordinary household nursing by members of the family; that a reasonable amount of discretion is vested in parents charged with the duty of maintaining and bringing up infant children; and that the standard is at what time would an ordinarily prudent person, solicitous for the welfare of his child and anxious to promote its recovery, deem it necessary to call in the services of a physician. But is it necessary that all of this should be set forth in the indictment? The indictment has alleged that the defendant unlawfully omitted to perform a duty imposed upon him, to furnish medical attendance for the child. If the medical attendance was not necessary, it was not a duty required of the defendant to furnish it; but, if it was necessary, then it was his duty to furnish it . . .

It is now contended that . . . the Penal Code does not, in terms or in effect, make it the duty of any one to furnish medical attendance to a minor child, and that under the common law it is not part of the duty of parents to provide medical attendance for their children . . . Under . . . the statute, the duty of parents to furnish medical attendance for their children is expressly provided for, and is made obligatory upon them, even if they were exempt from such duty under the common law . . .

We are thus brought to a consideration of what is meant by the term "medical attendance." Does it mean a regularly licensed physician, or may some other person render "medical attendance"? The foundation of medical science was laid by Hippocrates, in Greece, 500 years before the Christian era. His discoveries, experience, and observations were further developed and taught in the schools of Alexandria and Salerno, and have come down to us through all the intervening centuries, yet medicine, as a science, made little advance in northern Europe for many years thereafter—practically none until the dawn of the eighteenth century. After the adoption of Christianity by Rome, and the conversion of the greater part of Europe, there commenced a growth of legends of miracles connected with the lives of great men who became benefactors of humanity. Some of these have been cannonized by the church, and are to-day looked upon by a large portion of the Christian world as saints who had miraculous power. The great majority of miracles recorded had reference to the healing of the sick through Divine intervention, and so extensively was this belief rooted in the minds of the people that for a thousand years or more it was considered dishonorable to practice physic or surgery. At the Lateran Council of the Church, held at the beginning of the thirteenth century, physicians were forbidden, under pain of expulsion from the church, to undertake medical treatment without calling in a priest; and as late as 250 years thereafter Pope Pius V renewed the command of Pope Innocent by enforcing the penalties. The curing by miracles, or by interposition of Divine power, continued throughout Christian Europe during the entire period of the Middle Ages, and was the mode of treating sickness recognized by the church. This power to heal was not confined to the Catholics alone, but was also in later years invoked by Protestants and by rulers. We are told that Henry VIII, Queen Elizabeth, the Stuarts, James I, and Charles I, all possessed the power to cure epilepsy, scrofula, and other diseases known as the "king's evil"; and there is incontrovertible evidence that Charles II, the most thorough debauchee who ever sat on the English throne, possessed this miraculous gift to a marked degree, and that for the purpose of effecting cures he touched nearly a hundred thousand persons.

With the commencement of the eighteenth century a number of important discoveries were made in medicine and surgery, which effected a great change in public sentiment, and these have been followed by numerous discoveries of specifics in drugs and compounds. These discoveries have resulted in the establishment of schools for experiments and colleges throughout the civilized world for the special education of those who have chosen the practice of medicine for their profession. These schools and colleges have gone a long way in establishing medicine as a science, and such it has become to be recognized in the law of our land. By the middle of the eighteenth century the custom of calling upon practitioners of medicine in case of serious illness had become quite general in England, France, and Germany, and, indeed, to a considerable extent, throughout Europe and in this country. From that time on, the practice among the people of engaging physicians has continued to increase, until it has come to be regarded as a duty devolving upon persons having the care of others to call upon medical assistance in case of serious illness . . .

In England the first statute upon the subject [the Act of 1868] to which our attention has been called . . . made it the duty of persons having the care of infants to provide them with "medical aid". This statute was amended in 1894 . . . so as to read substantially the same as section 289 of our Penal Code . . . adopted as part of . . . the Laws of 1881 . . .

Formerly no license or certificate was required of a person who undertook the practice of medicine. A certificate or diploma of an incorporated medical college was looked upon by the public as furnishing the necessary qualification for a person to engage in the practice of such profession. The result was that many persons engaged in the practice of medicine who had acquired no scientific knowledge with reference to the character of diseases or of the ingredients of drugs that they administered, some of whom imposed upon the public by purchasing diplomas from fraudulent concerns and advertising them as real. This resulted in . . . several statutes upon the subject. The first . . . is chapter 513, p. 723, of the Laws of 1880, in which every person, before commencing to practice physic and surgery, is required to procure himself to be registered in the office of the clerk of the county where he intends to practice, giving the authority under which he claims the right to engage in the profession, either by diploma or license, and making a violation of the provisions of the act a misdemeanor.

The Laws of 1887 included "An act to regulate the licensing and registration of physicians and surgeons, and to codify the medical laws of the state of New York," which was amended and carried into the public health law of 1893,

in which there is an absolute prohibition to practice physics unless the person be a regularly licensed physician in accordance with the provisions of the act.

It will be observed that the provision of the Penal Code under consideration was first adopted in 1881, following the statute of 1880 prohibiting the practice of medicine by other than physicians duly qualified in accordance with the provisions of the act. This, we think, is significant. The Legislature first limits the right to practice medicine to those who have been licensed and registered . . . and then the following year it enacts the provisions of the Penal Code under consideration, in which it requires the procurement of medical attendance under the circumstances to which we have called attention. We think, therefore, that the medical attendance required by the Code is the authorized medical attendance prescribed by the statute . . .

And finally, did the statute violate the New York State Constitution's guarantee of "free exercise and enjoyment of religious profession and worship"?

The peace and safety of the state involve the protection of the lives and health of its children, as well as the obedience to its laws. Full and free enjoyment of religious profession and worship is guaranteed, but acts which are not worship are not . . . Children, when born into the world, are utterly helpless, having neither the power to care for, protect, or maintain themselves. They are exposed to all the ills to which flesh is heir, and require careful nursing, and at times, when danger is present, the help of an experienced physician. But the law of nature, as well as the common law, devolves upon the parents the duty of caring for their young in sickness and in health, and of doing whatever may be necessary for their care, maintenance, and preservation, including medical attendance, if necessary; and an omission to do this is a public wrong, which the state, under its police powers, may prevent . . .

We are aware that there are people who believe that the Divine power may be invoked to heal the sick, and that faith is all that is required. There are others who believe that the Creator has supplied the earth, nature's storehouse, with everything that man may want for his support and maintenance, including the restoration and preservation of his health, and that he is left to work out his own salvation, under fixed natural laws. There are still others who believe that Christianity and science go hand in hand, both proceeding from the Creator; that science is but the agent of the Almighty through which He accomplishes results; and that both science and Divine power may be invoked together to restore diseased and suffering humanity. But sitting as a court of law for the purpose of construing and determining the meaning of statutes, we have nothing to do with these variances in religious beliefs, and have no power to determine which is correct. We place no limitations upon the power of the mind over the body, the power of faith to dispel disease, or the power of the Supreme Being to heal the sick. We merely declare the law as given us by the Legislature.

Added Justice Cullen: "I concur . . . The state, as parens patriae, is authorized to legislate for the protection of children. [But as] to an adult, (except possibly in the case of a contagious disease which would affect the health of others), I think there is no power to prescribe what medical treatment he shall receive, and that he is entitled to follow his own election, whether that election be dictated by religious belief or other considerations."

Today, *Senior, Lewis* and *Pierson* remain the leading English, Canadian and U.S. decisions, respectively, on the question of parent liability in the "faith death" of a child. The fact of such liability is a "settled question." The many later cases reaching appellate courts have only defined more sharply the criteria for liability set down in 1899 in *Senior,* and in 1903 in *Lewis* and *Pierson.*

Pennsylvania's *Hoffman* case, also decided in 1903, established for that state, as did *Rex v. Lewis* for Canada, that Christian Science treatment was not a legal substitute for the medical attendance required by statute for a child. Hoffman's daughter became ill with scarlet fever. Instead of calling in a physician who was near at hand and available, Hoffman called in the elders of a Christian Science church, who prayed over the child and anointed it with oil. The girl received no medical attention or treatment, and died. The court held the omission to be criminal negligence, and that its being dictated by, or being consistent with, his religious belief, did not take away the criminal character of his neglect. In 1915, Pennsylvania's similar *Breth* case was similarly decided.

In Indiana, in 1899, the eight-month-old son of Joseph Chenoweth became sick. Both Chenoweth and his wife believed the infant had whooping cough. When it grew worse, neighbors advised Chenoweth to call a physician, but he refused: he believed in "Divine Healing." The "Word of God," he said, justified his course of conduct. On September 4, he procured an "elder" to come to his house, and the elder anointed the child with oil, and prayed to God for his healing. Chenoweth also communicated with John Alexander Dowie (Ch. 2), of Chicago, and procured him to pray, but on September 10 the boy died. A post mortem examination disclosed that the child had died of "double broncho-pneumonia." Joseph Chenoweth was indicted for involuntary manslaughter. On the trial, medical experts testified that, had a competent physician been called, and proper medicine administered, the life of the child would at least have been prolonged, but were unable to state whether, in case a physician had been called after broncho-pneumonia developed, its life could have been saved. Judge James V. Kent directed the jury to return a verdict of not guilty. The state appealed, but failed to file its bill within the authorized time, forcing the Supreme Court of Indiana to affirm judgment without considering the merits. In dictum, however, Chief Justice Jordan opined that, had the state carried its burden of proof, Chenoweth would have been guilty of manslaughter:

> It is certainly true that the conduct or acts of appellee in wholly refusing to secure the assistance of a physician, or to have any medicine administered to his helpless minor child in its sick condition, in order that its life might be either preserved or prolonged, should be condemned and punished by law. It is undisputed that medicine, as a science, is now, and had been for a long period of time, generally recognized by law, and the efficacy of medical treatment by a skilled and competent physician is universally conceded. The religious doctrine or belief of a person cannot be recognized or accepted as a justi-

fication or excuse for his committing an act which is a criminal offense under the law of the land.

The sordid *Beardsley* account leaves the question: to what extent is a husband criminally liable for failure to provide medical attendance for his wife? In Kentucky, Florence Westrup, "a woman of unusual intelligence," strongly believed in "the laws of nature" and was firmly opposed to medical treatment during childbirth. Her husband shared these convictions. In 1902 she gave birth to a child. Afterwards, though she had insisted that she could manage without aid, her husband became alarmed, and, believing her condition perilous, first called upon neighbors and then secured a physician. But Florence refused to accept the medicine prescribed, and died two hours later. The child survived. Arthur Westrup was indicted for involuntary manslaughter. At the trial, medical testimony established that death was due to a post-partum hemorrhage and that this (as of 1902) was nearly always fatal. Westrup was convicted, but on appeal, in 1906, judgment was reversed, the court holding the evidence of neglect not sufficient to support a conviction, and that such deaths frequently occurred even when medical assistance was given during the childbirth. As to a husband's liability in general:

> Where a husband neglects to provide necessaries for his wife or medical attention in case of her illness, he will be guilty of involuntary manslaughter if she dies, if she was helpless and unable to appeal elsewhere for aid, and her death, though not intended nor anticipated by him, was the natural and reasonable consequence of his negligence.

In Oklahoma, in 1925, Johnnie Beck, eleven, one day was seized with intense pain. His father, J. H. Beck, for several hours resorted to prayer, to no avail. Then, under pressure, Beck agreed to allow medical treatment. Two physicians eventually were summoned, the malady identified as lockjaw, and serum administered. But in spite of the treatment the boy died. Beck was indicted for misdemeanor. At the trial, medical testimony advised that the serum was administered "too late," and that if it had been given earlier the boy's life might have been saved. Beck was convicted, but on appeal judgment was reversed, the court holding that, in spite of the child's suffering, Beck had at first failed to understand the gravity of the situation—an honest mistake for which he should not be held criminally liable.

For sixty-odd years, then, it has been established that a parent who— though prompted by sincere religious conviction—denies his sick child the medical attention required by statute is guilty of misdemeanor; and that if the child dies, the parent is likely to be found guilty of involuntary manslaughter. Each case, of course, presents its own unique circumstances, but the general area of liability has been mapped out in this chapter. The reader may ask why it contains no account of such a prosecution following the death of Chicago's Thomas Grzyb, Jr. (Ch. 1) in 1954. The answer: following institution of the custody proceeding and its thwarting by the baby's death, the matter was dropped. One competent observer offered the author the following reasons why, afterwards, no charge of manslaughter was brought: 1) "a tendency toward a sympathetic attitude on the part of local juries"; and 2) "the condition of the child was such that it might have died anyway despite a transfusion, hence the failure to consent might not be regarded as the efficient cause of the death."

True, a conviction for misdemeanor undoubtedly could have been had, and that as well before the death as after. Such a prosecution, however, would in no way have worked toward saving the child's life. And that is the point: the action the state did take aimed squarely at saving the child's life. And having asserted and set in process this authority and having been forestalled in a way which still left no doubt that the same swift action could afterward be expected in any similar case—the state was satisfied.

For what an empty victory, after all, is the establishment of parent liability! What does society gain by so punishing the parent after his child is dead? Even the stern God of Israel, testing Abraham's faith (Gen. 22:12), stopped him from sacrificing his son Isaac to prove that faith. In our day, we are less and less disposed to stand aside while a fanatical parent completes the sacrifice of his innocent child upon the altar of his religion—and in Part IV we shall follow the enlightened steps already taken, under the doctrine of *parens patriae,* toward effective interference. But first there are other relevant "settled" questions to be inquired into: the conflict of the faith healer's right to practice with medical practice statutes; the unique status won by the Christian Science practitioner; the question of the ill adult's right to submit to the faith healer; the peculiar results in certain civil actions; the accessory liability of a pastor or other counsellor; and the question of fraud.

# 11

# The Right to Practice

Susie Jessel at 16 saw Jesus standing on a cloud. He told her: "Go and heal the sick." For 23 years—as reported by *Time* in 1953—she had prayed and passed her hands over the sick and crippled. She begins her 14-hour healing sessions with these words: "I dedicate my hands to the Lord . . . The Lord give me the gift, and He did not give it in vain. If he chooses at times to make it so they don't heal, we must remember that we cannot be a winner all the time." The patient, sitting on a stool, slips into one of Susie's prominent apron pockets a $1 bill, a "voluntary contribution." Her average night's take: $500. Oregon's medical practice act, like that of other states, has a clause which excepts from the licensing requirements those persons who endeavor to treat human ailments by prayer or spiritual means exclusively. Faith-healer Jessel, with no medical training, is therefore within her legal rights. "The medical people," she says, "do the operating, the cutting, the diagnosing, but with me it's His work." A California businessman, when doctors ($7,000 worth) failed to cure his crippling neuromuscular condition, came to Susie. After the first treatment he reported no improvement but said he would stay for more: "After all, a drowning man will grab at any kind of a straw." Susie's thousands of hopeful patients come from as far as Texas and Canada to spend their money in Ashland's booming motels, stores and restaurants. "She's the biggest business in town for everybody," said an enthusiastic local undertaker, who last year buried 18 of her patients.[1]

Medical practice acts have always been upheld as being within the state's police power. All such acts, however, have clauses excepting from the licensing requirements persons who treat human ailments by prayer or spiritual means *exclusively*. Only when the faith healer undertakes diagnosis, or treatment by other than spiritual means, and thus steps over into the area of medical practice as defined by the act, does he become liable to prosecution. We shall first note the statutes' un-

178 CRIME AND PUNISHMENT

questioned constitutionality, then examine some attempts to prosecute faith healers under them.

Upon first passage of a state medical practice act, a number of citizens were likely to be hurt. A man who in good faith had studied medicine, invested in equipment and worked up a practice was suddenly told his training did not come up to the requirements of the act, and found himself deprived of his livelihood. Such a man might with good reason contend that the act was contrary to the Fourteenth Amendment in that it abridged his privileges or immunities, deprived him of his property, and denied him the equal protection of the laws.

In 1876, one Dent, with a diploma from the "American Medical Eclectic College of Cincinnati, Ohio," engaged in the practice of medicine in Newburg, West Virginia. He soon enjoyed a "lucrative practice." Six years later, in 1882, the Legislature of West Virginia passed a statute requiring every practitioner of medicine to obtain a certificate from the State Board of Health to the effect that he was a graduate of a reputable medical college, or had practiced medicine in the state continously for ten years prior to March 8, 1881, or had been found upon examination by the Board to be qualified to practice. Dent accordingly presented his diploma and asked for his certificate. But the Board refused to give him one, saying that his college was not "reputable" as the word was defined by the Board. Dent presumably continued to practice. In 1882, he was indicted and found guilty of unlawfully engaging in the practice of medicine. The case eventually reached the U.S. Supreme Court, where in 1889 Associate Justice Stephen Johnson Field affirmed judgment, holding that the statute did not deprive Dent of his estate or interest in his profession without due process of law; that the state, in the exercise of its power to provide for the general welfare of its people, may require for the practice of medicine a degree of skill and learning upon which the community employing such services may confidently rely; and that, if the qualifications required were appropriate to the profession, and were attainable by reasonable study or application, then the validity of the qualifications was not subject to objection because of their stringency or difficulty.

Medical practice acts, wherever the question has been raised, have been held not to violate the right to religious freedom. In general, these acts set up licensing requirements and standards for the practice of medicine, and make it a criminal offense, usually a misdemeanor, to diagnose, treat, or prescribe any form of treatment of a disease or injury of a human being with the intention of receiving therefor, either directly or indirectly, any fee or compensation; or to attach any title or any word or abbreviation to one's name indicating that he is engaged in the treatment or diagnosis of the diseases or injuries of human beings, without first being properly licensed. But all of these acts have clauses which except from the licensing requirements persons treating human ailments by prayer or spiritual means exclusively. The problem then becomes, when is a minister or other "healer" using spiritual means, and when is he stepping over into the area of medical practice as defined by the act?

In New York, in 1917, one Vogelgesang, claiming to be an ordained spiritualist healer, maintained an office where he received patients and administered to them, applying ointments, patent medicines and "silent prayer." He was convicted of practicing medicine without a license. On appeal, it was held that his practice did not come within the exclusionary clause of the Public Health Law. Said Judge Cardozo:

> The meaning of the act is made plain . . . immunity is granted to those who practice their religious tenets, but always in such a form as to confine the exemption to spiritual ministrations . . . Through all this legislation there runs a common purpose. The law exacts no license for ministrations by prayer or by the power of religion, but one who heals by other agencies must have the training of the expert.

The distinction between the practice of religious belief as intended to be excepted from the operation of the medical practice act, and the commercial practice of medicine as intended to be brought under the act, was soundly made in the two cases which follow.

In the Colorado case of *Smith v. People,* decided in 1911, Smith was convicted of "practicing medicine without a license." On appeal, affirming conviction, the court said:

> The people's evidence shows that the defendant kept a place of business for healing the sick; . . . that there were signs in the windows reading: "Professor Smith, Healer." "Office hours 9 to 12, 2 to 6." A sign on the door reading: "Professor Smith, Healer." "Walk in." . . . He claimed his treatment was a natural one—a gift from the Almighty; claimed to restore people to health; said he could cure any disease a medical man could, and many they could not; could cure diarrhea, and stomach, spinal, nervous and throat troubles, and pneumonia; mentioned several cases of pneumonia he had recently cured that doctors had given up; said he diagnosed his cases and treated them without medicine.
>
> Defendant testified that he belonged to the church of "The Divine Scientific Healing Mission," a corporation; that he was a preacher of the gospel, and a healer of the sick; held services Sunday afternoons at Howe Hall, where he preached and cured the sick; said his church had branches everywhere; he occupied a couple of living rooms, not an office, where he lived and treated the sick and afflicted

without the use of drugs or a knife; some he charged, some he did not; never turned any one away; the signs had been there for over two years and spoke for themselves; did not practice medicine or diagnose diseases; people came to his rooms, told him what was the matter with them, and he treated them; could not tell whether patients had gout, smallpox or rheumatism, but could and did treat and cure them; "healer" means curing the sick.

The court quoted from the certificate of incorporation of "The Divine Scientific Healing Mission," offered in evidence but excluded by the trial court. Its objects were "Preaching, teaching and practising the gifts of healing, guided and directed by divine power, by laying on of hands, regardless of faith, creed, sect or race, to promote peace on earth, good will to men." Its tenets: "We believe in healing the suffering humanity by laying on of hands to be the gift of the divine spirit, and by sound reason we can comprehend its virtue."

It is the nature of defendant's business, not the objects of the corporation or the tenets of his church, that is in controversy. The evidence shows he was practicing medicine within the definition of the statute, and was using the title "healer," to his name, to indicate that he was engaged in the business of healing the sick. He treated in his office or place of business, for hire, persons suffering from disease, for the purpose of curing them. He held himself out to the public as a professional healer of diseases, and a practitioner of the healing art. The statute lays hands on commercial healing as a money-making occupation, business or profession, regardless of the method of treatment or curative agency employed. It concerns the public health, and should be liberally construed to accomplish the object of its enactment . . .

The statute does not interfere with the free exercise of religion or worship. Any persons, individually or collectively, any minister, or any church congregation may resort to prayer whenever they wish for the healing of the sick. No attempt is made to interfere with religion or religious devotions. This does not, however, authorize one under the cover of religion or religious exercise to go into healing commercially for hire, using prayer as the curative agency or treatment. Religion cannot be used as a shield to cover a business undertaking. Defendant was engaged in a business venture, not a religious exercise. The practice of medicine, defined by our statute, means the practice of the healing art commercially, regardless of the curative agency employed. The commercial practice of healing by prayer, followed as a money making venture or occupation, is the practice of medicine within the plain meaning of the statute . . .

In Kansas, in 1912, one Peters, a practitioner of "suggestive therapeutics," was convicted under the medical practice statute. As he explained his practice:

First had my attention called to healing people about 25 years ago from the study of the Bible. I supplemented that study by different branches. I have religious beliefs as to healing. I believe that the words of Jesus Christ in regard to healing can be carried out now just the same as they ever could. I believe from my study of the Bible and my supplemental study that I can carry out to some extent the healing as by Him practiced. My conviction is that I can do the work and ought to do it, and this has been my belief during the past three years, and it is my conviction that it is a duty I owe and must perform it. My supplemental studies have been psychology and suggestive therapeutics. I have studied the Weltmer system of suggestive therapeutics.

The president of the Weltmer Institute testified: "The fundamental principle in suggestive therapeutics is that the movement of the mind is the remedy in healing. Mind is both finite and infinite intelligence which governs all physical and mental actions, conscious and unconscious. Thinking is the mind's mode of acting. Then thought is the movement of the mind. Whatever other method is used is for the purpose of starting the mind of the patient into a state of activity in which the vibrations of his own mind will change the cell vibrations of his body. A movement of the mind that would have in it the constructive idea of replacing diseased tissue with healthy tissue would be a therapeutic thought. Anything that will induce this subjective intelligence to begin the process of healing is a therapeutic suggestion. Anything from the outside world that would secure a response from the suggestive mind would be a suggestion."

On appeal, affirming conviction, the court said:

The appellant was regularly engaged in soliciting, receiving, and treating patients for bodily infirmities, for fees charged and collected. This is within the statute . . . The claim of the appellant that he only practices a religious belief, within the exception which declares that nothing in the act shall be construed to interfere with any religious beliefs in the treatment of diseases, cannot be sustained. The only basis for this claim is the appellant's testimony that he believed the words of Jesus in regard to healing; that from Bible study and supplemental study of psychology and suggestive therapeutics he believes that he can carry out this healing practice to some extent, and that it is his duty to do so. Still, the fact remains uncontradicted that he diagnosed diseases and treated patients in a matter of fact way by manipulations and rubbing. He was thus treating people as a business for compensation, by outward physical means, and was not engaged merely in a religious observance, or, as counsel say, "practicing a religious belief." The place and value of suggestion in the treatment of disease need not be discussed, for, apart from this, the appellant engaged in the practice requiring an examination and certificate under the statute . . . The medical practitioner may entertain any belief his conscience approves, but this will not excuse him from a failure to observe the laws of the state regulating the calling in which he is engaged.

The many present-day cases of prosecutions of professed religious ministers all agree in holding that where religion and medicine are practiced together, the constitutional right to the practice of religion does not justify the concurrent illegal practice of medicine. The following are a few accounts of those whose administrations overstepped the statutory bounds of medical practice.

In Alabama, in 1916, one Fealy, a bishop and preacher of the Altrurian Church, was convicted of practicing medicine without a license, contrary to a Birmingham ordinance. He excepted to the court's instruction which left it to the jury to decide whether he was practicing a system of medicine or his religion, and on appeal, it was held that the instruction was erroneous, since it submitted to the jury a question of law as to what constitutes practicing medicine.

In North Dakota, in 1930, conviction of one Miller was affirmed for practicing medicine without a license. He had taken on the title of "Dr." and opened an office where he made diagnoses and gave treatment for a fee. He contended that he was an ordained minister of the Seventh Day Adventist Church and was practicing naturopathy, that this was one of his church's tenets, and that his practice therefore was within the exclusionary clause of the medical practice act; but it was held that he was practicing medicine as defined by the act.

In the State of Washington, in 1932, one Verbon prescribed various "drugs" which he contended were not "drugs" but "concentrates" of vegetables or herbs to be used as a diet supplement. He was a member of the Church of the Illumination, and contended that his acts were sanctioned by that church. He was convicted, and on appeal, affirming conviction, the court held that he was administering "drugs" within the meaning of the medical practice act.

In the Illinois case of *People v. Handzik,* decided in 1951, the defendant titled herself "doctor" and undertook to render medical diagnosis and treatment. Her treatment: certain breathing exercises, drinking two glasses of water—one "holy" and one "atomic"—laying on of hands, and prayer. A "donation" was accepted. On appeal, conviction was affirmed: the defendant's acts were not entirely spiritual.

And in Illinois, in 1952, William and Dora Estep organized the "Ministry of the Central Baptist Church of Chicago, Inc." and embarked upon a grandiose program for the training of "psycho-physicians," who set about to cure their patients through the use of various machines invented by Estep, and through prayer. The Esteps were convicted of conspiracy to violate the medical practice act. On appeal, affirming convictions, the court held that they were not within the exclusionary clause, and that it was a question of fact in each case whether or not a faith healer is legitimately exercising his religious freedom or merely using religion as a subterfuge to practice medicine illegally.

But all of the above are the exceptions. The "true" faith healers, like Susie Jessel, A. C. Valdez, Jr., the Rev. Jack Coe, and the Rev. Oral Roberts, who keep strictly and exclusively to "prayer or spiritual means," are specifically excluded from the requirements of the medical practice statutes. Likewise excluded, as we shall see in what follows, are the Christian Science practitioners.

When, to discredit her former student and defecting partner, prosperous practitioner Richard Kennedy (Ch. 3), Mrs. Glover, sometime between 1872 and 1875, renounced Quimby's "laying on of hands," she eliminated from her system the one element which later might have brought Christian Science under medical practice acts. The cases which follow only hint of the state by state, knock-down, drag-out fight between the medical societies and the Christian Science practitioners. The latter, for all their insistence upon the "unreality of matter," fought a most realistic battle in the courts, press and legislatures against the outlawing of their profitable trade. In 1894, they lost in Nebraska in *Buswell,* and again in 1905 in Ohio, in *Marble.* But in New York in 1916, after a five-year court battle, they won in *Cole*—under the typical excepting clause which *The New York Times* thereupon labelled "the bulwark of quackery."

But by then it had occurred to the Church leaders that, rather than fighting a series of such prosecutions, it would be simpler to pressure state legislatures into inserting a clause in the medical practice acts specifically exempting the practice of Christian Science. Indeed, by the time of the final Cole decision in 1916, they already had succeeded in doing so in ten states. In 1949, Ohio, the last state to do so, legalized the public practice of Christian Science as a healing art, its statute providing that "treatment of human ills through prayer alone by a practitioner of the Christian Science Church, in accordance with the tenets or creed of such church, shall not be regarded as the practice of medicine."[2]

In a Nebraska case decided in 1894, Buswell, a Christian Science practitioner, was indicted for practicing medicine without a license. At the trial, the judge instructed the jury that the defendant "could only be found guilty if he practiced medicine, surgery, and obstetrics as these terms are usually and generally understood." The jury brought in a verdict of not guilty, but on appeal, judgment was reversed. Chief Justice Ryan of Nebraska's Supreme Court first reviewed the defendant's brief:

> The defendant claimed that "to hold that the practices of the defendant are a violation of the law, would be to abrogate . . . the Constitution of this state, which provides that all persons have the natural and indefeasible right to worship Almighty God according to the dictates of their own conscience . . . The defendant, and those of the same faith with him, believe as a matter of conscience that the giving of medicine is a sin; that it is placing faith in the power of material things which belongs alone to Omnipotence. To the Christian Scientist it is as much a violation of the law of God to take drugs for the alleviation of suffering or the cure of disease as for a Methodist clergyman to take the name of his God in vain to relieve his overwrought feelings. It is as much the duty of the defendant as his conscience and understanding teach him his duty, to visit the sick and afflicted and relieve their distress of mind, as it is for the Presbyterian minister to go into his pulpit on Sabbath morning and preach the word of God according to the understanding of that denomination or visit the bedside of one of his sick parishioners and administer that religious consolation which is so dear to the heart of the Christian and which is apparently so necessary to their spiritual welfare. The act of the latter the eyes of all Christendom look upon in admiration as the performance of a Christian duty. Upon the former the able counsel of the state would have the world look as upon the act of a criminal.

In rebuttal, the court offered two Biblical accounts: that of Gehazi (II Kings 5), the servant of Elisha, who, after Elisha had cleansed Syrian captain Naaman of leprosy and afterwards refused any gift from Naaman, ran after Naaman and falsely represented that Elisha wished a talent of silver and two changes of garments, and was given two changes and two talents; for which sin, on Gehazi's return, Elisha brought Naaman's former affliction upon Gehazi. And that of Simon (Acts 8), the sorcerer of Samaria, who was converted by Philip and baptised, and who, afterwards, observing how, through the laying on of hands by apostles Peter and John, "the Holy Ghost was given, he offered them money, Saying, Give me also this power, that on whomsoever I lay hands, he may receive the Holy Ghost. But Peter said unto him, Thy money perish with thee, because thou hast thought that the gift of God may be purchased with money."

> In the light of these instances, cited from defendant's own authority, it is confidently believed that the exercise of the art of healing for

compensation, whether exacted as a fee or expected as a gratuity, cannot be classed as an act of worship. Neither is it the performance of a religious duty, as was claimed in the district court . . . Under the indictment, the sole question presented upon the evidence was whether or not the defendant within the time charged had operated on, or professed to heal, or prescribed for or otherwise treated, any physical or mental ailment of another. There was involved no question of sentiment nor of religious practice or duty. If the defendant was guilty as charged, neither pretense of worship nor of the performance of any other duty should have exonerated him from the punishment which an infraction of the statute involved.

But four years later, in 1898, in the Rhode Island case of *State v. Mylod,* it was held that Christian Scientists were not practicing medicine within the meaning of the statute, and were exempt from securing licenses because in exercising their religious liberty they healed by prayer. The court pointed out that the defendant not only did not attempt to treat disease, but denied its very existence.

In Ohio, in the early case of *State v. Evans,* decided in 1889, the court held that Christian Science practice did not come within the medical practice statute: "Freedom of thought and worship in matters of religion is a birthright of every citizen, and the legislature cannot take it away or abridge it in any way." Afterwards, however, the legislature amended the statute to make it more inclusive, and in 1905, the conviction of Christian Science practitioner Marble for practicing medicine without a license upon rheumatic Christ Hehl was affirmed:

> If its followers call it treatment, they ought not to be heard to say it is not . . . If the defendant prayed for the recovery of Hehl, that was the treatment he gave him for the cure of his rheumatism and for which Hehl paid him. He was practicing healing or curing disease. To assume that legislation may be directed only against the administering of drugs or the use of the knife is to take a too narrow view. The subject of the legislation is not medicine and surgery. It is the public health or the practice of healing . . .
> While the state may not deem it wise to go to the extent of requiring the individual to avail himself of the services of a physician, yet it may not wish to hasten his death and so to transfer to itself the burden of supporting those dependent upon him by making it possible for him to employ an empiric.* Again, where there is an infectious or contagious disease, the public welfare may be vitally affected by a failure promptly to recognize it, and so the state is interested in permitting to practice the art of healing only those possessing recognized qualifications. So that, regarding disease rather than the treatment of

---

* In the better—or least bad—sense, one who follows an empirical method; otherwise, a quack or charlatan.

it as the subject of the legislation, it is not necessary that the statute be preventive of particular practices, but it may make the right to undertake the treatment of disease dependent upon the possession of reasonable qualifications.

On Thursday, January 19, 1911, Mrs. Frances Benzecry, an investigator for the New York County Medical Society, entered the Brunswick Building, at 225 Fifth Avenue, Madison Square, New York City. She proceeded to the ninth floor and to an office door bearing the words *Willis Vernon Cole, Christian Scientist*.[3] In the reception room she waited her turn with others ("There were a number of men and women there, coming and going"), then went into the inner office.

> I asked him if he was Dr. Cole. And he said he was Mr. Cole, a Christian Science healer. He said, "Who recommended you here?" I said I read about him in the newspaper; that I called to see if he could cure my eyes, I had been troubled with eye trouble. And he said, "How long have you been wearing glasses?" I said, "Ten years." He said: "You understand I do not give any medicine; I only give Christian Science treatment." I said to him, "What is Christian Science?" He said, "I cure by prayer." He said, "You must have faith in God, that God don't make us to have any disease, that we must be all love and kindness, and that God would cure the infidel as well as the confirmed believer in his Divine Power." And I said, "What would be the fee?" And he said $2 for the first treatment and all subsequent treatments $1. [He] then said, "I will give you a treatment." So Mr. Cole had his chair facing mine, and he closed his eyes and raised his hands up to his face and remained in perfect silence for 15 or 20 minutes. He then said: "That will do for to-day's treatment." I said to him, "When will I come back again?" He says, "You come back on Friday any time." I paid him $2.

The next day, when Mrs. Benzecry returned:

> I went in and he said to me, "Why, you are looking very well." I said, "I feel about the same." After that he spoke about God is good, and we must have love and faith in God. And then he says he will give me a treatment. So then Mr. Cole placed his chair facing mine again, and closed his eyes and put his hands up to his face, and he remained in perfect silence there for 15 to 20 minutes.

Before this treatment she said to him:

> "Mr. Cole, I have a pain in my back." I then said that I had a porous plaster on my back at that time. I said to him what did he think about the pain I had in my back. He said it was some kind of disease, but he could not tell what it was. He said, "I can cure it."

He said, "You must now take off that porous plaster, because Christian Science cannot cure with plasters on." He said that I must take off my glasses as well as remove the plaster from my back; that I should have more faith and understanding; that I must have courage; that I should remove the glasses. I said I must keep my glasses as I cannot go without them. I told him I had worn them for 10 years. He said if I wanted to be cured by Christian Science I must remove the glasses. After he gave me the second treatment, I said, "How can you cure locomotor ataxia?" He said, "Just by prayer and having faith in God." He said, "When patients are given up by physicians, they always turn to Christian Science for help." He said he could cure locomotor ataxia* by Christian Science.

He told her to come back on Monday, January 23, and she did so:

He said, "You are looking very well." I said, "I removed the plaster that was on my back as you told me to." And he said, "I want you also to remove the glasses." I says, "I have to keep the glasses on." I said to Mr. Cole that when I eat bread and potato, I would distress my stomach very much. He said: "Leave your stomach alone. You go home and eat anything you want to, if you keep bothering your stomach." He said, "I can cure that by Christian Science." I said that I was suffering from delayed menstruation. He said, "I am glad you spoke about it, as it is all one cause; but I can cure it." He said, "I will give you a treatment." And the treatment was exactly like the treatment before.

On January 27 she returned for the last time, bringing along her ten-year-old daughter, who wore glasses.

I said to Mr. Cole that the child has been wearing glasses and she also has a cold. I said, "Can you cure her by Christian Science?" He said, "Absolutely." I said, "Well, will you cure her?" He said, "Absolutely." I said that the child had a pair of roller skates, and, wearing glasses, why, if she should fall she would injure herself. And he said, "You take the glasses off and let the child run and romp like other children; that mothers should not put such fear in children." He said: "I will give the child a treatment and you a treatment." Before he started the treatment, he said, "What is the child's first name?" I said, "Lucille." Then he closed his eyes and gave the treatment.

Q. "What did he say when he took his hands down and opened his eyes?"

---

* Progressive destruction of the spinal chord during the tertiary stages of syphilis, evidenced by a shuffling gait and later by paralysis of the legs. Progress of the disease can be arrested by treatment, but the damage already done to the nervous system before treatment is started cannot (at least to the author's knowledge) be repaired.

A. "He said that was enough for to-day."

I then said . . . "How is it that you cure cancer?" He said, "By prayer." I said I had a friend who was suffering from cancer and had visited Dr. Mason. [He] said, "Why, I know Dr. Mason." He said, "By all means send your friend to me for treatment." He said: "That is the way, when patients are given up by physicians, they always turn to Christian Science for help."

On February 18, 1911, the New York County Medical Society applied for a warrant charging Cole with practicing medicine without being duly licensed. At the preliminary examination in the Magistrates' Court, Virgil O. Strickley, First Reader of the local First Church of Christ, asserted that his faith would cure the ill without any other aid. "Christian Science teaches that Christ never commanded an impossible or an unnecessary thing. Christian Scientists obey Christ's words, 'Go forth and heal the sick.'" Asked if there was anything in the Bible authorizing such healers to charge a fee, Mr. Strickley's counsel replied, "The laborer is worthy of his hire." According to Mr. Strickley, it was even possible to raise the dead. And prayer, he said, was as efficacious in the case of animals as of human beings.

Cole himself testified that he had been practicing for nine years, and that in order to get his "card" listed in the Christian Science periodicals, it had been necessary to show that he had performed three cures. He himself had been cured by that method of three diseases commonly considered incurable. He had often treated animals, and had been particularly successful in the case of dogs.

Cole was tried in the Criminal Term of the New York Supreme Court. The only evidence taken: the testimony of Mrs. Benzecry and of Cole himself. On Mrs. Benzecry's cross examination:

Q. You have said . . . that Mr. Cole said, I will cure this, that, and the other. Did not Mr. Cole tell you on your first visit and reiterate it on subsequent visits that he had no power in and of himself? A. He said he did not have any power.

Q. That you had every bit of power that he had, did not he? A. Yes.

Q. That you could heal as well as he if you would study the Bible and rely upon its promises, and offer the prayer of understanding and faith? A. Yes, sir.

Q. That when Mr. Cole had explained to you that he had no power in himself, that all power came from God, and that you had every particle of power that he had, and that what you needed was faith in the Almighty, you understood by that that if he said "I can do this" or "do that," "I can cure," that it was through this means of prayer, did you not. A. Through Almighty God.

Q. . . . you stated in effect, did you not, that all diseases look alike to a Christian Scientist—that he said that? A. Yes.

Q. That Mr. Cole told you that. A. That Mr. Cole said that all diseases were alike.

Q. As a matter of fact, did not Mr. Cole explain to you that it was the teaching of the Bible and of Christian Science that God healed all diseases, and that He was the Great Physician, and that if you would be good and pure and honest and come to Him in sincerity and truth and ask Him for his power, that it would be given to you? A. Well, he said something very similar to it.

Q. He told you, did he not, that there was nothing mysterious about Christian Science, that you could learn all that he knew? A. Yes, sir.

Q. He even went so far as to ask you, to suggest, that you buy the book and study it in connection with the Bible? A. Yes, sir.

Q. And then you would know how to cure yourself and how to remain cured and well. A. Yes, sir . . .

Q. Did Mr. Cole look at your tongue? A. No.

Q. Feel your pulse? A. No.

Q. Test your temperature? A. No.

Q. Make any analysis of your blood? A. No.

Q. He undertook no diagnosis whatever, did he? A. No.

Q. Did he put you on a diet? A. No.

Q. Told you to eat what was set before you? A. He told me to eat anything I wanted to. He said that God never made us to have any disease.

Q. And that that was a mental—that the body itself had no power to feel, that it was the mind that suffered always, or words to that effect? A. Words to that effect.

Q. And that God was all mind, and that we were simply an idea of the Almighty—meant us to be well if we would trust Him, or words to that effect? A. Words to that effect.

Q. And that if we lived honest and pure and kind lives that we would remain well? A. Yes . . .

Q. Did he strike you as though he was greedy for money? A. No, he did not act that way to me . . .

Q. He never intimated to you on any of those visits that you should pay him. You always asked him what the charge was, did you not? A. Yes . . .

Q. Mr. Cole in all of your visits took pains to explain to you, did he not, that so far from being a mystery, so far from having any power himself, that this was a religion that everybody ought to know and practice, did he not? A. Yes.

Cole testified that he had been an authorized practitioner of the Christian Science Church for eight years; that he had maintained his office in the Brunswick building for five years in May; that when he received his first knowledge of Christian Science he was a sculptor, and a poet; that he had never studied medicine in any way; that his average income per year from his practice was about $5,000 or $6,000; and that he did not ask people for money for treating them. When they tendered it, he took it.

Q. Is it not one of the rules of the Church? A. I don't say there is any definite rule, but it is a practice to treat all who are honest and sincere whether they can pay or not, and that is a rule; we are to help every one.

Cole testified that he remembered the occasion on which Mrs. Benzecry first called on him:

She sat about four feet away from me, facing me. She told me that she had come to be treated for trouble with her eyes and stomach trouble. I informed her that Christian Science treatment was prayer to God; we did not believe in drugs, medical treatment, anything like that; and she asked me to give her treatment. Something was said in regard to the basis of Christian Science, and I told her substantially that Christian Science was the truth about God, and the truth about man, and the truth about man's relationship to God, and the truth of his birthright as a result of this relationship, which is the foundation of what we teach, and I told her that on this basis disease was no part of her birthright, or inharmony, and when she realized her oneness with God and got in harmony with God that this was the treatment and was what we would do. She sat there about 15 minutes. I covered my face with my hands, or sat with my head partially bowed for 15 minutes in prayer to God . . . Mrs. Benzecry asked me how much I charged for treatment, and I told her it was customary to pay $2 for the first treatment and $1 for any other treatments, and she paid me $2 . . .

At another interview she asked me if she should—spoke to me about taking off her glasses, and I said to her: "There is no reason that you should not take off your glasses. I took off mine and had not been wearing them for years." And then I started to tell her about the work and practice of Christian Science . . . I told her I had trouble with my eyes and had several other diseases, and that I had been to a number of physicians, and that I had been healed by Christian Science . . . I told her that Christian Science was prayer to God. I told her that Christian Science realized that God was omnipotent, or all-powerful, and that He was omniscient, or all knowing; that He was omnipresent, or ever-present; and that because God was omnipotent, omniscient, and omnipresent, and God was good, that it must follow that evil, disease, inharmony, sin, and discord were no part of His being and had no real existence, and I told her that man was the image and likeness of God, and was entitled to dominion, and that his birthright was dominion, and that he had the right to affirm and secure immunity from discord of whatever name and nature, and that disease was like a shadow that flees before the light . . . I prayed. Our whole interview took about 25 minutes. I remained all this time in silent prayer. That word "prayer" is a synonym for treatment. I sat in silence for about 15 minutes, and Mrs. Benzecry sat opposite me, and at the end of that time I took my hands—removed my hands from my eyes and spoke a few words, and she paid me for that treatment, paid me the sum of $1, and that was practically our interview.

Q. Well, at that interview or at the first interview did you tell Mrs. Benzecry that you could cure her?

I told her I could not cure her, that I had no more power to cure her than any one else, that God was the only power and the only healer. I remember one thing I did say to her. That God was no respecter of diseases and could cure one thing just as much as another, and especially when she told me about her delayed menstruation. She asked me about that . . . I said to her: "Mrs. Benzecry, God is no respecter of diseases, and through Christian Science, through prayer, can heal one thing just as readily as another." And I said substantially the same thing on the third interview when she asked me about the friend who had locomotor ataxia . . . I did say Christian Science cured locomotor ataxia through prayer to God. I told her that I had no more power than she did; that God had the only power. She asked me, I believe, if I cured cancer, or if Christian Science cured cancer. I told her that Christian Science cured all manner of diseases through prayer to God, and she told me, I remember at that incident, that she had a friend that had cancer, and this friend had consulted a physician, and I spoke to her in regard to Christian Science treating and healing diseases that the physicians had given up. I told her that there were a number of diseases that the physicians deemed incurable, and that such cases had been successfully treated in Christian Science.

Q. At the time of these interviews with Mrs. Benzecry you were practicing Christian Science with her, weren't you? A. I was.

Q. At the time of these interviews were you practicing or trying to practice any other system? A. None other.

Q. Of healing or religion or anything else? A. Nothing else.

On the third visit, according to Cole:

We discussed Christian Science and I picked up *Science and Health with Key to the Scriptures* by Mrs. Eddy which is recognized in Christian Science as the standard text-book; it is the original Christian Science text-book which we accept with the Holy Scriptures of which it is explanatory as the basis of our great religious truth. I asked her to procure a copy of this book.

He read to her from *Science and Health:* "To be 'present with the Lord' is to have, not mere emotional ecstasy or faith, but the actual demonstration and understanding of Life as revealed in Christian Science. To be 'with the Lord' is to be in obedience to the law of God, to be absolutely governed by Divine Love—by Spirit, not by matter. Become conscious for a single moment that Life and intelligence are purely spiritual—neither in nor of matter—and the body will then utter no conscious complaints. If suffering from a belief in sickness, you will find yourself suddenly well. Sorrow is turned into joy when the body is controlled by spiritual life, Truth and Love . . . Entirely separate from the belief and dream of material living is the Life Divine, revealing spiritual understanding and the consciousness of man's dominion over the whole earth. This understanding casts out error and heals the sick, and with it you can speak 'as one having authority.' "

Under cross-examination, Cole testified:

Q. Now you had an office, and in that office, as I understand, you held yourself out as being able to treat human diseases through the medium or by the means of the Christian Science doctrine of religion? A. Through prayer to God, yes.

Q. That is the means by which you held yourself out as being able to treat human diseases; is that correct? A. It is incorrect. It is incorrect on this basis that Christian Science does not recognize disease as a reality . . . The patients that come to us to be treated for sin and disease and other inharmonious, similar inharmonious conditions, are treated for those through prayer to God, and it is the function of the Christian Science practitioner to offer this prayer to God.

Q. You don't answer my question at all. Your office was a place in which you held yourself out as being able to treat those people that came to you for sin or disease by the means of the method that you thought was efficacious; was that correct? A. By the means of prayer to God.

Q. And that is the means that you considered efficacious? A. Yes.

Q. And you held yourself out as being able to treat them by those means or by that method; is that correct? A. To pray to God for them.

Q. I am taking now their state of mind, certain people resorted to your office for the purpose of being treated for sin or disease; is that correct? A. It is correct.

Q. And you used your office as a place where you held yourself out as being able to treat them for what they came to you by methods you thought were efficacious? A. Through prayer to God, yes.

Cole stated that he would have above 2,500 and 3,000 calls a year at his place. The number of calls were considerably over 3,000 to his best belief.

Q. And did you treat all patients that came substantially by the same method, and in the same way, all these 3,000 people by the same method of treatment? A. If you mean on that basis I will state I did, through prayer.

Q. I say did you treat them all by the same method, or did you employ different methods? A. One method.

Q. Now it has been testified here both by yourself, and I think by Mrs. Benzecry, you told her that through Christian Science and God all disease was the same: that is correct, is it not? A. Yes, sir.

Q. Therefore you would treat by this method anybody who came into your office, no matter with what disease they thought they were afflicted; is that correct? A. I would not say that . . .

Q. What diseases would you except from that statement? A. I would not say.

Q. Well, I ask you to say? A. There is no special disease that I do exempt.

Q. Then why do you say you would not treat them all? A. There might be cases that it would appear to be better not to treat.

Q. Well, I ask you what cases would you refuse to treat? A. For instance, it might be a case that a person would prefer to have medical treatment.

Q. I am not asking that; I am asking about people that came to you and wanted to be treated by you. Now, I ask you would you refuse to treat anybody? . . . Is there any disease or supposed disease you would not treat if a person came in to you and asked you to treat them? A. No.

Q. None whatever? A. No, sir . . .

Q. Does that include contagious diseases, or does it not? A. It is possible for Christian Science to heal contagious diseases.

Q. I will ask you to answer my question. A. I would treat any one that came to me who seemed honest and earnest and who wanted Christian Science treatment.

Q. Does that include contagious diseases, or so-called contagious diseases; yes or no? A. I don't think any one would come to me if they had a contagious disease.

Q. I am not asking you what they would do. I am asking you what you would do. Would you be ashamed to treat them? A. I would not be ashamed to treat them.

Q. Please tell me whether you would treat them? A. I have treated them . . .

Q. Suppose a person brought a child she said had pneumonia or pleurisy, would you treat it? A. Of course, I would pray to God for the child . . .

Q. Would you tell the parent of the child to take the child to a physician? A. Why, God is the Great Physician.

Q. Will you please answer my question. I did not ask you about God. A. I would not say to take a child to the physician if they had applied to me to pray to God for the child.

Q. That is just what I asked you. Would you or would you not tell them to take a child to the physician? A. I would not do so . . .

Q. Suppose she said she did want Christian Science treatment and then asked whether she should also take it to a doctor, what would you say then? A. I would say, "God is mightier than all the doctors."

Q. Would you advise her to take her or not to take her? A. If she asked my advice and was there for treatment, I would say not to take the child . . .

Q. Would you therefore tell the mother you advised her not to take the child to a doctor? A. No, I would not advise her not to take the child to a doctor. I would say, "That is for you to decide."

Q. But you would tell her if she wished to be cured by Christian Science in that case she should not take it? A. If the mother wishes Christian Science treatment, she should not rely on drugs.

Q. Or the doctor? A. Doctors, or other material things.

At the trial, evidence showing that healing by prayer had been accomplished was excluded on the ground that the question was not whether the treatment favored by the Christian Scientists was successful but simply whether Cole had practiced medicine without a license. Afterwards, the jury failed to agree. A second trial resulted in a verdict of guilty, and on March 30, 1912, judgment was entered against Cole. He was fined $100 and the fine was paid. His counsel, Samuel Untermyer, said he would carry the case to the highest courts. Two years later, on July 10, 1914, the Appellate Division affirmed judgment by a divided court. Said Justice Clarke:

. . . The language of the statute is "by any means or method." This covers the means or method used by him. While he denied the material existence of disease and said it was merely mental, yet he undertook to treat people he called patients for what they told him was the matter with them; in other words, what they thought were diseases . . . Whatever the believers in Christian Science may think about disease, the law regards it as a fact. It requires the vaccination of children; it requires the examination and quarantine of children admitted to institutions, and a certificate, where the child has diphtheria, scarlet fever, measles, whooping cough, or any other contagious or infectious disease . . .

The one question presented here is whether the defendant is permitted to do what he has done under the clause of the statute: "This article shall not be construed to affect . . . the practice of the religious tenets of any church."

Is the commercialized use of prayer for the avowed purpose of treating all persons seeking cure for all kinds of bodily ills the practice of the religious tenets of a church? . . . "Tenet" is defined by the Century Dictionary as "any opinion, principle, dogma, or doctrine which a person, school or sect holds or maintains is true." A man's right to hold and express such is unquestioned. But when he advances from the realm of thought to that of action, he must obey the law.

Though there was still the matter of an appeal to the highest court, the affirming of Cole's conviction by the Appellate Division brought many cheers. "Paid Prayer Curing Declared Illegal," crowed *The New York Times,* and on July 13, under the heading, " 'Healing' Made Profitless," editorialized: "This decision will be a stunning blow to the exploiters of the particular form of suggestion to which Mrs. Eddy gave vogue among the credulous and erratic. As Cole is of good and regular standing in the cult, its votaries cannot, as often, disclaim responsibility for him, and as his dealings with the detective were typical of what goes on daily in the offices of these 'healers,' all of them are declared to be violators of the Medical Practice Act and amenable to its penalties."

But two years later, under a dateline of October 3, 1916, the *Times* had stunning news from Albany. "Annuls Conviction of W. V. Cole, Healer," its captions read, "Court of Appeals Holds Practice of Christian Science is not Medical Practice," "New trial for Defendant," and "Following of Religious Tenets in Treatment a Factor—Case Fought 5 Years."

"The Court of Appeals decision," reported the *Times,* "holds that while the practice of healing by Christian Scientists would come within the definition of medical practice, the statute specifically exempts those who in the treatment of bodily ills follow out the tenets of any religion . . . "

At a meeting on October 9, the New York County Medical Society resolved to ask the next Legislature to amend the Public Health Law by striking out the excepting clause. George W. Whiteside, counsel for the Society, opined that because of that clause, any retrial of Cole at the present time would be useless. Bitterly he advised that any incompetent who wished to enter medical practice had first only to "organize some religious sect and meet in some building that might be designated as a church."

On October 11, the *Times* characterized the aim of the Society as "Desirable but Not Probable": "A long, hard fight, with victory rather to be hoped than expected, is that which the County Medical Society promises to make against the sentence in New York's excellent Medical Practice Act which forbids the application of its prohibitions and penalties to 'the practice of the religious tenets of any church.' That sentence is the bulwark of quackery . . . "

In handing down the opinion, Justice Chase said:

> Practicing medicine, when unaccompanied by acts that are in themselves evil, vicious, and criminal, is not a crime at common law. Practicing medicine is not *malum in se* * . . .
>
> It does not appear that the defendant attempted to diagnose the diseases which the investigator stated to him that she had; he not only in substance denied that she had any disease, but asserted that they rested in her imagination, or were mere evidence of a lack of true relation to her God. There was no inquiry on his part into the symptoms which the investigator claimed that she had as indicating the diseases. There was no laying on of hands, manipulation, massage, or outward ceremonial. His direction to her to remove her glasses and take off a porous plaster . . . were, as also asserted by him, simply to bring about complete reliance by her upon the power and willingness of God to heal her diseases . . . It was a test of her faith. He, however, testified that prayer was a synonym for treatment. He habitually termed his interposition by prayer a treatment, and such it would seem to have been in the ordinary meaning of the word . . .
>
> We are of the opinion that the defendant did "treat" the investigator by "any means or method," as the word is used in the general prohibition contained in the statute. The general and comprehensive definition of a person who practices medicine has an express exception . . . as follows:
>
> "This article shall not be construed to affect . . . the practice of the religious tenets of any church."
>
> The exception includes every person in the practice of the religious tenets of any church, and it is not in any way in conflict with the federal or state Constitution. The language quoted . . . is not in any sense an affirmative license. It is, we repeat, an exception to the general prohibition. Whether the practice of the religious tenets of any church should have been excepted from the general prohibition against the practice of medicine unless the practitioner is registered and authorized so to do, or whether the exception should

---

* I.e., not a wrong in itself, like larceny or murder.

be continued therein, is a question for the Legislature and not for the courts. The purpose of the general statute is to protect citizens and others of the state from being treated in their physical ailments and diseases by persons who have not adequate or proper training, education, or qualifications to treat them . . .

The exception in the statute is not confined to worship or belief, but includes the practice of religious tenets. If it was the intention of the Legislature to relieve members of the Christian Science and other churches from the provisions . . . of the Public Health Law to the extent of permitting them within the rules, regulations, and tenets of a church to maintain an office and there offer prayer for the healing of the diseases of those that might come to such church members for treatment, and the defendant had in good faith acted in accordance therewith, he is not guilty of the crime alleged in the indictment.

The Christian Science Church is in terms expressly excepted from the prohibition contained in the medical practice acts of many of the states. It is so expressly excepted in the statutes of Maine, New Hampshire, Massachusetts, Connecticut, North Carolina, North and South Dakota, Kentucky, Tennessee, and Wisconsin.

We think the exception in the statute in this state is broad enough to permit offering prayer for the healing of disease in accordance with the recognized tenets of the Christian Science Church. It may be said that if the exception is so construed, it will lead to numberless persons assuming to cure diseases in the name of a church for the purpose of thereby maintaining a business and securing a livelihood. The religious tenets of a church must be practiced in good faith to come within the exception. When such practice is a fraud or pretense it is not excepted from the general prohibition . . . When a person claims to be practicing the religious tenets of any church, particularly where compensation is taken therefor and the practice is apart from a church edifice or the sanctity of the home of the applicant, the question whether such person is within the exception should be left to a jury as a question of fact. In this case the court charged the jury:

"If you find from the evidence in this case that this defendant did engage in the practice of medicine as alleged in the indictment, within the definition which I have given to you, it is no defense that he did what he did from any sense of duty, or that he did these acts in the practice of the religious tenets of the Christian Science Church."

We are of the opinion that the court was in error in so charging the jury . . . the court, instead of charging the jury as stated, should have left to the jury the question whether the defendant was in good faith practicing the tenets of such a church within the meaning of the statutory exception.

Added Chief Justice Bartlett: "I concur in Judge Chase's construction of the statute. But I would go farther. I deny the power of the Legislature to make it a crime to treat disease by prayer."

And so stands the anomaly in child protection and medical practice acts today. True, the parent-liability decisions hold that the faith healer's and Christian Science practitioner's ministrations do *not* constitute "proper medical care" for a sick child. The parent who calls in such people instead of a qualified physician is punished. But there is no law enjoining these same faith healers and Christian Science practitioners from holding themselves out to parents as proper healers for their children. Afterwards, only the parents of the dead child are haled off to court, while the "healer," who urged upon them a trust in his methods and a distrust in those of the medical profession, goes free.

The hard fact is that today, from the lone operator like Susie Jessel to the corporate colossus of the Christian Science Church—all such, so long as they confine themselves strictly to prayer and spiritual means, are free to practice their profitable trade on children as well as on adults, and whether they live or die.

# 12

# The Right to Submit; Pastor Liability

Granting (reluctantly) that the sincere faith healer and Christian Science practitioner are by law free to practice, is the ill adult at the same time entirely free to submit solely to their ministrations? Or more practically, is the ill adult free to deny himself necessary medical aid? At least three circumstances occur. In one, the sick man, alarmed by his faith healer's failure, finally calls in a qualified physician and sumbits—often with the greatest embarrassment, and likely keeping the faith healer at his side—to the physician's treatment as well. Here, if the state had complaint before, it has none now. This happens regularly in the case of Christian Scientists. Here, the long-suffering physician is presented with a case which by inattention has already reached a late and perhaps inoperable or incurable stage, and when despite his desperate last-minute efforts death follows, the Christian Science organization triumphantly points out still another failure of medicine. Or, incredible as it may seem, if the doctor is successful, the religious practitioner, unfettered by medical ethics, blandly announces that it was his own continuing prayers, in the face of the medico's meddling, which in fact brought about the cure.

Quite different is the circumstance where the doctor-denying and perhaps disease-denying sick adult's illness proves not only real but contagious as well. Here the state, with its overriding interest in the public health and safety, brushes aside the sick man's claims to the constitution's guarantees of personal liberty and religious freedom, and at once steps in to apply quarantine regulations. Indeed, it has been sixty-odd years since the Supreme Court, in *Jacobson* (Ch. 8) upheld the state's right to go even farther, and, in the face of a threatened epidemic, force vaccination upon its *well* citizens, regardless of their personal feelings. Had tubercular Christian Scientist Cora Sutherland's condition (Ch. 3) been discovered earlier, there is no doubt that the state would summarily have forced her isolation to the extent that she no longer endangered the health of others.

But could the state then have gone farther, and forced Cora Sutherland to undertake proper treatment? This is the third circumstance. An
adult is seriously ill but not endangering others. Can he elect to deny
himself the medical aid without which it is clear to the law's "reasonable man" that he will die? At first glance (I will qualify this in a
moment) the question appears to reduce to a simpler form: is it unlawful to attempt suicide?

Suicide is a unique act in that the doer thereby effectively forestalls
prosecution. Even so, at common law the completed act was a felony,
and to attempt suicide—as to attempt any other crime—was a misdemeanor. In England at one time the dead offender was "punished" by
the shame of unmarked burial in the highway and by his heirs forfeiting to the king their right to the deceased's lands and goods. But
though this attempted punishment was abandoned, suicide thereafter
was still held, though not punishable, to be very much a crime—to the
practical end that *attempted* suicide should therefore remain a misdemeanor. This was desirable for other reasons than only to deter the
would-be suicide. Thus, if a man aimed and fired a gun intending to
kill himself but missed and killed a bystander, the former still would be
liable for manslaughter or murder, and one who persuaded another to
commit suicide would still be guilty of murder as principal or accessory.

Today, in at least eleven states, the common law of crimes, insofar
as it defines and punishes offenses, has been completely abolished and
replaced by statutes. In these states, no offense is punishable unless
made so by statute. Some odd results have followed when a state has
undertaken at one sweep to abolish the entire common law and replace
it by statutes. When Ohio abolished the common law as to defining
what acts were crimes, it failed to provide by statute for the punishment of a man having carnal knowledge of a girl under ten with her
consent. Consequently, in *Smith v. State,* the court was forced to hold
such an act not a crime.

Where a state does not risk such sweeping abolition, the question
may arise as to whether a certain statute, by implication, has repealed
some principle of common law. Here, in general, if there is no repug-
nancy between the statute and the common law, the common-law principle continues to operate. In Massachusetts, where at common law
attempted suicide was a misdemeanor, the legislature undertook to
define all "attempts" by statute. It made only those attempts punishable
where the offense so attempted was itself punishable by death, imprisonment or fine. Afterwards, in *Dennis,* a prosecution for attempted
suicide, the court held that, since suicide itself could not be punished

either by death, imprisonment or fine, the attempt was no longer indictable.

In Texas, the statute makes neither suicide nor furnishing the means a crime. In Iowa, where the statute does not make suicide unlawful, it was held not murder when a person was killed in trying to prevent another's suicide. But in Michigan, a man who furnished the means for his wife's suicide at her request, and was present, was held guilty of murder. And in Ohio, one who administered poison by request was convicted of murder. In other states, the common law has in some particulars been repealed or superseded by statute but in all other respects remains in effect. Under such a statute in Missouri, one who assists another to commit suicide is guilty of manslaughter . . .[1]

But I hear the reader's voice objecting:

"This is all no doubt very interesting, but I still have not quite managed to swallow your first premise—that refusal of necessary medical aid by an adult is identical with attempted suicide. In the former, where is the criminal intent?"

Granting the objection, I would reply that, even so, the excursion to here has yielded an answer in part. The answer: in those states where attempted suicide has been made lawful by statute or the lack of one, the adult's self-denial of necessary medical aid, whether equal to or less than attempted suicide, must be conceded to be lawful.

This leaves in question those states where the common law in this respect remains unchanged—where attempted suicide remains a misdemeanor. Here, I have no case to cite, and instead must submit a conjecture which leans upon the significance of the Wagstaffe trial. This inspired the first child protection statute, which in turn led to the sound establishment, in *Senior,* of the principle of parent liability regardless of belief.

In pre-Wagstaffe times, the faith-healing parent's religious belief negated any "negligence so gross and wanton as to be criminal," when he denied his child proper medical care. In post-Wagstaffe times, the child protection statutes created a positive duty for the parent to furnish such care, against which religious belief to the contrary was no defense. Again, then, in pre-Wagstaffe times could the ill adult who relied on faith and prayer for his own cure be found to entertain the criminal intent required to make up the crime of attempted suicide? I think not, for his only intent was to get well. And since no present-day "adult protection statute" has appeared to complete the parallel, this status of the ill adult must remain unchanged.

Would medical doctors favor the forced acceptance of their efforts by such an "adult protection statute"? An editor-physician wrote me:

> Refusal of medical advice is often foolish and may even be danger-
> ous. But we must never forget that freedom is based on the privilege
> to accept or reject. As a practicing physician I must defend the right
> of my patients to reject my advice. I would never condone anything
> forcing them to accept it. A free medical profession must accept this
> viewpoint or be subjected to the same destructive application of force
> which would be applied to others . . . I do not agree with those who
> let serious and preventable diseases develop by refusing medical
> advice, but I will staunchly defend their right to refuse . . . It is
> fundamental to freedom in America.

Though the answer clearly lies in the state's anciently asserted right
to a greater active concern for its infant than for its adult citizens, a
number of judges have been impelled to note, in asides or dicta, the
apparent or possible incongruity in requiring for the child what is not
required for the adult. In *Pierson:* "As to an adult (except possibly in
the case of a contagious disease which would affect the health of
others), I think there is no power to prescribe what medical treatment
he shall receive, and that he is entitled to follow his own election,
whether that election be dictated by religious belief or other considerations." In *Cole:* "There is no law in this state which compels an adult
person, suffering from disease, to obtain medical assistance." In *Marble:*
"The state might make it an offense . . . for any one to omit to furnish
medical attendance to those dependent upon him, and at the same time
leave him at liberty to die in any manner he may choose." In *Owens\*:*
"Under the law in this state, there is probably no way of reaching an
adult who refuses to accept medical aid for himself on his own responsibility." And in *Prince:* "Parents may be free to become martyrs
themselves."

Newspaper accounts appear to confirm this result. In Texas, in 1952,
Fred Newhouse was badly injured in such a manner that doctors dared
not proceed with a necessary operation without a blood transfusion.
When Witness Newhouse refused on religious grounds to allow it, the
law did not intervene.[2] In Missouri, in 1952, Ozarks minister J. J. Ivie
tried in vain to obtain a "revelation of God's will," then vowed to pray
and fast until God gave him a sign. After 51 days of fasting and praying, and still without the prayed for sign, he died. During his fast,
which received nationwide publicity, no attempt was made to stop him,
even though, towards the end, Ivie's religion-motivated determination
clearly was leading to his death.[3]

---

\* An Oklahoma case not described in this book.

Society, its legislatures and its courts seem to say: "We are determined that a child shall grow up safely and in good health, and we will intervene when his life or health is threatened by his parent's religious or other eccentricity. But having taken this trouble so to see him into manhood, why, if he thereafter chooses to endanger his own life—and does not at the same time endanger others—then we wash our hands of him."

Let us distinguish between crimes and civil actions. The law, Justice Oliver Wendell Holmes said, is simply "a statement of the circumstances in which the public force will be brought to bear upon men through the courts."[4] So far, we have been concerned with the law of crimes. Crimes, however, constitute only one of the three general areas of the law. The others: contracts and torts. In these two areas the "public force" is also brought to bear upon men, to the end that disputes between them may be settled fairly and without bloodshed. As was said in *Bridges,* "The right to sue and defend in the courts is the alternative of force. In an organized society it is the right conservative of all other rights, and lies at the foundation of orderly government." When two men make a contract and one breaks it, the other may resort to the courts for enforcing it. And when one man injures another's person or property—a tort—the courts offer the injured party the legal means of an action at law for obtaining from the other a fair payment of damages. To say it another way, in crimes, the quarrel is between the state and a citizen; in contracts and in torts—both "civil actions"—the quarrel is between two citizens.

This of course is not the whole story. In many disputes between citizens, the court's forcing one party to pay the other money would not fairly right the wrong. In such cases a "suit in equity," in which the court may order the two (or many) parties to make various readjustments, is much more *equitable.* Too, in many situations the state's punishing a citizen for a crime by its only means, fine or imprisonment, would not fairly right the wrong. Thus, fine and imprisonment of a parent for neglect does not save his sick child's life. And so, courts also provide an equity proceeding whereby such a child may be taken from the parent and placed in better hands, as we shall see in Part IV.

In what follows, I have lumped together a number of odd results in "civil actions," some bordering on the humorous, some not, where the rights and legal remedies of the parties have been affected by—or, what is just as important, have *not* been affected by—a religion-inspired aversion to medicine. Herein, too, is set down briefly the problem that today faces the physician, threatening him, as it does, with both civil and criminal liability—where his prospective Witness patient stipulates that he is not, under any circumstances, to be given a blood transfusion.

In Maine's *Wheeler v. Sawyer,* decided in 1888, the plaintiff, a Christian Science practitioner, after his patient died, brought suit against the heir for $30 worth of prayers owed by the deceased—and collected. A Maine statute provided that no one except a physician or surgeon should "recover any compensation for medical or surgical services unless previous to such services he had obtained a certificate of good moral character from the municipal officers of the town where he then resided." The plaintiff had received such a certificate. The court said the late patient had chosen that form of treatment and agreed to pay for it:

> We are not required here to investigate Christian Science. The defendant's intestate chose that treatment. There is nothing unlawful or immoral in such a contract. The wisdom or folly is for the parties, not for the court, to determine.

New Hampshire druggist Robinson's marriage was idyllic for two years. Then his wife became a "Doctor of Christian Science." Her practice caused him to be ridiculed. His business suffered, his health was impaired and he became morose and despondent. He begged her to give up only her practice—not her belief—but she refused. He then brought suit for divorce on grounds of extreme cruelty. In 1891, in declaring him entitled to a decree, the court held that his wife's conduct as a Christian Science "Doctor" came within the statute, since such behavior on her part had the effect of endangering the health and reason of her husband.

In the *Matter of Brush,* decided in 1901, a woman willed $20,000 to formidable Mrs. Augusta Stetson's First Church of Christ, Scientist, of New York City. After the woman's death, relatives sought to have this legacy set aside. They claimed she had lacked testamentary capacity— proved by her belief in Christian Science, which was an insane delusion. But the court decreed the legacy valid:

> However opposed these teachings may be to the beliefs or notions of others, they are founded on the religious convictions of those professing them. That being so, the court cannot say that those persons are mentally unsound.

In the New Hampshire case of *Spead v. Tomlinson,* decided in 1904, a middle-aged woman had an attack of appendicitis but dreaded a surgical operation. A Christian Science practitioner told her an operation was not necessary and that he could cure her. She accordingly employed him for several days, but her illness increased. She then engaged a physician, submitted to an operation, and was cured. Afterwards, she brought suit against the practitioner for malpractice and deceit. The evidence tended to show that the practitioner's "treatment" had been injurious, and that if he persisted in it, a cure would have been impossible. But the court found for the practitioner, holding his representations not fraudulent but merely a strong expression of religious opinion based on his apparently sincere belief in Christian Science.

In the Texas case of *Fort Worth & Denver City Ry. Co. v. Travis,* decided in 1907, the plaintiff's wife had been put off one of the defendant's trains. The plaintiff brought suit to recover damages for her resulting physical injuries and mental suffering. When the Company sought to cross-examine her to prove she was a Christian Scientist and therefore incapable of sustaining physical injury or mental suffering, the trial judge sustained the plaintiff's objection, and awarded $190 to the plaintiff. But on appeal, the court held the trial judge had erred in treating the inquiry as an immaterial one, since the testimony was pertinent:

> If she had such control of her feelings or thought she had, as to render her insensible to pain when she willed to be, we see no reason why that circumstance should not have been considered by the jury in determining the extent of her suffering and the compensation to be made on account of it.

When an adult is injured through the negligence or fault of another, he still must promptly obtain all necessary medical advice and treatment. If he does not, the law regards his failure as "contributory negligence." Such neglect by the injured party not only is likely to seriously aggravate the extent of his injury, but also may greatly reduce the amount of damages he may recover, or allow him to recover no damages at all.

In the California case of *Ash v. Barker,* decided in 1915, an apartment house manager fell and severely injured herself, but for forty days relied solely on a Christian Science practitioner's treatments. Then, because of unbearable suffering, she quit her job. Later, she submitted to the surgical operation which, as evidence later showed, she should have had immediately after the accident. In holding that she was not entitled to workmen's compensation, the Industrial Commission declared that Christian Science treatments were not such as

> may be reasonably required to cure and relieve where surgical treatment is indicated by the symptoms. In delaying such surgical

treatment for more than two months, applicant not only jeopardized her own interests, but the interest of her employer, and in fact slept upon her rights to demand medical and surgical treatment at the expense of her employer or her employer's insurance carrier.

A will contest, *In re Malvasi's Estate,* was decided in California in 1929. The question: whether or not the late Malvasi had been of sound mind. The jurors decided he had been, thus upholding the will. Afterwards, the opponents' counsel discovered that one juror, Mrs. Post, was a Christian Scientist, and moved for a new trial. Their argument: as such, she could not believe in the existence of unsoundness of mind, since unsoundness of mind was a human disease; therefore she was disqualified as a juror. In her affidavit, Mrs. Post deposed that Christian Science was a healing agency and that it at all times recognized the existence of human disease, including mental incompetency. The court denied the motion, holding that Mrs. Post, in her conception of Christian Science, "understood" it to recognize the existence of disease, including mental incompetency; therefore, 1) Mrs. Post was not disqualified as a juror; 2) she was "not chargeable with any misconduct for failure to volunteer information concerning her religious belief"; and, 3) appellant was not deprived of a fair and impartial jury.

In New Jersey's *Christian v. Canfield,* decided in 1931, Miss Christian, a confirmed invalid for over 25 years, died at 67. For several years prior to her death, she had relied exclusively upon treatments by the defendant, a "Christian Science healer." Her relatives brought suit to set aside two instruments made by Miss Christian conveying securities valued at $13,730 to the "healer," claiming they had been secured by fraud and undue influence. The evidence showed that the "healer" had had charge of Miss Christian's financial affairs, and that she had been under the influence of opiates at the time the instruments were executed. The court decreed in favor of the relatives:

At the outset, we start with the presumption against the bona fides of the transaction because of the confidential and fiduciary relationship, and the burden of showing the contrary is upon the beneficiary. That includes the burden of showing not only that the transfer was not procured by fraud or undue influence, but that the nature of the transaction was fully understood by decedent, and that she had independent advice.

What is a doctor to do when his patient stipulates that, no matter what happens, he is not to be given a blood transfusion? One state medical association wrote me of its attitude:

There is another problem we encounter from time to time, where the members of a religious sect (Jehovah's Witnesses) seek to secure the word of a physician that he will not administer blood as a part of his treatment. This occurs generally in obstetrical cases, where the prospective mother seeks an advance guarantee from the doctor that he will not administer blood to her, no matter what circumstances may arise. We have recently had two cases of this type and our advice to the attending physician has been that he must practice medicine in the most scientific way known to him and that, if the mother declines his services on this basis, he should decline to handle the case and tell her to seek professional services elsewhere. The doctor in such cases has a moral, professional, legal and ethical obligation which, no matter what the pleading of the prospective parent, he must observe. This attitude is designed to permit the physicians to practice their science in the best possible manner without denying the patient the right to his own beliefs. Generally speaking, the physician taking the attitude we suggest eventually finds cooperation on the part of the parents . . . I do not know that this is a nationwide attitude but in our opinion it is the only sound suggestion we could make to a physician. Doubtless, some doctors would accede to such a request but I imagine the overwhelming majority of physicians would continue to use their own professional judgment rather than sharing the treatment of a particular case with an untrained person who was motivated by **religious** rather than scientific beliefs.

The author cannot bring himself to agree with this attitude. If all doctors so held out for a free hand to administer strictly according to their own best judgment and without being hampered by the patient's stipulations, and if all Jehovah's Witnesses held firmly to their religious convictions—then no medical aid would be available to any Jehovah's Witness. At best, such an attitude has the physician stepping out of his proper role to engage in a theological argument. At worst, it has an organization of physicians saying to an organization of Jehovah's Witnesses: "Abandon your religious notion or you will get no doctoring from us." But the discussion probably is pointless: the fact is clear enough, even from the incidents reported in this study, that physicians *do* administer to Jehovah's Witnesses. Confronted with his patient's restrictions, the physician simply does the best he can.

It is the plainest law that a physician who administers a blood transfusion or performs any other operation upon an adult or upon the adult's child without the adult's express or implied consent, commits, 1) assault and battery, for which he is criminally liable; and 2) a trespass, for which he is liable in a civil action for damages.

When an adult patient, in his right mind, refuses blood transfusions or any other operation, the physician is absolutely obliged, legally, to respect the patient's wishes. The doctor, of course, must take what other measures he possibly can towards saving the patient's life. But if the patient then dies, the physician, in theory at least, incurs neither criminal nor civil liability. He would be very unwise, however, if he did not beforehand obtain the patient's stipulations in writing, properly signed and witnessed, against the possibility of a suit by the patient's heirs.

In the case of a child patient, the physician likewise is bound to respect the stipulations of that child's parent—so long as that parent remains in custody of the child. Here, when the parent denies the child necessary medical aid, the parent becomes a lawbreaker, and is, as we shall see in Part IV, likely to be deprived of that custody in short order. Certainly, the physician should waste no time in bringing the situation to the attention of the proper court. But afterwards, until that court acts, he still can do no more than the best he can under the parent's stipulations. The Labrenz (Ch. 15) and Grzyb (Ch. 1) accounts show how doctors have reasonably conducted themselves in such situations.

Not that the bringing of such a situation to the court's attention is the prerogative only of physicians. It is the right and moral obligation of *any* person who has reasonable grounds to believe that such a situation exists. Directions as to how to go about this are given in the last chapter of this book.

In criminal law it is basic that one who counsels another to commit a crime is also guilty as a principal or accessory. But as to accessory liability in connection with an adult's faith death, the answer by now is clear: if it is no crime for the adult to deny himself necessary medical aid, then it can be no crime for a faith healer, Christian Science practitioner or any one else to counsel such denial.

On Sunday, February 5, 1956, farmer James Grant of Englehart, Ontario, and wife were driving home from a Jehovah's Witness service when their car collided with a truck. Mrs. Grant, 29, mother of five, hospitalized, was told her life depended on immediate blood transfusions. She said she would agree only if Sadid Lionel Anyon, 29, appliance salesman and local Witness leader, approved. When doctors sent for him, Anyon advised her to refuse. She did, and died. Afterwards, her mother, Mrs. C. Rock, demanded an official investigation. "I am convinced," she said, "one word from Anyon would have changed her mind." While Ontario officials studied her complaint, many residents of Englehart were reportedly "openly outspoken" against Witnesses and in "an ugly mood." When the funeral was set for Wednesday, a family squabble arose, Mrs. Grant's mother and a sister wanting a separate Baptist funeral service. A Provincial Police constable was assigned to protect mourners. Two hours before the scheduled service, the coroner, after consulting the crown attorney at Haileybury, ordered the funeral postponed so that an autopsy could be performed, and ordered an inquest. Leader Anyon announced he was not bothered by townspeoples' threats of violence against him, and praised Mrs. Grant's decision: "She realized that if the transfusion had saved her life, she would have lost her life at Armageddon." No further development, at least to the author's knowledge, appeared in the news, so it is not likely that any legal basis for action was found. So long as Mrs. Grant was not thereby endangering others, she had the legal right to refuse the transfusions; and Anyon therefore had the legal right so to counsel her.[5]

What, then, of the faith healer or practitioner who counsels a parent to deny his child the necessary medical aid required by statute, whereby the child dies and the parent becomes criminally liable for manslaughter?

In England and in the United States, the mere soliciting or inciting of another to commit murder, arson or other felonies has usually been held an indictable offense. Canada's *Criminal Code* (below) is clearcut on this point. Some states have also held it a misdemeanor to solicit another to commit a misdemeanor.[6] But in such states one looks in vain for any blanket indictment of churches whose teachings plainly solicit or incite parents to deny their children the necessary medical aid required by statute. There is, however, an uncomfortably close parallel in the historic prosecution of a church by the United States, described in Chapter 6.

Suppression of such churches by a state could be justified only where their teachings had become a "clear and present danger" to the state. They have not, and in the face of our general aversion to any action which even hints of religious persecution, the state only reluctantly proceeds against the occasional faith-healing parent whose unattended child has died, and even more reluctantly against the pastor or practitioner as well.

In the United States, no Christian Science practitioner has ever been convicted, to the author's knowledge, as an accessory before the fact in such a situation. In Canada, the attempt was made in *Beer* and *Elder*. Since the indictments in both prosecutions included counts charging malpractice—improper treatment of disease—these cases show Canada's stand on that point as well.

In Toronto, in 1895, Percy Robert Beck, six, complained of a mild sore throat. His parents formerly had had the services of a reputable doctor, but two years before had been converted to Christian Science. Accordingly, they called in a "practitioner," Mrs. Mary Ellen Beer. Her treatment consisted "in simply sitting by the bedside, rarely saying anything, never prescribing, nor in any way touching the child, or making any examination or otherwise diagnosing the patient." But that same day, Percy died. A post mortem revealed "diphtheria of a non-malignant character, a disease rarely fatal." According to later medical testimony, the boy probably would have recovered if the disease had been properly treated; also, his death definitely had been accelerated by his not receiving proper medical attendance.

Criminal law in Canada comes under the jurisdiction of the Dominion Government. The *Criminal Code* is applicable to all of the Provinces. Mrs. Beer was indicted for manslaughter under the Code, and prosecuted on two theories: 1) for improper treatment of disease, and 2) as an accessory or accomplice, in that she counselled or procured, or aided and abetted the father in his disregard of his legal duty to provide the child with medical attention.

As to the first theory, the statute provided that everyone who undertakes, except in case of necessity, to administer surgical or medical treatments is under a legal duty to have and to use reasonable knowledge, skill, and care in doing any such act. Judge Falconbridge held, however, that Mrs. Beer had not been retained, nor was she expected to, nor did she, come in as a medical attendant, and that the failure to examine the child in the manner in which a doctor would do, and which was the negligence relied on by the prosecution, was exactly what was expected of her as a Christian Science practitioner. As to the second theory, Judge Falconbridge first refused to accept the defense contention that there could be no accessory to manslaughter:

> It is laid down [by the defense] as a general principle there can be no accessary before the fact to manslaughter, because manslaughter necessarily implies absence of malice, absence of premeditation . . . I do not subscribe entirely to the general principle, because I think sometimes there may be an accessary before the fact.

I shall take up this important point below. But the court failed to find any evidence of "counselling or procuring," and further opined that it was impossible to "aid and abet" in another's doing *nothing*, i.e., failing to provide medical attention. Mrs. Beer therefore was acquitted.

Percy's father apparently was not indicted. True, he was under a statutory duty to provide the "necessaries of life." But under the apparent condition of "a mild sore throat" it could hardly be proven that he was under a positive duty to provide medical aid. At the same time, this did not bar prosecution of Mrs. Beer, because under the *Code,* "everyone is guilty of an offense who counsels another to commit it, whether the person so counselled actually commits the offence or not."

As to the argument in 2, above, it should be noted that the defense counsel's concept was solely of *voluntary* manslaughter, while Judge Falconbridge, *circa* 1895, was groping toward the different notion of *involuntary* manslaughter, where there may indeed be accessories before the fact, as will be seen below.

John Rogers of British Columbia was a Zionite (Ch. 2). In 1902, two of his children, both under six years of age, contracted diphtheria. Rogers knew the disease was dangerous and contagious, and could afford the services of a doctor. But because of his religious belief, he, with the counsel of one Brooks, refused to call in medical attendance. Both children died. At Rogers's trial for manslaughter, it was proved that the disease caused the children's deaths, and that the ordinary remedies Rogers had denied them not only would have prolonged their lives but probably would have resulted in their recovery. He was convicted, and the Supreme Court of British Columbia held that in such circumstances he was bound, regardless of his religious belief to the contrary, to furnish medical attendance, both under the statute and at common law.

Brooks—whether he was Rogers's pastor or only a friend does not appear—at the same time was indicted for manslaughter as an accessory to the father's neglect. The indictment charged Brooks with being present, "unlawfully aiding, abetting, assisting, counseling and procuring John Rogers not to regard his duty to provide his child with medical attention, by reason of which neglect the child died." In affirming Brooks's conviction, the Supreme Court noted that under the *Code,* Brooks could just as well have been prosecuted as a principal.

In Winnipeg, Manitoba, one Friday in the Fall of 1924, the ten-year-old son of Mr. and Mrs. Robert Watson, Christian Scientists, became ill with a headache. Mrs. Watson asked William Elder, a Christian Science practitioner, to treat him. Elder did, and the boy recovered. The following Wednesday, November 5, their daughter, Doreen Watson, twelve, complained of a headache. That evening, Mrs. Watson met Elder at a prayer meeting and asked him to "help" Doreen, meaning that he should give her Christian Science treatment. By Thursday, November 6, Doreen was no better and a swelling had started in her neck. That morning, Mrs. Watson so informed Elder. She telephoned him again in the afternoon; there was no improvement and Doreen's nose was stuffed. The same conditions continued on Friday, and her breathing became difficult. Mrs. Watson told Elder of these symptoms and he undertook to treat them. On Saturday the girl was much the same; there was some improvement in her breathing. But on Sunday evening, after church, Mrs. Watson told Elder that there was not much improvement and asked him to come and see her. Elder did so, looking at Doreen for about two minutes. He did not touch her or speak to her. After leaving the bedroom, he told Mrs. Watson he would continue the treatment.

On Monday morning, November 10, Elder telephoned Mrs. Watson that Mr. Robb, who had been her special Christian Science practitioner, had returned to Winnipeg. She then telephoned Robb and suggested that a medical practitioner be called in, as the improvement in Doreen's condition had not come as quickly as in the boy's case. Robb suggested calling in Dr. Fraser, who was known to Mr. Elder, for a diagnosis. As Mrs. Watson later testified: "We did not know what the trouble was, and we wanted to know. I never heard of a Christian Scientist diagnosing any case."

On Tuesday evening, November 11, Dr. Fraser came with Elder to the Watson home. Dr. Fraser was a duly registered physician and had been for some years the physician of the Workmen's Compensation Board at Winnipeg, but was occasionally consulted by former patients. According to Dr. Fraser's later account, Mr. Elder that day asked him to see a case he was treating in order to make a diagnosis; Dr. Fraser made no enquiries as to the nature of the case or whether it was an adult or child. At 7:30 p.m., when Elder came for him, Dr. Fraser made some enquiry as to the nature of the case. Hearing that it was a little girl with a sore throat, he took a swab with him.

On arrival, they were taken upstairs to the girl's bedroom. The doctor was given the particulars of her illness, the date when she was taken ill and the fact that her brother had been ill. Doreen's condition, as described by Dr. Fraser: her nostrils were completely obstructed so that she could not breathe through them. Her lips and mouth were dry and cracked. There was an irritating discharge from the nostrils, which were red and irritated. Her breath was exceedingly offensive. The glands of her neck on each side under the jaw were quite swollen and prominent. Both tonsils were covered with a dense, heavy, gray membrane which extended across the uvula and up in the nasal cavities. Where her throat was not covered with membrane it was red and inflamed. Her lungs and heart were normal. Her pulse was 90; her temperature 99½. Dr. Fraser took a swab of the child's throat.

When they went downstairs, Dr. Fraser told Mr. and Mrs. Watson that the child had nasal and pharyngeal diphtheria, a very serious attack, and that she was dangerously ill. He advised that antitoxin treatment be given at once and that she be sent to the hospital immediately. Dr. Fraser told them antitoxin was a remedy for the treatment of diphtheria all over the world and that, if given in time, was a specific for the disease. He pointed out the danger of delay in the administration of antitoxin, and how with every day's delay the danger increased and the mortality from the disease was greater. He also emphasized the need for hospital care, rest and quiet and the importance of having a trained nurse and house surgeons in constant attendance. He was asked by Mr. and Mrs. Watson if he could guarantee that antitoxin would cure the disease. (No doctor "guarantees" to cure anything.) He pointed out the danger of the delay that had taken place, and urged that antitoxin should be administered and the girl receive hospital care. Mr. and Mrs. Watson declined to consent. Mrs. Watson said, "I have no fear." She told of having suffered for years by having attacks of quinsy and of being cured by Christian Science treatment. Mr. Watson also strongly objected to antitoxin treatment of diphtheria. Dr. Fraser gave statistics of the reduction of mortality from diphtheria by the use of antitoxin. Elder claimed that much of the credit for the reduction in the mortality from diphtheria in the last twenty years must be given to Christian Science treatment.

Elder also stated to Mrs. Watson that he would immediately take steps to break up the disease and stated he would phone Mr. Robb. Dr. Fraser left Elder at the Watsons' house. The following morning, November 12, he took the swab to the bacteriological laboratory in the city health department for a report. About eleven or twelve o'clock that morning he telephoned Elder that the smear of the swab was reported suspicious, and to go carefully or he would have a tragedy on his hands. Elder said he was going carefully. The next morning, Dr. Fraser informed Elder that he had a positive report on the swab, which confirmed the diagnosis of the case as diphtheria. Elder replied that he was no longer in charge of the case; he had turned it over to Robb.

At about five o'clock that afternoon, Robb called upon Dr. Fraser at his office and both of them went to the Watsons' house. The doctor examined the child and found her temperature had risen to 100. Her pulse was 102 as against 90 on the 11th. There were also other symptoms which led him to believe that her condition was worse than on his previous visit. The doctor left alone and did not see the child again until after her death. On Friday, November 21, a few hours before she died, Doreen was propped up in bed and allowed to amuse herself painting. The immediate cause of death seems to have been a slight exertion she made in bed while her mother was ill in another room and unable to go to her assistance.

During the morning in which Doreen died, Mrs. Watson was taken ill. A Dr. Moody examined her and pronounced her illness to be diphtheria. He ordered that antitoxin should be administered to her. This was done, she was taken to the St. George Hospital, and after treatment there she recovered.*

The child had been dead about half an hour when Dr. Fraser examined the body. He found the swelling of the neck had disappeared, the throat had become clear, one nostril had opened up and the membrane had cleared away. Dr. W. P. McCowan made a post mortem examination. He found the bacillus of diphtheria in the dead child's nose, throat and vocal chords. There was also a condition of acute dilation of the heart and a fatty degeneration of that organ which, as Dr. McCowan later testified, occurs in fatal cases of diphtheria. His opinion was that her death had been caused by that disease. Afterwards, a police constable named Hull interviewed Elder.

William Elder was indicted for manslaughter on five counts: 1) for having actively (unlawfully), aided, abetted, counseled, or procured Robert Watson to omit his duty to supply Doreen Watson with the necessaries of life; 2) the same, substituting "necessaries" for "necessaries of life"; 3) for being under a legal duty to have and to use reasonable knowledge, skill and care in administering surgical and medical treatment, but omitting to do so; 4) for having held himself out as possessing competent skill to deal with Doreen's life and health but treating her with criminal inattention and gross neglect; and 5) for unlawfully killing and slaying Doreen Watson.

At the trial, evidence was given by Dr. Finkelstein, bacteriologist of the Winnipeg health department, by Dr. Alexander, medical superintendent of the King George and Municipal Hospital, and by Dr. Douglas, the health officer of Winnipeg. All medical testimony was in agreement that the only cure for diphtheria was antitoxin and that it should be accompanied by absolute rest in bed, careful nursing and the treatment of any condition that might arise. It was agreed that antitoxin, if administered within twenty-four hours after the disease manifests itself, will cure practically every case of diphtheria. It was stated that even in the later stages of the disease antitoxin will be beneficial and may effect a cure, but the longer its administration is delayed the less become the chances of recovery. Medical opinion was that if antitoxin had been given on November 11, when Dr. Fraser first saw Doreen and prescribed that remedy, the child might have recovered. The same opinion showed that, owing to the effect of diphtheria upon the heart, absolute rest on the part of the patient was essential, so that no stress might be put upon

---

* Will the reader please go back to the beginning of this short paragraph and read it again, slowly and aloud?

that organ. The evidence showed that Doreen Watson had not been kept absolutely quiet.

Robert Watson stated very frankly his antipathy against serums, vaccines and antitoxins: "From my study I have objected to the pure blood streams of any child of God being polluted with what I consider pus, filth, or a part of the poisoned blood of a lower animal . . . A beast is a beast in my mind, and a man is a man, and I object to the mixing of the two in that form." ("Steadfast in his opinions," commented Judge Perdue, on appeal, "he would not hearken to medical advice and was prepared to risk the life of his child in deference to his prejudices.")

The trial judge, Justice Dysart, directed the jury to bring in a verdict of *not guilty* on the third count (presumably following *Beer*). The jury returned a verdict of *guilty* on the first, second and fourth counts, and of *not guilty* on the third and fifth, but on appeal, Elder went free over a point of evidence. Chief Judicial Magistrate Perdue delivered the judgment of the Manitoba Court of Appeal:

> However much respect may be paid to the honest belief of certain religious sects that medicine and medical treatment are of no avail and that prayer, and prayer alone, can cure disease, the adherents and devotees of these sects must bear in mind that the provisions of *The Criminal Code* are binding upon them . . . Professed religious belief or ignorance of the law will not protect them, if they offend against a provision of that *Code*.
>
> Making due allowance for Mr. Watson's personal prejudice as shown . . . he should have bourne in mind that the consensus of medical testimony and the experience of the great majority of persons are opposed to his views on the subject. If unfortunately his opinions should be generally adopted, smallpox would soon become as general and as virulent, and diphtheria as deadly, as these diseases were before the means of combating them were discovered. The opinion is general that Jenner's discovery and introduction of vaccination for smallpox, over a century and a quarter since, was one of the greatest boons ever conferred upon the human race. Prior to that discovery, as history tells us, whole communities of persons were decimated by smallpox, and the victims who escaped were marred and disfigured by the disease. The much more recent discovery of antitoxin as a cure for diphtheria is only less beneficial in degree than vaccination, because diphtheria was never so general or so readily communicable and contagious as smallpox . . .

Judge Perdue then took up counts 1, 2 and 4 of the indictment:

These counts are founded upon secs. 69, 241, 242, 244, 246 of *The Criminal Code*, which are as follows:

"69. Every one is a party to and guilty of an offence who,

(a) actually commits it; or

(b) does or omits an act for the purpose of aiding any person to commit the offence; or

(c) abets any person in commission of the offence; or

(d) counsels or procures any person to commit the offence . . .

"241. Every one who has charge of any other person unable by reason either of detention, age, sickness, insanity or any other cause, to withdraw himself from such charge, and unable to provide himself with the necessaries of life, is whether such charge is undertaken by him under any contract, or is imposed upon him by law, or by reason of his unlawful act, under a legal duty to supply that person with the necessaries of life, and is criminally responsible for omitting, without lawful excuse, to perform such duty if the death of such person is caused, or if his life is endangered, or his health has been or is likely to be permanently injured, by such omission . . . "

It has been held by the Supreme Court of Canada that under sec. 69 everyone is guilty of an offence who counsels another to commit it, whether the person so counselled actually commits the offence or not . . .

In *Rex v. Lewis* . . . it was held . . . that the term "necessaries" in sec. 241 of *The Code* (then sec. 210) included medicine and medical treatment, in cases where ordinarily prudent persons would obtain them. It was held in the same case that a conscientious objection to medical treatment, because of a belief in the doctrines of the sect known as "Christian Scientists" is not a "lawful excuse" for omitting to provide medicines and medical aid under the above sec. 241 of *The Code*. In the present case it is necessary to prove that Elder counselled and abetted Watson in omitting so to provide medicines and medical aid for the child Doreen Watson . . .

After careful perusal of the evidence, the only part of it which directly bears upon the charges in the indictment of counselling and abetting is that of the witness Hull, the police constable who interviewed Elder on November 22, 1924, respecting the death of Doreen Watson. Elder was not under arrest at the time and was not warned. He made a statement to Hull which was taken down in a note book. Hull then went to the detective department of the police and dictated the statement to a person who typed it on a typewriting machine. The note book was lost and could not be produced. Hull could not repeat what Elder had said without referring to the typewritten document . . .

There is no evidence that the copy was at any time compared with the original notes, or that it was read over by the witness and found to be a correct transcript, while the contents were still fresh in his memory. I think that the evidence of the witness Hull as to the statements made by the accused at the interview in question should have been rejected. Apart from Hull's evidence as to admissions made by Elder there is nothing to implicate the latter with aiding, abetting and counseling the parents of the child in omitting to provide her with necessaries, that is, proper medical attention . . .

Upon this ground the conviction should be quashed.

It is clear that, in Canada, criminal liability attaches to the pastor or other adult who actively counsels a parent against furnishing his child with necessary medical care. The conviction of Christian Science practitioner William Elder was reversed on a question of evidence; there was no question as to the law. A Winnipeg attorney, Mr. Roy St. George Stubbs, writing in the *Canadian Bar Review* and referring to what I had called the U.S. anomaly of convicting the parent while letting the pastor go free, indicates that *Rex v. Brooks* is followed in Canada today:

> No such anomaly exists in Canadian law. If a pastor persuades one of his followers to rely on prayer, to deny medical aid to his child, and the child dies, and it can be established in evidence that the child would have survived under proper medical care, the pastor may be convicted of manslaughter—not as an accessary before the fact, which Mr. Cawley seems to think he is, but as a principal.

In the United States, I find no such case reaching the higher courts. Though Sandford, in the Maine case (Ch. 5), was a minister, he also had custody of the boy, so the case turned on parent liability. I find, in fact, only one such attempt at a conviction, and this ended in the trial court.

In Los Angeles, in 1938, Mrs. Lillian Volstad, a widow, attended a "mission" run by Apostolic preacher Wilbur W. Alvis. In August, Mrs. Volstad's son Francis, nine, became ill. Their family physician, Dr. Frank J. Gaspard, diagnosed appendicitis and urged an immediate operation. Instead, Mrs. Volstad and Alvis resorted to prayer. Five days later, officers with a Juvenile Court order authorizing immediate surgical treatment arrived to remove the boy to the General Hospital. Mrs. Volstad was not at home. She was found at the mission, where others were praying and chanting, "He will be cured, he will be cured!" On August 8, Francis was removed to the hospital, but died there of a ruptured appendix before the operation could be performed.[7]

Both Mrs. Volstad and Alvis were charged with manslaughter. The papers in the case file, which I later examined, did not reveal the particular theory on which Alvis was prosecuted. The complaint merely set out briefly that the pair—as I now recall it—"did wilfully, unlawfully, feloniously and without malice kill one Francis Volstad, a human being."

At a hearing before Superior Judge Kincaid on September 2, both denied that the boy's death was due to negligence because they had resorted to prayer instead of an operation in an effort to cure him. They pled not guilty and were ordered to stand trial. Their attorney indicated that their defense would rest on the established right of a parent to control medical treatment of a child. The trial opened on November 17, before Superior Judge A. A. Scott, who heard the case without a jury. Referring to the time of Dr. Gaspard's diagnosis and recommendation, the deputy district attorney asked: "In your opinion, would the child have survived if operated upon then?"

"He would have, in my opinion," Dr. Gaspard replied. He testified that Mrs. Volstad had objected to an operation because she knew of a similar case a short time before wherein the patient died, and that the cost of the surgery was also a deterrent. Next day, Mrs. Marjorie Mares, Francis's aunt, testified that shortly before he was removed to the hospital, one of his final wishes was: "I would rather die than go to the hospital. Please send Mr. Alvis to pray for me." And she told how, while Francis lay critically ill, she had visited Mrs. Volstad at Alvis's mission and urged her to return home. A police officer testified that when Francis was taken to the hospital, Mrs. Volstad refused to accompany him in the ambulance, and the boy's grandmother went in her place.

The following Monday, the defense attorney argued for dismissal of the manslaughter charges on the grounds of lack of evidence and the right of a parent to dictate treatment for a child. He told of Francis's expression of faith, two days before his death. At that time the boy had said, "I want Mr. Alvis to pray for me." After a praying session at the Volstad home, the boy said, "Mother, I am healed. I felt as though an electric shock ran through me," and after that, he rested easily until his removal to the hospital. At the counsel table, Mrs. Volstad and Alvis wept so convulsively that Judge Scott was forced to call a recess.

On November 28, Judge Scott gave his decision:

Her [Mrs. Volstad's] actions are very hard to explain. Her sister, Mrs. Marjorie Mares, found her at the mission after the officers arrived at the home with an order from the Juvenile Court to remove the boy to the hospital, and pleaded with her to come home. She advised her . . . that her son was crying for her; but, did she come home then? No. She waited some two hours or more. The boy is placed on a stretcher and the defendant invited by the officers to ride in the ambulance to the hospital; but, does she accept? She does not. And so we have the sorry spectacle of a little boy, scared and worn out by the ravages of the dreaded peritonitis, deprived of the company of his mother on his last ride, and turns his little prayers to his grandmother to please ride with him to the hospital . . . There can be no question as to the efficacy of prayer and the wonderful results that have been obtained thereby . . . But had this boy been removed to the hospital in the first instance, he would be alive today.

Judge Scott convicted Mrs. Volstad of manslaughter, holding that her negligence caused the death of her son Francis. At the same time, he acquitted Rev. Alvis, but excoriated him for his conduct:

> It is not the intention of this court to criticize any person who, in good faith, regardless of religious belief, attempts to pray and ask the good Lord to heal the sick and afflicted, if it is His holy will. But this court cannot countenance the tactics used by this defendant Alvis, a self-ordained minister who belongs to that group of religious racketeers of whom there are too many in this small world of ours.

Both Mrs. Volstad and Alvis had been at liberty on their own recognizance. Mrs. Volstad was permitted to remain free without bail pending a probation hearing. After that hearing, she was placed on probation.

At first thought, one might suppose that there never could be an accessory before the fact to manslaughter, since manslaughter implies lack of premeditation; and this is true for *voluntary* manslaughter. But it is not true for the *involuntary* manslaughter, arising from criminal negligence, with which we are concerned here, for one may incite another to criminal negligence. This is the distinction towards which, in 1895, Judge Falconbridge was groping in *Reg. v. Beer*. Clark and Marshall make the point:

> . . . if two men drive separate vehicles at a furious and dangerous speed along the highway, each inciting and abetting the other, and one of them drives over and kills a person, the one thus causing the death is guilty of manslaughter as principal in the first degree, and the other is guilty as principal in the second degree . . . If one should incite another to so drive, and should be absent when the latter runs over and kills a person, he would be guilty of manslaughter as accessory before the fact.[8]

One might ask, too, "Where a statute establishing a crime imposes punishment only on the person who actually commits the crime, and not in general terms upon those who are guilty according to common law rules, are mere aiders and abettors within the act?" One Kentucky case held not, but this later was overruled, and the rule established that, unless it is plain from the statute that its intent is to affect only the party actually committing the offense, aiders and abettors are punishable.[9] It would be hard to defend the premise that one who leads another to commit a crime should himself incur no liability. But if the principles of law are sound, one still must consider that a state's criminal laws are prosecuted on only a county-wide scale, by the state's attorney for that county, who previously has faced the problem of getting himself elected by the voters of that county, and who later may be a candidate for reelection. His lack of enthusiasm for initiating all-out prosecutions in this religion-mixed area of the law is understandable.

The situation in the United States today, then, is this: that all manner of faith healers are allowed to run around loose, free to persuade parents to rely on prayer alone for their children's ills, and free of liability for the tragic results. I submit that here is the glaring anomaly in our law: that the parent who denies a child medical aid is punished, while the pastor who counsels that denial goes free. Here, in this area, it is time to reassess our existing legal boundary between religious freedom and fanatical religious irresponsibility.

# 13

# The Question of Fraud

*Whoever, having devised or intending to devise any scheme or artifice to defraud or for obtaining money or property by means of false or fraudulent pretenses, representations, or promises, . . . shall, for the purpose of executing such scheme or artifice or attempting so to do, place, or cause to be placed, any letter, postal card, package, writing, circular, pamphlet or advertisement, whether addressed to any person residing within or outside the United States, in any post office . . . of the United States . . . to be sent or delivered by the post office establishment of the United States, . . . or shall knowingly cause to be delivered by mail according to the direction thereon, . . . any such letter, postal card, package, writing, circular, pamphlet, or advertisement, shall be fined not more than $1,000, or imprisoned not more than five years, or both.*
*—Criminal Code, § 215, 18 U.S.C.A. § 338.*

*If two or more persons conspire . . . to commit any offense against the United States . . . and one or more of such parties do any act to effect the object of the conspiracy, each of the parties to such conspiracy shall be fined not more than $10,000, or imprisoned not more than two years, or both.*
*—Criminal Code, § 37, 18 U.S.C.A. § 88.*

Guy W. Ballard (1878–1939) by his own account was a mining engineer until his encounter upon California's Mount Shasta, in August of 1930, with a young man who asked for his cup. Ballard handed it over. Instantly it was filled with a creamy liquid. "Drink it," the young man advised. Ballard did, and was electrified. He had, the young man explained, drunk Omnipresent Life. "It is subject to our conscious control and direction, willingly obedient, when we Love enough . . . Whatsoever I desire manifests itself, when I command in

221

Love. I held out the cup, and that which I desired for you appeared. See! I have but to hold out my hand and, if I wish to use gold—gold is here." Instantly, there lay in his palm a disc about the size of a ten dollar gold piece. Ballard, it appeared, already had a certain Inner Understanding of the Great Law, but, as the young man explained, "you are not outwardly aware of It enough to produce that which you desire direct from the Omnipresent Universal Supply." He then instructed Ballard as to certain daily exercises which shortly would result in his feeling with deep, deep *intensity* the Tremendous Activity, Power, and Perfection that abides and is forever active within the Light. The young man then changed into a Magnificent Godlike figure in a white jeweled robe: he was Saint Germain.*

Saint Germain, it developed, had come from the planet Venus over two and a half million years before, and had had his eye on Guy for some time. He now showed Ballard how to leave his body and travel through space and time. They went back 70,000 years to a civilization on the then tropical Sahara Desert, where Germain was king, Ballard and his son Donald (as Amen Bey) were priests, and Guy's wife, Mrs. Edna W. Ballard, was Lotus, a beautiful young girl with hair like spun gold. There, Perfection was maintained without army or navy, under the direction of fourteen Ascended Masters of Light—the same who, in the 1930's, luckily were watching over and guarding the United States. ("America! We, the Ascended Host of Light, love and guard you. America! We love you.") The pair in like manner afterwards visited the ancient civilization of the Incas, where it appeared that the three Ballards had also stood high in the royal priesthood. By now, it was hardly surprising to learn that, at still another time, Guy, Mrs. Ballard and son Donald had been George Washington, Joan of Arc and Lafayette, respectively. The Great Ascended Masters, Ballard was told, "have guided the expansion of the Light in humanity on this planet from the beginning . . . The Ascended Master is an individual who by Self-Conscious effort has generated enough Love and Power within himself to snap the chains of all human limitations, and so he stands free and worthy to be trusted with the use of forces, beyond those of human experience."

After more such travels in time and space, Ballard got down to the practical business of precipitating gold from the Omnipresent Universal Supply. He studied the methods of operator Edwin J. Dingle, originator of the "Mentalphysics" cult in Los Angeles, and those used by Frank B. Robinson of Moscow, Idaho, leader of the fantastically profitable mail-order "Psychiana" movement. After Ballard's conference with

---

* Germanus the Deathless, Bishop of Auxerre, d. 448.

the latter, Robinson was reported to have told him "not to infringe my copyright. I just warned him to keep off my stuff."

Ballard offered to his prospective followers release from all their shortcomings, infirmities, complexes and failures. He also undertook to straighten out, with the help of the Ascended Masters, all industrial labor troubles and other national and international problems, including international war. The "Great I Am Movement" was intensely patriotic; as soon as enough Americans became I-Am-ers, America would be saved. In the meantime, in one crisis of which the general public was unaware at the time, Saint Germain himself personally saved the nation by destroying an offshore fleet of hostile submarines, using gaseous K-17 God-fire.

As of 1938, the Saint Germain Press of Chicago, Illinois offered the following volumes, all with green covers titled in gold: "Unveiled Mysteries—Volume I," by Godfré Ray King (Ballard's penname) price $2.50 ("Containing the first group of the author's experiences"); "The Magic Presence—Volume II," price $2.75 ("Containing the second group of the author's experiences"); "The 'I Am' Discourses—Volume III, by the Ascended Master, Saint Germain," price $2.75 ("Containing thirty-three Discourses explaining the Ascended Masters' application of the "I AM," with three color plates"); "The 'I AM' Adorations, Affirmations and Decrees—Volume V*, by Chanera," price $1.75 ("A selection of powerful adorations, affirmations and Decrees of the 'Mighty I AM Presence'"); "Ascended Master Discourses—Volume VI, by various of the Ascended Masters," price $2.75 ("Containing twenty Discourses dictated before hundreds of students, with three color plates"); "Ascended Master Light, by the Great Cosmic Beings, Volume VII**"; "'I AM' Adorations and Affirmations, by Chanera," price $1.00 ("Vest Pocket Edition of powerful Adorations and Affirmations"); and "'I AM' Decree Booklet, by Chanera," price $1.00 ("A paper bound booklet, containing a collection of "I AM" Decrees which everyone can use to bring Freedom to the individual, America and the world"); as well as volumes I, II and III, above, in Braille at $5.25, $7.75 and $6.75 respectively.

Also offered: a chart of "The Magic Presence," suitable for framing, 12x20, $1.00, also large size, 30x48, for Study Groups and individual use, at $15.00: hand colored steel engravings of etchings by Charles Sindelar, 12x16, "Picture of the Ascended Master, Jesus," and "Picture

---

* No Volume IV was offered at that time, nor could I discover in Volumes I, II, III, VI or VII, which I have gone through, any reference to such a Volume IV.
** This volume, the largest—536 pages—is printed in an eerie lavender ink but my first impression that it would glow in the dark proved false.

of the Ascended Master, Saint Germain," at $2.00 each; hand colored steel engraving of etching by Robert A. Aguilar, 12x16, "Picture of the 'Old Man of the Hills,' " $2.00; a new "Song Book," containing "many new and original songs for which music will be published through the Saint Germain Press," at 50¢; three "Songs with Music," at $1.00 each, including "Ascended Master Youth of America." Another, "Goddess of Liberty," was also available in a 21-piece Band arrangement at $2.00. Priced at one dollar: "A Group of Songs—Music and lyrics by Godfré Ray King. These are especially charged with powerful healing activity."

Ten phonograph records were available at $2.50 each, including "RR-1247—Harp Meditation ('Nearer My God to Thee') Mrs. Ballard." For $3.00 per year, followers received *The Voice of the "I Am,"* a monthly magazine containing articles explaining "the Law of Life; Discourses by the Ascended Masters and other important subjects." Directors of radio broadcasting stations could write to the Press in Chicago regarding transcriptions of "A series of Broadcasts available for use, containing explanation of the Law of Life; also protection for America." And for $12 one could wear a "Great I Am" ring.

"There is no commercialism in all this," the leaders advised, "no money or political schemes in or back of this Educational Activity . . . We give all and ask nothing in return." But when Dr. Mead (below) wrote for free literature and information, he got back only a price list and the admonition that "our business is conducted on the cash basis only, as such is Saint Germain's wish. Therefore we kindly ask for remittance with all orders. Yours in the Source of the Light . . ."

According to Dr. Frank S. Mead:

The Ballards did well. They toured the country in cream-colored limousines, with Mrs. Ballard's harp hitched on a rear bumper; they used only the best hotels. "Daddy" Ballard dressed like a Brummel, Mrs. Ballard graced meditative meetings in stunning evening gowns ablaze with jewels. They were definitely Big Time. When Ballard died in December, 1939, son Donald took over the helm, but the heir's ship fouled early. His beauteous young wife detoured from the Light long enough to sue him for divorce, asking $1,200 a month alimony and claiming he had a monthly income of $2,000. [She settled out of court.]

The appeal of the Great I Am is not to the poor, who couldn't afford it. It promises not so much pelf and prosperity as a boost toward power for those who crave it and can't seem to get it elsewhere. There are more complexes and submerged egos and baffled faces in an I Am meeting-room than you'll find concentrated anywhere else on earth. The Movement appeals to those so well off in

**MASSACHUSETTS SUPREME JUDICIAL COURT JUSTICE HENRY NEWTON SHELDON**//In *Purinton v. Jamrock:* "The first and paramount duty is to consult the welfare of the child."

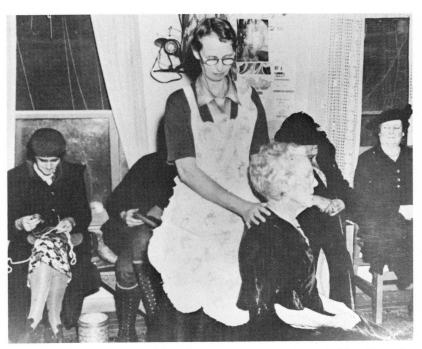

Susie Jessel places her "Healing Hands" on a patient. Ashland's undertakers were happy. (U.P.I.)

Mrs. Edna Ballard, leader of the fabulous "I AM" cult, after her indictment with 23 others on mail fraud and conspiracy charges. Federal officials accused the group of operating a gigantic religious racket, one of the most ruthless frauds on record. The large picture is of Guy W. Ballard; the small one was claimed to be a posed picture of St. Germain. The "crystal cup" was a highly prized symbol of the cult. (U.P.I.)

SUPREME COURT JUSTICE ROBERT H. JACKSON//"The price of freedom of religion or of speech or of the press is that we must put up with, and even pay for, a good deal of rubbish . . . I would . . . have done with this business of judicially examining other people's faiths."

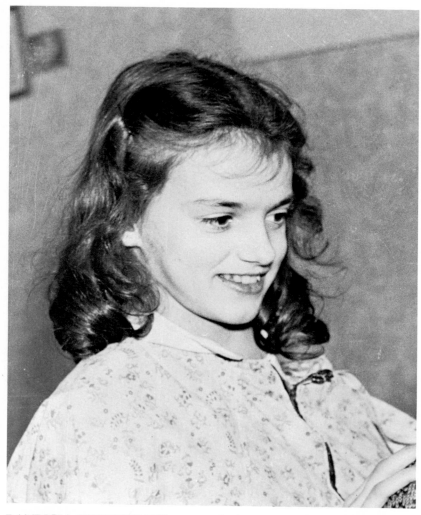

PATRICIA HUDSON//She wanted the operation. (Seattle Post-In-
telligencer.)

Leroy Mitchell is held by his sister while his mother prays aloud in court after Judge William Cramer decreed that Leroy be submitted to medical examination and treatment. (Wide World)

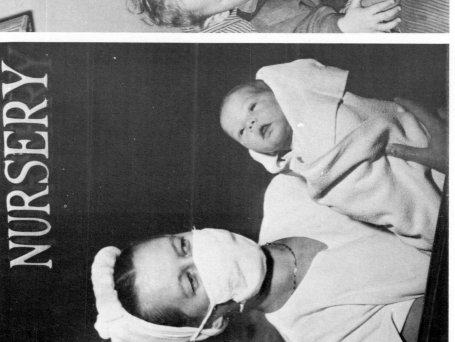

Cheryl Linn Labrenz (left), six days old, with nurse. Jehovah's Witness parents Darrell and Rhoda Labrenz (right) with son Kit. "The sanctity of the blood is a thing we cannot tamper with." (Wide World)

ILLINOIS SUPREME COURT JUSTICE WALTER V. SCHAEFER //"Neither rights of religion or rights of parenthood are beyond limitation." (Illinois State Bar Association)

FLOYD L. SPERRY, COMMISSIONER//Kansas City Court of Appeals//"We believe that every human being is endowed by God with the inalienable right to live." (Missouri Bar)

THE DECLARATION OF INDEPENDENCE//From a rough draft written by Thomas Jefferson in June of 1776 and edited by Benjamin Franklin and John Adams.

the world that they have nothing to aim at but the exhibition of their inhibitions.

Guy W. Ballard died before the return of a Federal indictment charging some 24 I Am leaders with using the mails to defraud, and with conspiring to use the mails to defraud. The government charged that the I Am leaders had mulcted their followers of some $3,000,000 by claiming that adherents of the cult could conquer old age, disease and poverty; and by predicting the end of the world and urging members to withdraw their funds—which they therefore would not need—from banks, investments and insurance policies, and to present such funds as "love gifts" to the leaders. Ballard's death necessitated a certain awkward rewording of the indictment.

Counts 1 to 11 alleged that the accused and Guy W. Ballard had devised a scheme to defraud and for obtaining money and property by means of false pretenses, representations and promises, and that the scheme was, in substance, that the accused and Guy W. Ballard would:

(a) Create, organize and operate a movement known as the "I Am" movement and, by means of the representations hereinafter set forth, solicit, induce, encourage, persuade and entice persons to become members and followers thereof.

(b) Form, organize, dominate and control a corporation known as the Saint Germain Foundation and arrange for the election of Donald Ballard as president, Paul Potter as vice president and Edna W. Ballard as secretary and treasurer thereof.

(c) By means of the representations hereinafter set forth, solicit, induce, encourage, persuade and entice persons to give money and property to the Saint Germain Foundation.

(d) Form, organize, dominate and control a corporation known as the Saint Germain Press and arrange for the election of Donald Ballard as president, Paul Potter as vice president and Edna W. Ballard as secretary and treasurer thereof.

(e) By means of the representations hereinafter set forth, solicit, induce, encourage, persuade and entice persons to purchase from defendants and Guy W. Ballard books, charts, pamphlets, magazines and other matter published by the Saint Germain Press.

(f) By means of the representations hereinafter set forth, sell pictures, charts, paraphernalia and other articles.

(g) Arrange for, establish and maintain branch offices, meeting rooms and reading rooms* in cities and towns throughout the United

---

* Copies of Ballard's books in the Boston Public Library bear a small sticker on the inside cover reading "From 'I AM' Reading Room, 127 Tremont St., Boston, Mass."

States, and arrange for and conduct meetings, classes and lectures at such offices and rooms for the instruction of persons in the principles, precepts and doctrines of the "I Am" movement.

(h) Arrange for and conduct radio programs and broadcasts over radio stations in the United States for the instruction of persons in the principles, precepts and doctrines of the "I Am" movement.

(i) In such meetings, lectures and broadcasts and by means of letters, books, pamphlets and other written and printed matter, make the following representations:

(1) That Guy W. Ballard had attained a supernatural state of self-immortality, which enabled him to conquer disease, death, old age, poverty and misery.

(2) That Guy W. Ballard, now deceased, alias Saint Germain, Jesus, George Washington, and Godfré Ray King, had been selected and thereby designated by the alleged "ascertained masters," Saint Germain, as a divine messenger; and that the words of "ascended masters" and the words of the alleged divine entity, Saint Germain, would be transmitted to mankind through the medium of the said Guy W. Ballard.

(3) That Guy W. Ballard, during his lifetime, and Edna W. Ballard and Donald Ballard, by reason of their alleged high spiritual attainments and righteous conduct, had been selected as divine messengers through which the words of the alleged "ascended masters," including the alleged Saint Germain, would be communicated to mankind under the teachings commonly known as the "I Am" movement.

(4) That the Ballards had, by supernatural visitation, been accorded a supernatural state of self-immortality of body and had been appointed messengers of divine entities and "ascended masters," and that it was only through them that the teachings and principles of such divine entities and "ascended masters" would be transmitted to mankind.

(5) That the teachings, precepts, doctrines and principles of the "I Am" movement were the only channels through which the spiritual teachings or words of Saint Germain and other "ascended masters" would be given to the world, and that said words and teachings were essential to the salvation of mankind.

(6) That the Ballards had attained a supernatural state of self-immortality, which enabled them to be entirely free from ailments common to man and to conquer disease, death, old age, poverty and misery, and that they could and would transmit that supernatural state to others willing to pay therefor.

(7) That Guy W. Ballard, during his lifetime, and Edna W. Ballard and Donald Ballard had, by reason of supernatural attain-

ments, the power to heal persons of ailments and diseases and to make well persons afflicted with any diseases, injuries, or ailments, and did falsely represent to persons intended to be defrauded that the three designated persons had the ability and power to cure persons of those diseases normally classified as curable and also of diseases which are ordinarily classified by the medical profession as being incurable diseases; and did further represent that the three designated persons had in fact cured either by the activity of one, either or all of said persons, hundreds of persons afflicted with disease and ailments.

(8) That the Ballards had, by reason of divine origin, acquired a great healing power, and that followers of the "I Am" movement could acquire such power, achieve perfect bodies and heal themselves of all human ailments by giving implicit obedience to the precepts, principles, teachings and doctrines of said movement.

(9) That the Ballards had a divine and supernatural ability to bring forth from a supernatural state money, riches and other things necessary to mankind and could transmit that ability to others willing to pay therefor.

(10) That books published and sold by the Ballards were the result of divine visitations and dictations to them by Saint Germain and other supernatural entities, that said books contained divine instructions for the salvation of mankind, and that the Ballards actually encountered the experiences related in said books.

(11) That magazines, booklets, circulars, letters, "edicts," "decrees" and musical compositions published, circulated and sold by the Ballards were divinely inspired and dictated by supernatural entities or "ascended masters" and were a part of the medium through which salvation could be obtained.

(12) That it was solely by reason of the Ballards' teachings and their embodiment in the "I Am" movement and by reason of the Ballards' divine power and influence that the United States was saved from destruction; that, by divine inspiration, there had been accorded to the Ballards the ability to maintain the sovereignty and general welfare of the United States; and that, by reason thereof, complete obedience to their teachings, commands and decrees was absolutely necessary for the safety, welfare and sovereignty of the United States and for divine justice to be had in governmental and industrial activities.

(13) That a certain picture, reproductions of which were sold by the Ballards, was an actual picture of Saint Germain and was the result of a visitation by Saint Germain to Charles Sindelar, and that the purchase of reproductions of said picture by followers of the "I Am" movement was "desirable in their aim and hope to achieve salvation."

(14) That the purchase of certain charts, phonograph records and other articles from the Ballards by followers of the "I Am" movement would bestow upon the purchasers "great blessings and rewards in their aim to achieve salvation."

(15) That there would be, in one or more places in the United States, an actual visitation of "ascended masters" or divine entities, and that said divine entities would then and there appear in physical form before the assembled followers of the "I Am" movement.

(16) That a cataclysm or the end of the world was approaching, that there was therefore no necessity to provide for the future or to save money or other things of value, and that followers of the "I Am" movement, instead of saving their money, should give it to the Ballards.

(17) That any person who criticized or questioned the teachings of the Ballards would be denounced or punished by "ascended masters."

(18) That persons who followed the principles, doctrines and precepts of the "I Am" movement and the teachings of the Ballards would not die, but would "ascend" in their physical, tangible bodies, associate with divine entities and "ascended masters" and be able thereafter to return to earth at will, and to "reascend" if they so desired.

Counts 1 to 11 alleged that all of the aforesaid representations were false, and that the accused and Guy W. Ballard "well knew" they were false.

And here I had best ask the reader's leave to go back and underscore the last statement, for the case turns on it: the government alleged that, 1) the representations *were* false; and that, 2) the accused *well knew* they were false. And each count described a specific letter, check or magazine mailed for the purpose of executing the scheme. Count 12 alleged that the leaders had conspired to commit the offenses charged above, and set forth fourteen alleged overt acts.

In 1940, in Los Angeles, a Federal grand jury indicted leaders Edna W. Ballard, Donald Ballard, Betty Mundy, Paul Stickell, Louise Majerus, William J. Cassiere, Charles Sindelar—see item "(13)" above —his wife, and Frank von der Hoya on the above charges. Before trial was held, trouble came from another direction.

On November 20, 1940, the Borden Publishing Company of Los Angeles and Leslie Robert Oliver brought suit against the "I Am" leaders for alleged infringement of copyright. They charged that Ballard's "Unveiled Mysteries" had been written under the pen-name of "Phylos" by the late Frederick S. Oliver and copyrighted in 1894. Leslie Oliver, the author's son, claimed to own the renewed copyright. Borden and Oliver set forth that some two million copies of "Unveiled Mysteries" (price $2.50; postpaid $2.75) had been sold, and sought an injunction against the "I Am" group and an accounting of all profits derived from the sale of the book.

Two weeks later, on December 3, the mail fraud case went to trial before Federal District Court Judge Leon R. Yankwich. On January 20, 1941, after almost four days of deliberation, the jury acquitted Charles Sindelar, his wife, and von der Hoya. The jury, however, was unable to agree as to the others, and a new trial was ordered.

Meanwhile, on February 13, 1942, the Post Office Department in Washington issued an order denying the use of the mails to the "Mighty I Am" cult, saying that the "scheme which the order was intended to suppress consisted in the sale through the mails by Edna W. Ballard, her son Donald, and certain associates" of a set of books called the "Saint Germain Series," subscriptions to a monthly magazine known as the "Voice of I Am," and various other publications, trinkets and paraphernalia relating to what the Ballards called the activity of the "Mighty I Am."

The second trial was held before Judge J. F. T. O'Connor. Before the Government had finished putting in its case, Judge O'Connor, for reasons which do not appear, made the following statement to the jury which later was assigned as error:

Now, Gentlemen, here is the issue in this case: First, the defendants in this case made certain representations of belief in a divinity and in a supernatural power. Some of the teachings of the defendants, representations, might seem extremely improbable to a great many people. For instance, the appearance of Jesus to dictate some of the works that we have introduced in evidence, as testified to here at the opening transcription, or shaking hands with Jesus. To some people that might seem highly improbable. I point that out as one of the many statements. Whether that is true or not is not the concern of this Court and is not the concern of the jury—and they are going to be told so in their instructions.*

As far as this Court sees the issue, it is immaterial what these defendants preached or wrote or taught in their classes. They are not going to be permitted to speculate on the actuality of the happening of those incidents. Now I think I have made that as clear as I can. Therefore, the religious beliefs of these defendants cannot be an issue in this court. The issue is: Did these defendants honestly and in good faith believe those things? If they did, they should be acquitted. I cannot make it any clearer than that. If these defendants did not believe those things, they did not believe that Jesus came down and dictated, or that Saint Germain came down and dictated, did not believe the things they wrote, the things they preached, but

---

* Between the case reports—which state they were made to the jury—and the tenor of the words, the author can only surmise that Judge O'Connor is addressing counsel while the jury looks on.

used the mail for the purpose of getting money, the jury should find them guilty. Therefore, gentlemen, religion cannot come into this case.

During the course of the trial, count 1, *re* a certain check mailed to Edna, was dismissed. She was convicted on counts 2, 3, 5, 7, 8, 11 and 12, and acquitted on counts 4, 6, 9 and 10. Donald Ballard was convicted on counts 2 to 7, 9 and 10. Mundy, Stickell, Majerus and Casiere were acquitted on counts 2 to 12. Edna W. Ballard and Donald Ballard were sentenced, and appealed.

In San Francisco, on June 21, 1943, the Circuit Court of Appeals held that the restriction of the issue in question to that of good faith was error, and that the question of the truth of the representations concerning the respondents' doctrines or beliefs should also have been submitted to the jury. The Court accordingly reversed the Ballards' convictions and remanded the case for a new trial. But before this was done—and after denial, on September 29, 1943, of a petition for a rehearing—the question was taken to the Supreme Court on a petition for a writ of *certiorari,* which was granted, on January 3, 1944, "because of the importance of the question presented."

In Washington, on April 24, 1944, with the court divided five to four, Justice William O. Douglas delivered the majority decision, ruling that it was not necessary for the trial jury to have considered the truthfulness of the defendants' religious views, and reversing the order of the Circuit Court of Appeals. This in effect sustained the convictions of Edna and Donald, and in principle reaffirmed that courts have no power to pass upon the truth of any religious doctrine, no matter how incredible it may appear to others, or how fraudulently it may have been used. As to this main issue, both dissents showed agreement with the majority opinion: Justices Stone, Roberts and Frankfurter would have reversed the appeals court and affirmed the original verdict; Justice Jackson would have reversed the appeals court, voided the sentence and dismissed the indictment. Said Justice Douglas:

> We do not agree that the truth or verity of respondents' religious doctrines or beliefs should have been submitted to the jury. Whatever this particular indictment might require, the First Amendment precludes such a course, as the United States [i.e., the prosecution] seems to concede. "The law knows no heresy, and is committed to the support of no dogma, the establishment of no sect." . . . The First Amendment has a dual aspect. It not only "forestalls compulsion by law of the acceptance of any creed or the practice of any form of worship," but also "safeguards the free exercise of the chosen form of religion . . ." "Thus the Amendment embraces two concepts—free-

dom to believe and freedom to act. The first is absolute but, in the nature of things, the second cannot be." . . . Freedom of thought, which includes freedom of religious belief, is basic in a society of free men . . . It embraces the right to maintain theories of life and of death and of the hereafter which are rank heresy to followers of the orthodox faiths. Heresy trials are foreign to our Constitution. Men may believe what they cannot prove. They may not be put to the proof of their religious doctrines or beliefs. Religious experiences which are as real as life to some may be incomprehensible to others. Yet the fact that they may be beyond the ken of mortals does not mean that they can be made suspect before the law. Many take their gospel from the New Testament. But it would hardly be supposed that they could be tried before a jury charged with the duty of determining whether those teachings contained false representations. The miracles of the New Testament, the Divinity of Christ, life after death, the power of prayer are deep in the religious convictions of many. If one could be sent to jail because a jury in a hostile environment found those teachings false, little indeed would be left of religious freedom. The Fathers of the Constitution were not unaware of the varied and extreme views of religious sects, of the violence of disagreement among them, and of the lack of any one religious creed on which all men could agree. They fashioned a charter of government which envisaged the widest possible toleration of conflicting views. Man's relation to his God was made no concern of the state. He was granted the right to worship as he pleased and to answer to no man for the verity of his religious views. The religious views espoused by respondents might seem incredible, if not preposterous, to most people. But if those doctrines are subject to trial before a jury charged with finding their truth or falsity, then the same can be done with the religious beliefs of any sect. When the triers of fact undertake that task, they enter a forbidden domain. The First Amendment does not select any one group or any one type of religion for preferred treatment. It puts them all in that position . . . So we conclude that the District Court ruled properly when it witheld from the jury all questions concerning the truth or falsity of the religious beliefs or doctrines of respondents.

Chief Justice Harlan Fiske Stone submitted a dissenting opinion in which Justices Owen J. Roberts and Felix Frankfurter concurred:

I am not prepared to say that the constitutional guarantee of freedom of religion affords immunity from criminal prosecution for the fraudulent procurement of money by false statements as to one's religious experiences, more than it renders polygamy or libel immune from criminal prosecution . . . I cannot say that freedom of thought and worship includes freedom to procure money by making knowingly false statements about one's religious experiences. To go no further, if it were shown that a defendant in this case had asserted as a part of the alleged fraudulent scheme, that he had physically shaken hands with St. Germain in San Francisco on a day named, or that, as the indictment here alleges, by the exertion of his spiritual power he "had in fact cured . . . hundreds of persons afflicted with diseases and ailments," I should not doubt that it would be open to the Government to submit to the jury proof that he had never been in San Francisco and that no such cures had ever been effected. In any event I see no occasion for making any pronouncement on this subject in the present case.

The indictment charges respondents' use of the mails to defraud and a conspiracy to commit that offense by false statements of their religious experiences which had not in fact occurred. But it also charged that the representations were "falsely and fraudulently" made, that respondents "well knew" that these representations were untrue, and that they were made by respondents with the intent to cheat and defraud those to whom they were made. With the assent of the prosecution and the defense the trial judge withdrew from the consideration of the jury the question whether the alleged religious experiences had in fact occurred, but submitted to the jury the single issue whether petitioners honestly believed that they had occurred, with the instruction that if the jury did not so find, then it should return a verdict of guilty. On this issue the jury, on ample evidence that respondents were without belief in the statements which they had made to their victims, found a verdict of guilty. The state of one's mind is a fact as capable of fraudulent misrepresentation as is one's physical condition or the state of his bodily health . . . There are no exceptions to the charge and no contention that the trial court rejected any relevant evidence which petitioners sought to offer. Since the indictment and the evidence support the conviction, it is irrelevant whether the religious experiences alleged did or did not in fact occur or whether that issue could or could not, for constitutional reasons, have been rightly submitted to the jury. Certainly none of the respondents' constitutional rights are violated if they are prosecuted for the fradulent procurement of money by false representations as to their beliefs, religious or otherwise.

Obviously if the question whether the religious experiences in fact occurred could not constitutionally have been submitted to the jury the court rightly withdrew it. If it could have been submitted I know of no reason why the parties could not, with the advice of counsel, assent to its withdrawal from the jury. And where, as here, the indictment charges two sets of false statements, each independently sufficient to sustain the conviction, I cannot accept respondents' contention that the withdrawal of one set and the submission of the other to the jury amounted to an amendment of the indictment . . .

On the issue submitted to the jury in this case it properly rendered a verdict of guilty. As no legally sufficient reason for disturbing it appears, I think the judgment below should be reversed and that of the District Court reinstated.

"This is magnificent [Justice Robert H. Jackson's separate dissent, which follows], and some of it is law," commented *The Christian Century,* afterwards. "In the part which is law, it passes lightly and inconclusively over the question as to whether it is possible, as the rest of the court holds it to be, to prove bad faith and financial fraud in the propagation of opinions without proving the falsity of the opinions. It concurs with the court's decision and with the other dissenting opinion in holding that the truth of a doctrine, however absurd to most minds, cannot be submitted to determination by a jury. This is another seal upon our charter of religious liberty. And it should stir the minds of men who think they have a sane and true religion to consider how they may make it serve the needs of those whose normal hungers seek abnormal food in these fantastic cults."

Said Justice Jackson:

I should say the defendants have done just that for which they are indicted. If I might agree to their conviction without creating a precedent, I cheerfully would do so. I can see in their teachings nothing but humbug, untainted by any trace of truth. But that does not dispose of the constitutional question whether misrepresentation of religious experience or belief is prosecutable; it rather emphasizes the danger of such prosecutions.

The Ballard family claimed miraculous communication with the spirit world and supernatural power to heal the sick. They were brought to trial for mail fraud on an indictment which charged that their representations were false and that they "well knew" they were false. The trial judge, obviously troubled, ruled that the court could not try whether the statements were untrue, but could inquire whether the defendants knew them to be untrue; and, if so, they could be convicted.

I find it difficult to reconcile this conclusion with our traditional religious freedoms.

In the first place, as a matter of either practice or philosophy I do not see how we can separate an issue as to what is believed from considerations as to what is believable. The most convincing proof that one believes his statements is to show that they have been true in his experience. Likewise, that one knowingly falsified is best proved by showing that what he said happened never did happen. How can the Government prove these persons knew something to be false which it cannot prove to be false? If we try religious sincerity severed from religious verity, we isolate the dispute from the very considerations which in common experience provide its most reliable answer.

In the second place, any inquiry into intellectual honesty in religion raises profound psychological problems. William James, who wrote on these matters as a scientist, reminds us that it is not theology and ceremonies which keep religion going. Its vitality is in the religious experiences of many people. "If you ask what these experiences are, they are conversations with the unseen, voices and visions, responses to prayer, changes of heart, deliverances from fear, inflowings of help, assurances of support, whenever certain persons set their own internal attitude in certain appropriate ways."[2]

If religious liberty includes, as it must, the right to communicate such experiences to others, it seems to me an impossible task for juries to separate fancied ones from real ones, dreams from happenings, and hallucinations from true clairvoyance. Such experiences, like some tones and colors, have existence for one, but none at all for another. They cannot be verified to the minds of those whose field of consciousness does not include religious insight. When one comes to trial which turns on any aspect of religious belief or representation, unbelievers among his judges are likely not to understand and are almost certain not to believe him.

And then I do not know what degree of skepticism or disbelief in a religious representation amounts to actionable fraud. James points out that "Faith means belief in something concerning which doubt is still theoretically possible."[3] Belief in what one may demonstrate to the senses is not faith. All schools of religious thought make enormous assumptions, generally on the basis of revelations authenticated by some sign or miracle. The appeal in such matters is to a very different plane of credulity than is invoked by representations of secular fact in commerce. Some who profess belief in the Bible read literally what others read as allegory or metaphor, as they read Aesop's fables. Religious symbolism is even used by some with the same mental reservations one has in teaching of Santa Claus or Uncle Sam or Easter bunnies or dispassionate judges. It is hard in matters so mystical to say how literally one is bound to believe the doctrine he teaches and even more difficult to say how far it is reliance upon a teacher's literal belief which induces followers to give him money.

There appear to be persons—let us hope not many—who find refreshment and courage in the teaching of the "I Am" cult. If the members of the sect get comfort from the celestial guidance of their "Saint Germain," however doubtful it seems to me, it is hard to say that they do not get what they pay for. Scores of sects flourish in this country by teaching what to me are queer notions. It is plain that there is a wide variety in American religious taste. The Ballards are not alone in catering to it with a pretty dubious product.

The chief wrong which false prophets do to their following is not financial. The collections aggregate a tempting total, but individual payments are not ruinous. I doubt if the vigilance of the law is equal to making money stick by over-credulous people. But the real harm is on the mental and spiritual plane. There are those who hunger and thirst after higher values which they feel wanting in their humdrum lives. They live in mental confusion or moral anarchy and seek vaguely for truth and beauty and moral support. When they are deluded and then disillusioned, cynicism and confusion follow. The wrong of these things, as I see it, is not in the money the victims part with half so much as in the mental and spiritual poison they get. But that is precisely the thing the Constitution put beyond the reach of the prosecutor, for the price of freedom of religion or of speech or of the press is that we must put with with, and even pay for, a good deal of rubbish.

Prosecutions of this character easily could degenerate into religious prosecution. I do not doubt that religious leaders may be convicted of fraud for making false representations on matters other than faith or experience, as for example if one represents that funds are being used to construct a church when in fact thay are being used for personal purposes. But that is not this case, which reaches wholly dangerous ground. When does less than full belief in a professed credo become actionable fraud if one is soliciting gifts or legacies? Such inquiries may discomfort orthodox as well as unconventional religious teachers, for even the most regular of them are sometimes accused of taking their orthodoxy with a grain of salt.

I would dismiss the indictment and have done with this business of judicially examining other people's faiths.

*Part IV*

# THE RIGHT TO LIVE

# Parens Patriae

Regarding the primary concern of this study—the right of children to live—Judge Walter V. Schaefer of the Supreme Court of Illinois, in *Labrenz* (Ch. 15), noted the "responsibility of government, in its character as *parens patriae*\* to care for infants within its jurisdiction and to protect them from neglect, abuse and fraud." Such jurisdiction, "of ancient origin," was codified for Illinois in its Juvenile Court Act, "which expressly authorizes the court, if circumstances warrant, to remove the child from the custody of its parents and award its custody to an appointed guardian."

In overruling the parents' objection that the action taken under this statute violated the parents' freedom of religion, Judge Schaefer said "Because the governing principles are well settled, this argument requires no extensive discussion." The basic such principle was one which had carried over, logically and without much argument, from that established in the historic *Senior, Lewis* and *Pierson* decisions—which last, in turn, was based upon *Reynolds*—that religious belief is no defense to prosecution of a parent under a child protection statute.

In what follows, we shall first see the state, by punishment or the threat of it, coercing the parent (and a company) to attend to the child's long-term welfare to the extent prescribed by statute. We witnessed in Part III the establishment of the state's right to coerce the parent in the area of "denial of medical aid because of religious belief." But in emergency situations in this area, where the child's life or health is immediately threatened, such action, being indirect, likely succeeds only in "avenging" a by then dead child.

And so we shall go back to the turn of the century or before, and follow the fortunes of courts dealing not in law but in equity—the juvenile, family and children's courts—as they proceed with their

---

\* "Parent of the country"; the state, as to its sovereign power of guardianship over persons under disability—such as minors and insane and incompetent persons.

attempts to secure directly the well-being of live children, rather than
to leave it to other courts to punish, afterwards, the parent of a dead
child. In these cases, the question of the propriety of interference with
the rights of parenthood is at first hard enough by itself; the additional
problem of religious freedom does not appear for some time. When
it does, we shall no longer be surprised to find this question—one largely
concerned with the parent's beliefs rather than the considered welfare
of the child—being dealt with rather shortly.

We shall first examine some decisions not of juvenile-type courts,
but which had to do generally with the welfare of children. In the first
of these, *Ewer,* Justice Gray's remarks are important in setting forth
the state's sentiments, *circa* 1894, as to the justifiable extent of its active
concern for child welfare. The following briefly described cases represent
other battle-markers on the field of clash between the parent's claimed
right to control his child and the state's claimed right to interfere,
sometimes with an appeal beyond the state to claimed rights of freedom
under the federal constitution.

At the Broadway Theater in New York City, in 1893 or before,
Mildred Ewer, aged seven, billed as "La Regaloncita" and wearing a
short dress and purple tights, "danced upon the stage to the music of
an orchestra, elevating her legs, moving upon her toes, and posturing
with her figure." Her mother, Charlotte Ewer, was arrested upon a
police magistrate's warrant, charged with violating section 292 of the
New York Penal Code, which made it a misdemeanor for the parent of
a female child under the age of fourteen years to procure or consent to
the employment or exhibition of the child as a dancer. Being held, she
sued out writs of *habeas corpus* and *certiorari,* alleging that there were
no sufficient grounds for holding her and that the statute was unconstitutional, since it deprived the parent of the right to custody and service
of the child, and deprived the child of the right to follow a lawful occupation. The writs were dismissed and she appealed. The Court of Appeals of New York, though all of its judges were satisfied with the
decision, felt that "the range taken by the arguments of counsel seemed
to call for a brief expression by us of our view of the principle of state
interference."

In affirming conviction, Justice Gray said:

> This question falls within those which are classified under the head
> of the police power of the state. The extent of the exercise of that
> power, with which the legislature is invested, and which it has so freely
> exerted in many directions, within constitutional limits, is a matter
> resting in discretion, to be guided by the wisdom of the people's
> representatives . . . The proposition is indisputable that the custody

of the child by the parent is within legislative regulation. The parent, by natural law, is entitled to the custody and care of the child, and its natural guardian is held to the performance of certain duties. To society, organized as a state, it is a matter of paramount interest that the child shall be cared for, and that the duties of support and education be performed by the parent or guardian, in order that the child shall become a healthful and useful member of the community. It has been well remarked that, the better organized and trained the race, the better it is prepared for holding its own. Hence it is that laws are enacted looking to the compulsory education by parents of their children, and to their punishment for cruel treatment, and which limit and regulate the employment of children in the factory and the workshop, to prevent injury from excessive labor . . . It is true enough that if the court could say that this legislation was an arbitrary exercise of the legislative power, depriving the parent of a right to a legitimate use of his child's services—that, while ostensibly for the promotion of the well-being of children, in reality it strikes at an inalienable right or at the personal liberty of the citizen—it would be its duty to so pronounce, and to declare its invalidity. But this legislation has no such destructive effect or tendency. It does not deprive the parent of the child's custody, nor does it abridge any just rights. It interferes to prevent the public exhibition of children, under a certain age, in spectacles or performances which, by reason of the place or hour, of the nature of the acts demanded of the child performer, and of the surroundings and circumstances of the exhibition, are deemed by the legislature prejudicial to the physical, mental, or moral well-being of the child, and hence to the interests of the state itself . . . Its application is to all public exhibitions or shows. That any and all such shall be deemed prejudicial to the interests of the child, and contrary to the policy of the state to permit, was for the legislature to consider and say.

When Sheridan Bailey "neglected, omitted and refused" to send his child, Vory Bailey, to school, he was charged upon affidavit before a justice of the peace with violating the compulsory education law of Indiana. He was convicted before the justice, and appealed from that judgment to the circuit court of Jay County, which quashed the affidavit. The state appealed. On October 29, 1901, the Supreme Court of Indiana reversed judgment, upholding the constitutionality (under the state constitution) of the compulsory education act against the claim that it invaded the natural right of a parent to govern and control his own children.

Arthur Beauchamp, actually between fourteen and sixteen, represented he was over sixteen to secure employment with Sturges & Burn Manufacturing Company. There, while operating a punch press, he was injured. Through "next friend" he brought an action in Cook County Superior Court for the damages sustained, counting on the Illinois statute prohibiting employment of children under sixteen in hazardous occupations such as his own. The trial court directed the jury that, if Beauchamp was in fact less than sixteen, then in spite of his deceit the company was guilty of violation of the statute, and he was entitled to recover. The case reached the Supreme Court, where, in 1913, judgment was affirmed. Said Justice Hughes:

> The Federal question presented is whether the statute, as construed by the state court, contravenes the 14th Amendment. It cannot be doubted that the state was entitled to prohibit the employment of persons of tender years in dangerous occupations [but it] is urged that the [company] was not permitted to defend upon the ground that it acted in good faith relying upon representation made by Beauchamp that he was over sixteen. It is said that, being over fourteen, he at least had attained the age at which he should have been treated as responsible for his statements. But, as it was competent for the state, in securing the safety of the young, to prohibit such employment altogether, it could select means appropriate to make its prohibition effective, and could compel employers, at their peril, to ascertain whether those they employed were in fact under the age specified.

In 1922, in the case of Rosalyn Zucht, the Supreme Court declined to question the validity of a San Antonio ordinance which allowed no child to attend any public or private school without first presenting a certificate of vaccination. Said Judge Brandeis: "Long before this suit was instituted, *Jacobson v. Massachusetts* . . . had settled that it was within the public power of a State to provide for compulsory vaccination."

In Nebraska, in 1920, one Meyer taught a child of ten in a parochial school to read in German. He was convicted of violating a state law forbidding the teaching in any private, denominational, parochial or public school of any modern language other than English to any child who had not attained and successfully passed the eighth grade—a law undeniably inspired by hatred toward anything German after World War I. On appeal, the United States Supreme Court in 1923 held that, both in denying an instructor the right to follow a lawful occupation and in denying a child the right to receive teaching in languages other than the nation's common tongue, the law invaded liberties guaranteed by the Fourteenth Amendment, and therefore was unconstitutional.

And in 1925, in *Pierce v. Society of Sisters,* the Supreme Court held that, while a state may compel parents to send their children to school, it may not require that all children be educated in *public* schools, and that the parent may choose instead to send the child to a private school, where it may receive religious along with secular schooling.

In *Hamilton v. Regents of the University of California,* certain minors, because of their religious convictions, had refused to take the University's course in military science and tactics required by statute. The board of regents accordingly refused to admit them. The Supreme Court in 1934 upheld the statute, even though the state university afforded "opportunity for education such as may not be had at any other institution in California except at a greater cost which these minors are not able to pay," holding that the state may provide services on a condition which may be contrary to the religious scruples of some of its citizens.

In 1948, both the questions of the propriety of a vaccination statute and whether it infringed on religious freedom were raised in the New Jersey case of *Sadlock v. Board of Education.* Said Justice Eastwood: " . . . the question of the desirability or efficacy of compulsory vaccination . . . is strictly a legislative and not a judicial question . . . So, too, with respect to the guaranty of religious freedom, the constitutional guaranty of religious freedom was not intended to prohibit legislation with respect to the general public welfare."

Charles Heinemann, a "simple journeyman mechanic," lived in Pittsburgh, Pennsylvania, with his wife and five children. Heinemann was a convert to the exanthematic method of healing discovered by Dr. Carl Baunscheidt—the "Baunscheidt system"—and practiced it by himself. In December of 1879, his eldest child, about nine, became ill with diphtheria. He accordingly began pricking its skin on different parts of its body with an instrument composed of about thirty needles and operated with a spring. The parts thus pricked he afterwards rubbed, in the Baunscheidt manner, with an irritating oil. But on December 22, despite this salutary treatment, the child died.

Meanwhile, Heinemann's wife also had come down with diphtheria. Nothing daunted, he gave her the same treatment; she died on December 27. Shortly thereafter, a second child died, and some months later the youngest child also died, both of the same disease and under the same treatment. During the illnesses of his wife and these two children, Heinemann refused to call in any physician or to provide any medical treatment except his own panacea, though finally he did call in an allopath when "death was at the door." This left the father, then in "indigent circumstances," with only two young sons, Osmar, eight, and Eugene, five. The children "had some estate," and it was necessary to support them out of it.

To Catherine Reineman, the boys' maternal grandmother, it appeared quite likely that, should Osmar or Eugene become ill with diphtheria or any other serious disease, they would receive the same treatment from their father, and likely with the same fatal result. She accordingly petitioned the Orphans' Court of Allegheny County, praying that the court appoint a guardian—herself—for the two boys, and setting forth that their father, Charles Heinemann, by reason of indolence, ignorance, stubbornness, or some other cause unknown to herself, had neglected and refused to provide for his children. This was in accordance with a statute enacted May 4, 1855, authorizing the Orphans' Court to appoint a guardian for a child, "its mother being dead, whose father shall, for any cause, neglect or refuse to provide for it." Charles Heinemann filed an answer to the petition, denying its allegations. But after testimony was taken, the court entered a decree appointing Catherine Reineman as Osmar and Eugene's guardian. On appeal, the Supreme Court of Pennsylvania affirmed the decree. Said Judge Trunkey:

> The general rule is, that the father is entitled to the custody of his infant children, that right growing out of the obligation to maintain and educate them. But this is not on account of any absolute right in the father, but for the benefit of the infant . . . It is a mistake to suppose that the father has an absolute, vested right to the custody of the infant . . . When a court is asked to appoint a guardian of the person of a child, it will investigate the circumstances and act according to a sound discretion, the primary object being the good of the child . . .
>
> An examination of the testimony shows that the appellant's conduct towards his family would have been the moving cause for the decree. While the evidence reveals that he had no faith in allopathic physicians, it also reveals that he had neglected to call any others for his wife and three children who died within less than seven months prior to the hearing. He may have been an affectionate husband and father and have done what he thought was best, yet according to the evidence they were shamefully neglected as regards medical treatment.

Mr. Tuttendario was a street cleaner for the city of Philadelphia. His wife had borne him ten children; seven had died. Of the three surviving, one was older and one younger than Tony. In June of 1912, Tony Tuttendario was seven and one-half years old; for six of those years he had been afflicted with rickets. By then, he had a resulting deformity which could be cured by an operation, but which, without an operation, probably would leave him a cripple all his life. Dr. di Stephano, who had attended the family, had examined Tony and had advised an operation. A Dr. Cortese also had attended the boy and had advised that the best thing was an operation. But the mother refused, saying they were afraid of hospitals and afraid Tony would die, because she had lost seven other children.

The year before, after receiving complaints from school authorities, the Society for the Prevention of Cruelty to Children had urged the Tuttendarios to permit the operation, which would be performed without expense to them, or that Tony be given some treatment. They refused. Other persons who knew the family urged the father and mother to have the operation performed, but to no avail. In February of 1911, David J. Terry, an officer of the Society, applied to Judge McMichael of the District Court of Philadelphia County for an order committing the boy to them for the purpose of having the operation performed, but the judge dismissed the case. That July, the Society presented a second petition to the Court. This was left under consideration for some time, in the hope that the father and mother might be induced to consent.

Finally, on June 15, 1912, the hearing was held. Professor H. Augustus Wilson, an expert on that branch of medicine and surgery, testified that Tony was suffering from rachitis, otherwise known as bow-legs and knock-knees; that the disease was curable by operation upon the bones, and that the operation had been very extensively performed; that it could be cured in no other way; that if it was not cured the victim could get along in life, but that the deformity tended to increase; that it interfered with a person making a livelihood in anything that required standing or walking, but that any occupation that could be attended to sitting down would not be interfered with; and that the disease did not in any manner tend to shorten life if not cured.

Mrs. Tuttendario testified that she would never permit an operation to be performed upon her son, saying that he was not born in that condition, and, therefore, she would not have him operated on, nor would her husband. The court held that there was no evidence that the parents had inflicted physical or moral injury upon the child with malicious intent—the only grounds under the applicable statute, for forfeiting their natural guardianship—and dismissed the petition. Said Judge Sulzberger:

The case is one of great interest. The Society for the Prevention of Cruelty to Children, actuated by a highly benevolent and charitable purpose, desires to give this boy a better opportunity in his future life than he can have if the disease is not cured. The father and mother, apprehending possible fatal results from an operation, dread it to such an extent that they refuse their consent to its being performed. This refusal by the child's natural guardians, its parents, is the basis of the petitioner's charge of cruelty, and the foundation for its prayer that it be appointed the legal guardian of the child for the specific purpose of having the operation performed.

Judge Sulzberger outlined Pennsylvania's concern for children in its

Crimes Act of 1860, its Act of 1879 (which penalized the "employment of children under twelve in any underground works or mine") and the Act of 1893.

This legislation during the last half century shows the anxious care with which the general assembly has from time to time considered the subject. It shows, too, that the natural right of parents to the care and custody of their children has been abridged only in cases where they have been guilty of inflicting physical or moral injury upon their offspring with malicious intent . . . The case before us is of an essentially different character. The parents here are charged with allowing their unreasonable apprehension of injury to their child to outweigh the reasonable judgment of professional experts that the danger, whatever it is, should be incurred . . . We are . . . asked to supersede the child's natural guardians on the sole ground that their judgment is impaired by natural love and affection . . .

We see no warrant in the statutes for granting this request. We have not yet adopted as a public policy the Spartan rule that children belong, not to their parents, but to the state . . . In the case before us, the parents fear that the operation will result in their child's death. There is ever present to their minds the fact that of ten children born to them seven died at an early age. It may be neither absurd nor illogical to argue from this that there is an inherent constitutional weakness in the family which increases the peril of a serious operation and tends to put the patient in the class of those who succumb. At all events, such a conclusion is not so patently wrong that a court would or ought to interfere with it.

Having regard to all these considerations and to the fact that the child's present condition involves no danger to its life, and that, even if uncured, he is still capable of a reasonable amount of activity in all ordinary affairs, we do not think that this is a case in which we can displace the natural guardians on the ground of cruelty.

John Vasko, born in Czechoslovakia, immigrated with his wife Mary to the United States. They lived in Bayonne and Passaic, and afterwards in a flat on Ridge Street in Hastings-upon-Hudson, a few miles above Yonkers. In the spring of 1933, their daughter Mary was eleven; the twins, Anna and Helen, were two. At that time, Helen's left eye appeared infected, and Mrs. Vasko began treating it with drops of an herb medicine obtained from a man in Pennsylvania. At that time, too, John Vasko, unemployed, was a patient in Grasslands Hospital, at Eastview. When Mrs. Vasko took Helen to visit him, physicians noticed her infected eye and became greatly alarmed. Dr. E. C. Wood, head of the hospital's eye department, diagnosed the "infection" to be in fact a glioma, a malignant tumor on the retina. Already, Helen was totally blind in that eye, and the growth was one whose inevitable course was to spread to the brain and cause death. He urged the mother to permit the hospital to remove the child's eye. She refused.[1]

The Westchester Children's Association then became interested, but Mary Vasko was adamant against the pleadings of the Association, physicians, Catholic priests and the Children's Court. After all other attempts failed, the Association applied for a court order directing the operation.

In March of 1933, at a hearing before Judge George W. Smyth in Westchester Children's Court, Dr. Angelo J. Smith, a Yonkers eye specialist, testified that the child would have about an even chance to survive such an operation, but that she certainly would die unless the eye was removed. He said a malignant growth eventually would affect the child's brain and cause a "disagreeable death." Mrs. Vasko was then asked if she would rather have her child die than undergo the operation. She replied: "No one knows whether my child is diseased. If she is going to die naturally, probably she would be better than she is now . . . God gave me the baby and God can do what he wants." Afterwards, Judge Smyth signed an order—which he then stayed pending appeal— permitting physicians to remove Helen's eye and part of the optical nerve. He then appointed Francis R. Fay, a Yonkers attorney, as Helen's special guardian *ad litem* and counsel for the parents, and ordered him to appeal the decision to the Appellate Division. And he appointed Maurice Zucker, an attorney of White Plains, as *amicus curiae,* to appear for the court.

Later, Hastings neighbors informed police that Helen had a new ailment, and on Wednesday evening, April 12, Dr. Michael Bender was sent to see her; he found she had a cold and a temperature slightly above 100 degrees. No similar case had ever been decided by a New York court, and by now it had attracted national attention; Attorney Fay reported being deluged with letters from "self-styled humanitarians." Newspapermen, photographers and crowds of curious townsfolk flocked to Ridge Street to watch developments in the controversy. The front of the Vasko flat was level with the road but the rear overhung a steep hill; the frightened family therefore moved into the rear rooms, which were inaccessible to the curious, and locked all doors and windows. Next morning, when Dr. Bender returned, he was unable to gain admittance but, not considering the child seriously ill, did not assert his right to obtain police assistance.

That same day, attorneys Zucker and Fay submitted their briefs to the Appellate Division. Zucker declared that "the public policy of protecting wards of this State is more important than the peculiar belief or personal convictions of the parents when the life of a child is in danger," and urged that the operation be permitted immediately:

A public wrong would be committed if the parents of the child could, by refusing to give their consent to the operation, prevent this court from ordering the operation under the authority vested by the Constitution and the statute of this state. The public policy of the State does not require that the court sit idly by and permit the child to die when, by the exercise of the powers conferred upon it by the Legislature, it can step in and prevent the tragedy which the penal law declares to be a crime when committed by the parents. The crime should be prevented in advance—save the child's life as far as possible, rather than let nature kill the child and then hold the parents criminally responsible . . .

Fay pointed out that "there is no certainty that the operation will arrest the malignant growth," and that "it is extremely doubtful if a person of ordinary prudence would deem it advisable to resort to such a drastic operation when the result is so speculative."

That evening, the Vaskos' parish priest visited them, but afterwards reported that his entreaties had failed to move the mother. She continued to place her faith in God, and had told him that Helen would live or die in accordance with God's will, not medical treatment. But the priest caused John Vasko to yield a point. Friday morning, he opened his barricaded front door and told a waiting group of newspaper men that, though his wife still had not changed her mind, he was ready to place the responsibility in the hands of the law: "The law knows best. If the law says the child must lose its eye, I will say all right."

It was Easter weekend. Mr. Vasko, who was receiving emergency relief employment, had Friday off; during the day he occasionally came to the front door, muttered imprecations at the crowd and directed a menacing foot toward the constant group of photographers and reporters. Finally he became so annoyed that he threw one reporter out of the entrance and threatened bodily harm to others. The next day, Saturday, when Andrew Lesko of Passaic, whose wife was Mary's sister, came with members of his family to visit, he found the Vaskos had disappeared.

Later, James Brody, a Yonkers milkman, reported that he had seen them leave by a circuitous route shortly after 5 o'clock that morning. Local police, fearful that Helen had been removed from jurisdiction, began a search in behalf of the Children's Court. Monday evening, April 17, John Vasko returned alone to Hastings, went to Police Commissioner Frederick Charles' home and asked for police protection against reporters and curious intruders. He explained that his wife was on the verge of a nervous breakdown, and that they had been staying with a cousin over the weekend. Charles promised to place a guard at the Vasko home, beginning the following morning. Vasko then said he would bring his family back at that time. In Brooklyn, on Tuesday, April 18, the Appellate Division by unanimous decision ( dated April 13) affirmed the Children's Court order. Said Associate Justice Hagarty:

> The order appealed from adjudges the infant-appellant to be a neglected child, as defined by the Children's Court Act of the state of New York (Laws 1930, c. 393), in that the parents have neglected and refused to provide necessary medical and surgical care for said child . . . While the question now before us has never been presented to an appellate court in this state in so far as I am able to determine, power in the court to act rests upon ample authority.
>
> Prior to the adoption of the Children's Court Act of the state of New York in 1922 (Laws 1922, c. 547), resting upon constitutional edict, there existed no affirmative statutory power to exercise direct control over the physical welfare of a child. Action was indirect, by punishment of those vested with responsibility for neglect of the health of children in failing to furnish medical attendance when needed, in violation of the Penal Law . . . Such a law remains upon our statute books (Penal Law § 482), and provides that one who, under a duty to furnish medical or surgical attendance to a minor, willfully omits to perform that duty, is guilty of a misdemeanor. That provision of the Penal Law is not inconsistent with the act controlling here, which goes further, and, instead of punishing those guilty of neglecting children, which procedure conceivably might be entirely abortive, permits the state to assume the obligation and responsibility, and in the interest of the child and for its present and future welfare renders unto it the necessary medical or surgical treatment . . . The learned court has acted in this case not only in strict compliance with the law, but with scrupulous care and moderation and upon ample and competent proof. His discretion should not be disturbed.

The day of the appellate decision, John Vasko had returned to work for the Westchester County Emergency Work Bureau, on the Saw Mill River Highway. When he saw newspaper photographers approaching, he fled into the woods and was not seen again that day. The following day, it was discovered that the Vasko family had disappeared again.

Late Thursday afternoon, April 20, Judge Smyth issued a statement to the press: "My efforts would be greatly facilitated if the newspapers would call off the reporters and cameramen so that the parents may feel secure against further invasion of their privacy and may feel at liberty to get in touch with me. I realize the news value of the case from the standpoint of the papers, but I do hope that where a child's life is at stake I may count on their cooperation." Through relatives, attorney Fay suggested to the Vaskos that, if they were not satisfied with the previous medical opinions, he would take them to other authorities. They then agreed to allow Helen to be examined, provided it did not mean an immediate operation. The Columbia University Presbyterian Medical Centre was selected.

Shortly after noon on Friday, April 21, the Vaskos, with Helen wrapped in a blue blanket and tightly held by her mother, met Fay in front of their home. In Fay's car, accompanied by an interpreter and a police escort, they sped to the Medical Centre. There they were taken to the offices of Dr. J. M. Wheeler* and were met by his assistant, Dr. John Hughes Dunnington, professor of opthalmology at the College of Physicians and Surgeons of Columbia University, who also was in charge of the centre's Eye Institute. Aided by several other physicians, Dr. Dunnington examined Helen for more than an hour, then said that he would confer with the other physicians and then send a full report to Mr. Fay. The parents, with Helen, left for a "hiding place"—later revealed to be the home of Judge Smyth's secretary, Theodore Murin, in Yonkers.

Saturday, Fay received the report. Dr. Dunnington and two other eye specialists supported the earlier diagnosis by Dr. Angelo J. Smith and others; an immediate operation was needed to keep the malignant tumor from spreading into the brain, where it would cause certain death. But that night, when Fay reported this to the Vaskos, they said they wished to consult with relatives before giving their decision. Sunday night, after several such conferences, the Vaskos asked Fay to allow them more time to consider. The father, who previously had expressed his willingness to follow the advice of the physicians, now said that the final decision rested with his wife. Fay replied that he would insist on a decision Monday.

In Judge Smyth's chambers, about 8 o'clock Monday evening, after a conference of three hours between the parents, who had brought Helen with them, and Mr. Fay, Judge Smyth and some of his staff, Mrs. Vasko consented to the operation and surrendered Helen to the Children's Court. Helen was taken to St. John's Hospital, in Yonkers, which the mother had selected, for temporary care, and reporters "learned" that preparations were being made to perform the operation within 24 hours at Grasslands Hospital.

Tuesday, April 25, shortly after noon, Theodore Murin and Mrs. Mary Miner, a nurse, drove Helen to the Presbyterian Medical Centre— the report of preparations at Grassland apparently had been a ruse to

---

* Who previously had operated on the King of Siam during the latter's visit to the United States.

divert the curious. They reached the Eye Institute just before one o'clock, and carried Helen to the children's ward. Neither parent was there; both were ill at home. Helen was operated on at 4:25 P.M. by Dr. Dunnington. The operation was completed in thirteen minutes, the diseased eye and a section of the eye nerve being removed. Afterwards, Helen's condition was reported as "entirely satisfactory." At the same time, however, it was admitted that because of the delay, the child had only an even chance to recover.

That day, Deputy Sheriff Frank Cherico, who with Deputy Sheriff Fred Roscoe had been present at the conference in Judge Smyth's chambers, told a different version of it: "I feel terrible about it. Mrs. Vasko just kept saying, 'I'm the child's mother. Let me take her back to Czechoslovakia,' and she wouldn't permit the operation. So then Judge Smyth nodded to us and said we had to follow the court's order. So we took the baby away and carried her to the hospital." Judge Smyth denied this to have been the case. Wednesday, Dr. Galdston reported that Helen "passed a very comfortable night and was visited for a few moments by her father, who was very much relieved to have the operation over with."

That day, John Vasko stayed at his home in Hastings with his wife, who had been prostrated by the strain of separation from her child. "My wife is sick in bed and I cannot leave her," he told reporters. "I can't see the baby because I've got to watch my wife. She says if baby die, she die too. I'm afraid the baby won't get well. They said the baby was blind, but she played so well. She could see everything. She would pick up little pins from the carpet. Her eyes seemed all right." He denied that he and his wife had consented to the operation: "No, no! That's not true. The judge he talked for three hours. Then my wife she got to go home to our other children. Then the judge said to three big men, 'Take her!' and the men took her away. They broke my wife's heart. She's been sick ever since. My wife told the judge there were hundreds of people in the city with no arms, no legs, no eyes; but the government doesn't take them and make them have an operation. They beg on the street. Why must they take my happy baby? They told my wife the baby would die. Well, everybody has to die some time. The baby belonged to its mother and it is not for the judge to decide what's best." Later, Fay said: "The judge did the right thing," and declined to comment further.

Thursday, April 27, Helen appeared to be doing well. She sat up in bed, played with her toys and dolls and appeared content. She had no temperature and no untoward symptoms. Late that afternoon came another bulletin from the Medical Centre: "The pathological laboratory of the Eye Institute reports that a microscopic examination of the diseased eye of Helen Vasko reveals that the growth did not extend into the optic nerve. This finding renders the prognosis favorable." Helen was expected to live.

Friday, Helen left her bed to play with other children in the ward. That day, her father visited her. Back home, afterwards, he indicated that he was willing to forget his charge as to the judge's forcibly separating Helen from her mother. And Fay said that both parents were glad the operation was over and had dropped their attitude of opposition. Saturday, Helen was up and playing in the ward much of the time, and appeared to be progressing satisfactorily in her recovery. Her mother was still ill in bed at home. A week later, on Saturday, May 6, Helen was returned to her home, the hospital authorities saying that she was in "excellent condition" and need not return for further treatment.

Three months later, a reporter visited the Vaskos in Hastings. Helen, twin sister Anne and older sister Mary were playing happily together on the doorstep. Helen was plump and content, and appeared to be in the best spirits of all. Mrs. Vasko refused to be interviewed. "Everybody was interested in Helen," John Vasko said. "It was Helen this, Helen that. Now nobody cares. I have no job, I get $5 a week relief, we owe for the rent. You see, Helen has no glass eye yet. I think maybe she ought to have one. But we have no money."

Publication of this interview created the erroneous impression that the Children's Court had neglected to fulfill all of its obligations in connection with the operation. As a result, Miss Nina Webster, an NRA captain living in New York City's Barbizon-Plaza Hotel, ordered the eye-making firm of Mager & Guggelman to make a glass eye for Helen and send the bill to her. She wanted, she said, "to make the little girl happy." On August 9, Judge Smyth wrote Miss Webster, thanking her for her offer, advising her that Helen continued under his supervision, that the eye had not been forgotten, and that it was not yet time for her to have it. She was too young. No eye would be supplied, he noted, until he ordered it. In a later statement, he said: "I am deeply appreciative of Miss Webster's kind offer. She has consented to abide by my wishes that when the time comes for the new eye to be put in she may defray the expenses if she still desires to do so. In the meantime, we are trying to get her father, John Vasko, a position as gardener."

Two years later, Mrs. Mary Vasko made the headlines in the different role of Judge Smyth's champion. In August of 1935, a Yonkers truant officer discovered that Anthony Spiak, an employee of a carpet company, had a son, Henry, fourteen, who had never been to school. Nine years earlier, the boy had been crippled, apparently hopelessly, by infantile paralysis. Now, he could not sit up without assistance, and had never learned to read or write. Upon investigation, it appeared to Judge Smyth that, with an operation, Henry might be able to walk. But the father would not permit the operation. On August 11, 1935, when it was reported that the Court might call upon Mr. and Mrs. Vasko in an effort to convince Spiak, Mrs. Vasko made the following statement to the press:

"If I had known what doctors can do, I never would have fought so long in the court. I'm glad now that Helen was operated upon. Before she was always sick and I never knew what was the matter. I didn't think doctors could do anything. Now she is well and happy. I would like to tell the father of that boy that he can rely on the doctors."

Later, Spiak reluctantly consented to having his son hospitalized. Two years later, in May of 1937, young Henry, though still in Yonkers General Hospital, was reported well on the mend. By then, after a series of operations, he was able to walk with crutches. Whether he eventually would be able to discard the crutches was not then known, but by that time he had gotten the rudiments of an education, had become expert in making billfolds, pocketbooks and other articles, and was well on his way towards useful citizenship.

In Seattle, Washington, on August 8, 1930, Patricia Hudson[2] was born with a left arm nearly as big as the rest of her body. This monstrous arm, ten times normal in size and weight, and useless, continued to grow with her at the same rate. It hung almost to her ankle. At nine, she was taken to an orthopedic hospital in Seattle, where amputation was advised. But her father, an invalid, "bowed to the will of his wife," and the mother, Mrs. Nora Hudson, because of the risk, chose to do nothing. As the court later opined, she simply sought to shirk her own present duty by shifting the responsibility of decision to the child at some future date. At 11, Patricia was frail and weak, her chest and spine were becoming deformed from carrying the extra weight, and in nourishing the arm her heart was seriously overworked. The mother never had obtained any medical or surgical treatment for her, though for four years she employed a "Divine Healer" who undertook to cure the deformity by prayer—with obvious unsuccess.

On January 3, 1942 an adult sister complained to the juvenile court that Patricia was in need of medical care. On January 7 a hearing was had but no testimony taken. Patricia's mother consented to the entry of an order that the child be taken to an orthopedic hospital in Seattle for examination and observation, and this was done. Afterwards, on January 28, the chief probation officer of the juvenile court filed a petition alleging that "according to the recommendations of the attending physicians, the said child is in imperative need of operative treatment and amputation of her left arm; that the parents, Claude E. and Nora Hudson, refuse to provide such treatment and refuse to grant permission for such treatment to be given."

On January 30, a hearing was had on the petition before Judge William J. Long of the Juvenile Court of Seattle. The parents were present and represented by counsel. Patricia was represented by an attorney whom the court appointed as her guardian *ad litem*. Mrs. Hudson testified that she did not have any religious scruples against the amputation but that she opposed the operation because she thought there was "too much of a chance on her life." Asked if she would ever consent and, if so under what circumstances, she testified: "Well, if as the child grows older, and if she is not happy about it, I would then consent to it, because then I would feel that she had done it herself, and not me. This way I think it is too much of a thing to decide for her. And another thing, as the doctor stated, there is quite a chance on her life and I feel this way, that if I do consent to it, and her life is taken, I feel that I will be responsible."

Patricia's seven brothers and sisters, all adults except Dwane, testified. Said Dwane, fifteen: "Many times when I have been with my sister with that always like it is, it gave me a kind of a funny feeling. And then many times she has told me, she said she wished she had the arm off, because then she could wear clothes like the other girls could. And mother won't allow her to wear a skirt or sweater, and that is what she wants done. And she says that this is an awful load on her body, and she wishes it was off. She has cried many times on account of that."

A sister, Mrs. Delpha Clyde, twenty, testified: "Well, I have always felt that Patty was handicapped. I have a son of my own and I know how mother feels. But I believe if it was my own son I would consent, because I think that every child is entitled to a normal life, and her chances apparently are more than 50–50, and I can't see why—I think that she would be so much better off, even though she did not live, than she is handicapped the way she is."

Maude Bucklin, thirty, a sister, said: "Well, only that I never have seen how the child could possibly live a normal life like she is, and if nothing could ever be done, nothing can be done with that arm to bring it down to make it less conspicuous, I would be inclined—well, I think it should be amputated. There is no question. I am willing to take the doctors' word that the chances are better life minus the arm than the way she is."

Another sister, Leona Salgot, 30, was asked: "What is your attitude toward this situation?" She testified: "Well, I certainly think that the arm should be amputated, if that is the only thing the doctors found they could do. I don't know that any other opinion should be relied on more than theirs, and it seems to me that their opinion should be something that we could count on. And inasmuch as it is impossible for Patty to live a normal life, and anyone who has seen the little child— I live at home, and once in a while she is allowed the freedom of going without her wrap, and if there is a knock on the door she runs like an animal to get in her smock before anyone can see her, because she is so horrified about it. And the truth of Patricia being out of school is because she was jeered at by the other children in the school, and she could not stay there, because the teachers cannot be bothered with a thing like that. And she stayed out of school. And it keeps her out of life, and it will keep her out of everything eventually, because she cannot help taking that with her in life. And as far as her happiness is concerned, I think that anyone knows that a person does not want sympathy but happiness."

Claude Hudson, the father, testified: "I will tell you, I don't want to stand in the way at all of helping the child at all . . . I don't want to take—I don't want to take and hold her back and pin her down. So that I realize in the condition she is in at the present time nothing can be done with her . . . Somebody will have to stay with her and will more or less have to take care of her all her life. That is, she will never be able to be out on her own . . . It is up to—I am leaving it in the Judge's hands. I am leaving it right there. You can take my place Judge. You know your testimony . . . And if the rest of them think that is the only thing, that is you know more about it than I do."

Dr. Edward LeCocq of the Seattle Children's Orthopedic Hospital testified that he had examined Patricia "A year or two ago, and then . . . this week."

Q. If nothing is done for her, what is the prognosis? A. Well, I feel that the prognosis for life is not nearly as good as it would be if she did not have to nourish this enormous thing with her own little body. And I think that her general condition would be much improved if it is removed. If it is not removed, I think that she is going to remain in such a rather weakened condition that perhaps some infection or intercurrent infection, which might be, say pneumonia, or something of that sort—she would be an easy prey for anything of that sort. The heart, of course, is burdened a great deal by reason of having to pump blood through this large extremity."

Dr. Darrell G. Leavitt of the same staff had briefly examined Patricia: "This is not an unknown thing at all. It is a thing that we have seen in various portions of the body quite frequently. It may involve a large toe, such as a toe that cannot be put in a shoe. Under those circumstances in my experience I have seen those things trimmed down to a point where function was more nearly normal . . . I believe that the risk that would be involved in removing the extremity would be well worth while in this girl's own opinion, were she able and old enough to choose."

Q. Do you know what the cause of that condition is, doctor? A. Hypertrophy of an extremity can be caused by more than one thing . . . However we know that some disturbance or variation in the degree or amount of circulation to the limb or extremity can have a great deal to do with the rate of growth of the extremity. So that inside of this there is a communication between the artery and the vein of an extremity, called a congenital arteriovenous aneurysm, which is an abnormal shooting of blood between the artery and the vein, and the circulation of the extremity is so impaired that there is congestion, and the congestion permits abnormal growth in the size of the bone and the soft tissues. And it is also known in the presence of some of these aneurysms the life of the individual is remarkably shortened often because of the abnormal stress placed upon the circulatory system . . .

Q. Is there any known method of treatment other than surgery for such a condition as this?   A. Not of this condition in this case.

The court found Patricia Hudson to be a "dependent child" and made an order directing amputation of the child's left arm, then insisted, because of the gravity of its decision, upon a review. The Supreme Court of Washington treated this as an appeal, and in Olympia, on June 8, 1942, in a 6 to 3 ruling, reversed the order. Associate Justice Millard delivered the majority opinion:

> Respondent court specifically found that neither parent is guilty of bad faith or any neglect, other than failure to submit their minor child to an operation for removal of the child's deformed left arm which, considering the present and future welfare of the child, in the opinion of the court should be amputated, and which the parents "of excellent character, deeply concerned for the child's welfare, honest and sincere," are unwilling to authorize because of their fear that the operation will imperil the life of the child.
>
> The court stated that it was quite possible that the child might not survive the operation. As we read the evidence it is admitted by all concerned that there is a grave possibility that the child may not survive the ordeal of amputation; nevertheless, every one except the child's mother is willing, desirous, that the child be required to undergo the operation. Implicit in their position is their opinion that it would be preferable that the child die instead of going through life handicapped by the enlarged, deformed left arm. That may be to some today the humane, and in the future it may be the generally

accepted, view. However, we have not advanced or retrograded to the stage where, in the name of mercy, we may lawfully decide that one shall be deprived of life rather than continue to exist crippled or burdened with some abnormality. That right of decision is a prerogative of the Creator.

Justice Simpson strongly dissented:

. . . since Patricia is in need of medical and surgical attention, a necessary of life, she is destitute within the meaning of [the statute] and thus a dependent child. Being a dependent child, the juvenile court possessed power to order the required medical and surgical treatment . . . The decision of the majority seems to be based on the reasoning that under the common law and our juvenile court law any parent who is of excellent character and morally fit cannot be deprived of the custody of its child; that appellants were of excellent character and morally fit; and that, therefore, appellants cannot be deprived of the custody of their child.

In my estimation, this major premise is an inaccurate statement . . . By allowing their personal interests to affect their judgment in making a vital decision respecting the health and well-being of their daughter, appellants made themselves unfit as parents notwithstanding their excellent character. Therefore by virtue of [the statute], the juvenile court had the power to declare Patricia Hudson a dependent child; . . . the court also had the power to enter an order requiring the amputation of the girl's deformed arm . . .

I have no doubt that Mrs. Hudson is a kind and loving mother intensely interested in the welfare of her children. That fact, however, should not stand in the way of rescuing her child from the dreadful life which she faces. The courts should come to the child's rescue. She has no other friend able to assist her.

From the Volstad-Alvis account it would appear that by 1938 California already had quietly accepted the principle that a court can order an operation for a child whose life is in danger and summarily enforce it. In 1941, a New York court extended the *Vasko* holding to a case where not life but well-being was at stake. The question of religion was not involved.

In 1937 or before, Ida Rotkowitz had been stricken with poliomyelitis. The disease induced a deformity in the lower part of her right leg. When she was six, doctors advised an operation—not a serious one—to prevent the deformity from growing worse. Ida's mother strongly favored the operation but her father stubbornly opposed it. When Ida was ten, with her condition worsening but her father's attitude unchanged, her mother petitioned New York City's Domestic Relations Court, charging the father with neglect and asking the court to order the operation.

After a hearing on February 28, 1941 the Court found Ida Rotkowitz to be a neglected child, and ordered that the operation be performed. Said Judge Panken:

The question presented is, Has this Court the power to order an operation for this child in face of the opposition of her father? . . . It is doubtful that under the common law, the courts had the powers now conferred upon them, to order treatment for children to the extent even of a surgical operation or to require of parents to do that which is promotive of the interests and is protective of the rights of a child . . .

Under the Act establishing this Court, it has the power, where children have been neglected by parents or others, to place them in foster homes or institutions to afford these children proper surroundings, helpful atmosphere, training and a life-giving environment. That is done with or without consent of parents.

This Court has the power to require that children be examined psychiatrically, tested psychologically and physically examined so that the Court may be aided in determining what is best for the child . . . A child who is deprived of the use of its limb which becomes progressively worse cannot have a sense of security. It feels different from others. It suffers from a sense of rejection. It cannot take its proper place in the group in which it lives. To the extent that medical science can correct the deformity or the limitation of the use of a limb, that service should be accorded.

When the Legislature clothed this court with the power to make an order for surgical care, it cannot be said that an order is to be made only in case where the parents consented to such order. I must conclude that it was the intention of the Legislature to give power to the Justices of this Court to order an operation not only in an instance where the life of the child is to be saved but also in instances where the health, the limb, the person or the future of the child is at stake . . .

The father of the child testified and said, in so far as it was possible for him to make himself articulate, that he was opposed to the operation. He gave no reason why he is opposed. The mother testified that she is very anxious that the child be operated on. The situation is that one parent is in favor of the operation; the other opposed. The one who has the intelligence to be concerned about the future of the child wants the operation; the other who is either unconcerned or has no capacity to be concerned, is opposed to it. That creates a situation almost parallel to the two women, each of whom claimed to be the mother of a child, and when King Solomon said he would give each half of the child, the true mother was ready to give the whole child to the one who was not the mother.

Upon all of the testimony submitted, there is no doubt that a successful operation will correct the condition in so far as correction can be had of the child's foot. That would affect a stabilization of the foot. Presently, the foot is deformed and hangs, as I have observed it.

The hospital authorities refuse to perform the operation without the consent of both parents, unless ordered by the Court.

The question before this Court is whether an order should be made for such operation. It is my opinion that the best interests of the child now and for the future require an order to be made regardless of the opposition of the father. Such an order would be permissive in the face of opposition of both parents.

The Court acquired jurisdiction of the child on a petition of the mother charging neglect. The child was found neglected—neglected by the father.

Leroy Mitchell of Dallas County, Texas was normally alert and energetic up to August of 1946. At that time, when he was about twelve, he grew ill, and his illness progressively grew worse. His right knee swelled, his face became pale, and he moved about with difficulty, using crutches. His father was dead, and his mother refused to obtain medical treatment for him. She believed in "Divine Healing" and had absolute faith in the power of religion to overcome all physical ailments and disease.

During the first six weeks of his 1946 fall term, Leroy attended school about half the time; the last six weeks not at all. Mrs. Albrech, his school nurse, several times visited him at home. She observed that he moved about apparently with much pain, that he had lost considerable weight, was thinner, paler, and his eyes red-rimmed. His knee and ankle were greatly swollen; and he did not appear alert, energetic or interested. On November 26 she spoke to Mrs. Mitchell about medical treatment: "I asked her if she had consulted a doctor . . . and she said she hadn't and furthermore she didn't think it was necessary so long as she was praying for him . . . She told me it started last summer . . . and at times it was far worse and I should have seen him sometimes when he was in far worse condition that that; that sometimes he couldn't get out of bed and they prayed and when she and the child prayed he had strength to get up and go and sometimes he would be out playing and come in crying, in the mother's words, 'with tears streaming down his face,' and asking her to pray and do something for him and at one time she was sewing at the sewing machine and he sank to the floor and begged her to do something and she got down on her knees by the side of the child and prayed."

Dallas County Chief Juvenile Officer Sam Davis and others brought suit against Leroy "by next friend" to declare him a neglected child, alleging that he was seriously ill and that his life was in danger. After filing of suit but before trial, Mrs. Mitchell called in Dr. Bumpass, their family physician. As he later testified, he at that time advised

Mrs. Mitchell that Leroy probably was suffering from arthritis or complications following rheumatic fever; but that no positive diagnosis could be obtained without complete clinical tests and medical observation. He advised her to secure the services of an orthopedist. Instead, she took Leroy first to a chiropractor and then to an osteopath. Neither was able positively to diagnose his condition and both failed to recommend or suggest a cure or course of treatment.

At the trial, Mrs. Mitchell refused to permit a commitment of the boy to a hospital where he could receive diagnosis and treatment by the family physician free of charge. Afterwards, the jury found Leroy to be a neglected child. The court then awarded custody to the probation officer so that Leroy might "receive proper medical care, education and maintenance . . . subject to the further orders of this court."

Upon application, the judgment was superseded and an appeal prosecuted by Leroy through next friend. On October 17, 1947, the Texas Court of Civil Appeals affirmed judgment. As to the points of the appeal, Justice Young first stated that the action was properly predicated upon the dependency or neglect statute; the proof not only was sufficient but disclosed a "statutory cause of action" against the mother, as well—i.e., the mother could have been prosecuted for misdemeanor.

As to quibbling over the wording:

These allegations, though short, were to the effect that the parent was failing and refusing to provide medical treatment for the child in its serious and continuing illness. The Commission of Appeals has held that pleadings are of little importance in a child's custody hearing and that the trial court's efforts to exercise broad, equitable powers in determining what will be best for the future welfare of the children should be unhampered by narrow technical rules. Any pleading which shows upon its face that the welfare of a minor child requires that an order be made in regard to his custody is sufficient.

Was Mrs. Mitchell's right to freedom of religious worship infringed? In answer, Judge Young quoted *Reynolds*.

. . . Onerous as this order of custody may appear to the parties herein complaining, its entry was solely in the interest of appellant. It is not irrevocable, yielding always to changed conditions. The medical treatment outlined and recommended by the mother's own physician, followed by a reasonable cooperation on her part with juvenile authorities in the matter of appellant's physical welfare, will doubtless conclude this unhappy incident and result in his restoration to the usual routine of family life.

## 15

# The Right to Live

*But flesh with the life thereof, which is the blood thereof,*
*shall ye not eat.*

*—Gen. 9.4.*

Darrell Labrenz[1] and his wife Rhoda had been childhood sweethearts in Dalton, Wisconsin. In 1950 they joined the Jehovah's Witnesses and with their first child, Kit, moved to Chicago. There, in Bethany Hospital, on April 11, 1951, was born their second child, Cheryl Linn. Soon afterwards, it appeared that Cheryl had an "Rh" blood condition which threatened her life. But Rhoda, 20, refused to consent to the only known remedy, a blood transfusion. "The baby is in grave danger," Dr. William W. Wieand, who attended the birth, stated to reporters later. "Unless there is transfusion we must stand by and see its life ebb away."

When Dr. Herman Bundesen, Health Commissioner for the City of Chicago, was told, he called in Darrell and urged upon him the seriousness of the infant's condition and the need for immediate action. But Darrell, 25, also refused to consent, explaining: "The sanctity of the blood is a thing we cannot tamper with. Everybody knows that blood is the life force and we do not have control of life. Only Jehovah has that. Transfusion, which is a form of drinking or eating blood, is forbidden to us who are Jehovah's Witnesses." Darrell remained adamant against all the Commissioner's pleas; afterwards, Dr. Bundesen could only report the matter to the office of John S. Boyle, State's Attorney for Cook County.

Tuesday noon, April 17, First Assistant State's Attorney Edward T. Breen, Brief Department head John T. Gallagher and others conferred with the Chief Administrator of the Family Court of Chicago—a branch of the circuit court of Cook County, replacing the Juvenile Court. Their problem: to determine what action could be taken, and how quickly, to prevent what seemed to be the inevitable death in a matter of hours of six-day-old Cheryl Linn Labrenz.

They examined the statutes. The Illinois Criminal Code, Section 95, makes it unlawful for any person having the care or custody of any child wilfully to cause or permit the child to be injured or placed in such a situation that its life or health may be endangered. Section 95 of the Family Court Act provides that, when the health or condition of any child found to be dependent, neglected or delinquent requires, the court may order the guardian to place the child in a public hospital or institution which will receive it for like purposes, without charge to the public authorities. As against this, Article II, Section 3 of the Illinois Constitution of 1870 provides that *"the free exercise and enjoyment of religious profession and worship, without discrimination, shall forever be guaranteed."* Section 3, however, also provides, "But the liberty of conscience hereby secured shall not be construed to . . . excuse acts of licentiousness, or justify practices inconsistent with the peace or safety of the State." The crucial question: if Family Court action was forced, would a constitutional defense be interposed?

There was only one way to find out. Quickly a probation officer prepared a petition alleging the child dependent because she was without proper parental care and guardianship, and filed it in Family Court. Hearing was set for the following morning. It was then 2 P.M.; service had to be obtained within the next few hours. The State's Attorney placed a police officer and squad car at the probation officer's disposal. The Health Commissioner was notified; he promised to be present in court. A subpoena was served on the attending physician at the hospital. Summonses were served upon the parents and on the superintendent of the hospital. By four o'clock, the completed summonses had been returned.

The case at once received wide publicity in every local newspaper; by Wednesday morning, April 18, a battery of cameras and sound recorders was set up and reporters swarmed outside the courtroom. At the opening of court, Darrell and Rhoda Labrenz, red-eyed and distraught, sat in the second row, each with a Bible in hand. The Honorable Jerome Dunne, presiding judge of the Family Court, promptly called up the matter for hearing. Karl M. Milgrom, attorney for the parents, first moved for a continuance; Judge Dunne took the motion under advisement. Milgrom then presented a motion to dismiss, setting up that the contemplated action was contrary to the Constitution. Judge Dunne also took this motion under advisement, and the trial proceeded.

Two doctors testified that, unless a transfusion was administered, Cheryl was certain to die. A third, Dr. Morton Andelman, health department pediatrician, said, "Without a transfusion, I will say absolutely, this child cannot live; or, if it should, could not live without permanent brain injury." The gist of the medical problem: Cheryl suffered from the disease known as erythrobastosis fetalis—the "Rh" blood condition. Cheryl's blood, like her father's, contained the Rh (for rhesus) factor; her mother's did not. As a result, antibodies, or poisons, picked up from her mother were destroying Cheryl's red blood cells. (As often happens in cases of Rh incompatibility, there had been no such trouble with first child Kit.) Since birth, Cheryl's blood count had steadily dropped. The normal count for an infant her age is about 5.00 million; by then, Cheryl's count was only 1.95 million. And since her blood-supplying system could not manufacture red cells fast enough to overcome the condition, only a blood transfusion could save her life.

What degree of risk was involved in such a blood transfusion? One doctor testified that there would be no more hazard than in taking an aspirin. But all three conceded that, since it is never possible to eliminate completely the chance of human error, there must always remain the risk that diseased or mistyped blood might accidentally be used. All three agreed that, if properly conducted, a transfusion would involve no serious hazard. "The one chance this baby has," said Commissioner Bundesen, "is to get a transfusion."

At the conclusion of this evidence, defense attorney Milgrom moved to dismiss the petition. The motion was overruled. The parents testified that their refusal to consent was based upon religious grounds. An attempt to enter in evidence the Witness magazine *Awake* was denied.

"It is my belief," said Darrell, "that the commandment given us in Genesis, Chapter 9, Verse 4, and subsequent commandment of Leviticus, Chapter 17, Verse 14, and also in the testimony after Christ's time and recorded in Acts, 15th Chapter, it is my opinion that any use of the blood is prohibited whether it be for food or whether it be for, as modern medical science puts it, for injections into the blood stream and as such I object to it. The life is in the blood and the life belongs to our father, Jehovah, and it is only his to give or take; it isn't ours, and as such I object to the using of the blood in connection with this case."

Said Rhoda: "We believe it would be breaking God's commandment to take away blood which he told us to eat of the flesh but should not take of the blood into our systems. The life is in the blood and the blood should not be drained out. We feel that we would be breaking God's commandment, also destroying the baby's life for the future, not only this life, in case the baby should die and breaks the commandment, not only destroys our chances but also the baby's chances for future life. We feel it is more important than this life."

The state's attorney asked Darrell and Rhoda only one question: "Will you now agree to a transfusion?" Both refused. At the conclusion of all the evidence, Milgrom again moved to dismiss the petition, again was overruled. Judge Dunne then overruled the two motions under advisement. The whole hearing had taken less than an hour.

Judge Dunne found against the parents and promptly appointed Colonel Harry Hill, the Court's chief probation officer, to be guardian of the person of Cheryl Linn Labrenz, directed him to consent to a blood transfusion, and retained jurisdiction for the purpose of making further orders for the child's welfare. An emergency ambulance was waiting; Hill rushed Cheryl to Michael Reese Hospital, where transfusion apparatus already had been set up. There, he presented a certified copy of the order of his appointment and executed his consent. Within three hours, Cheryl was given a transfusion of five ounces of negative blood. Within forty-eight hours, her red blood cells appeared to be winning; afterwards, her condition steadily improved. At the end of three days she was reported to be out of danger.

After the trial, Darrell Labrenz remained stubbornly opposed to all that had been done. "Those who forced the issue," said he, "are the ones who are responsible for sinning." But Rhoda said, "Of course I want my baby to live. And I pray that she does." And there was still the question of whether, during the week that the transfusion had been delayed, Cheryl's brain might have been seriously damaged. "We won't be able to tell a thing about that for eight or nine months," said Dr. Wieand.

Two weeks later, on May 4, without waiting for the parents to act, the State presented a further petition describing Cheryl's improved condition and asking that the guardianship order be modified. After the hearing, Judge Dunne entered an order retaining guardianship but releasing Cheryl from the hospital into the custody of her parents, and providing that a doctor should examine her every two weeks until June 15—at which time he promised to inquire into the facts and make whatever further orders were necessary. Too, the order specified that there were to be no further transfusions unless ordered by the court upon a proper showing.

At home with her parents, Cheryl continued to improve. Medical reports submitted at the two subsequent hearings were even more reassuring. Accordingly, on June 15, on the State's motion, Judge Dunne entered a final order discharging the guardian, releasing Cheryl to her parents, and dismissing the proceedings. But the matter was far from ended.

Late in the morning of April 18, at the same time that newly appointed guardian Hill was rushing Cheryl to Michael Reese Hospital for her transfusion, Defense Attorney Milgrom also was rushing—to the Chicago chambers of Justice Walter V. Schaefer of the Illinois Supreme Court. There, armed with certified copies of Judge Dunne's order and the short record, Milgrom applied for a writ of error and asked that this be made a *supersedeas* to stop the contemplated action. But Justice Schaefer, after hearing the arguments on the application, denied the writ.

Later, the Clerk of the Circuit Court of Cook County was served with a *praecipe* for the record for review in the Supreme Court of Illinois, where the case was brought on a writ challenging the propriety of the Family Court's action on constitutional grounds. The following year, on March 20, 1952, Justice Schaefer handed down his decision. He first considered the State's contention that because the blood transfusion had long since been administered, the guardian discharged and the proceeding dismissed—the case was moot and should be dismissed.

Because the function of courts is to decide controverted issues in adversary proceedings, moot cases which do not present live issues are not ordinarily entertained . . . But when the issue presented is of substantial public interest, a well-recognized exception exists to the general rule that a case which has become moot will be dismissed upon appeal . . . Among the criteria considered in determining the existence of the requisite degree of public interest are the public or private nature of the questions presented, the desirability of an authoritative determination for the future guidance of public officers, and the likelihood of future recurrence of the question.

Applying these criteria, we find that the present case falls within that highly sensitive area in which governmental action comes into contact with the religious beliefs of individual citizens. Both the construction of the statute under which the trial court acted and its validity are challenged. In situations like this one, public authorities must act promptly if their action is to be effective, and although the precise limits of authorized conduct cannot be fixed in advance, no greater uncertainty should exist than the nature of the problems makes inevitable. In addition, the very urgency which presses for prompt action by public officials makes it probable that any similar case arising in the future will likewise become moot by ordinary standards before it can be determined by this court. For these reasons the case should not be dismissed as moot.

As an additional reason for retaining the case for decision, [the parents] suggest that the determination below, even though standing unreviewed, would nevertheless bar a subsequent action to recover damages for a violation of the rights of the parents or of the child . . . Because we hold that the public interest requires that the case be retained for decision, we do not decide this issue.

The Court then turned to the merits of the case and to the question: did Chicago's Family Court lack jurisdiction because, as argued by the parents, Cheryl was not a "neglected" or "dependent" child within the meaning of the statute? The Court's answer:

> The jurisdiction which was exercised in this case stems from the responsibility of government, in its character as *parens patriae*, to care for infants within its jurisdiction and to protect them from neglect, abuse and fraud . . . Historically exercised by courts of chancery . . . it is "of ancient origin." . . . That ancient equitable jurisdiction was codified in our Juvenile Court Act, which expressly authorizes the court, if circumstances warrant, to remove the child from the custody of its parents and award its custody to an appointed guardian . . .
> So far as here pertinent, the statute defines a dependent or neglected child as one which "has not proper parental care." . . . The record contains no suggestion of any improper conduct on the part of the parents except in their refusal to consent to a blood transfusion. And it is argued that this refusal on the part of the parents does not show neglect, or a lack of parental care . . . We entertain no doubt that this child, whose parents were deliberately depriving it of life or subjecting it to permanent mental impairment, was a neglected child within the meaning of the statute. The circuit court did not lack jurisdiction.

He then considered the parents' argument that they had merely exercised their right to avoid the risk of a proposed hazardous operation and that their choice did not indicate a lack of proper parental care:

> The short answer is that the facts here disclose no such perilous undertaking, but, on the contrary, an urgently needed transfusion—virtually certain of success if given in time—with only such attendant risk as is inescapable in all of the affairs of life. The argument, based upon such cases as In re Hudson . . . and In re Tuttendario . . . which deal with operations involving substantial risk of life, is obviously not in point.

Did the Juvenile Court Act, if held applicable, deprive the parents of freedom of religion and of their rights as parents, in violation of the fourteenth amendment to the Constitution of the United States and of section 3 of article II of the Constitution of Illinois?

> This contention is based upon the parents' objection to the transfusion because of their belief that blood transfusions are forbidden by the Scriptures. Because the governing principles are well settled, this argument requires no extensive discussion. Concededly, freedom of religion and the right of parents to the care and training of their children are to be accorded the highest possible respect in our basic scheme . . . But "neither rights of religion or rights of parenthood are beyond limitation." . . .

Indeed, the early decision in the Reynolds case, upholding a Mormon's conviction for bigamy against the defense of interference with religious freedom as guaranteed in the first amendment, leaves no doubt about the validity of the action here taken . . . The recent Prince decision reinforces that conclusion . . . We hold, therefore, that neither the statute nor the action of the court pursuant to the statute violated the constitutional rights of plaintiffs in error.

Finally, did the trial court commit prejudicial error in excluding from evidence the religious magazine, *Awake*?

The contention is without merit. Except as it might bear upon the good faith of the parents' belief in the Scriptural prohibition against blood transfusion, it was inadmissible as hearsay. And since the sincerity of the parents' religious beliefs was not questioned, the exclusion of the magazine was not error.

The Court accordingly affirmed the judgment of the Circuit Court of Cook County. Afterwards, a petition was filed for a writ of *certiorari* to be issued by the United States Supreme Court directing the Supreme Court of Illinois to send to it all of the record and proceedings, before verdict, with its certificate to the correctness and completeness of the record, for review. On October 13, 1952, the Family Court was notified by the clerk of the United States Supreme Court that the writ had been denied: i.e., the Supreme Court did not question the constitutionality of the decision.

And what of Cheryl, afterwards? Two years later, in April of 1954, the following note was included in a communication to the author from one of the parties involved: "Today Cheryl Linn Labrenz is living a normal life with her parents, and is a fine, healthy child."

Janet Lynn Morrison[2] was born in Kansas City on October 8, 1951. Next day, she developed symptoms of erythroblastic anemia, with extreme jaundice and a perilously dropping blood count. But when Dr. Esther Winkelman, who delivered the child and attended her, told the parents of the need for an immediate blood transfusion, they refused to consent: it was contrary to their religious belief and convictions. On October 12, when Janet Lynn was twelve days old, the chief probation officer filed a complaint in Juvenile Court, praying that Janet Lynn be declared a neglected child. The cause was heard the same day before Justice John F. Cook of the Circuit Court, Juvenile Division—there was no one-day delay as required in Illinois.

At the hearing, Esther Winkelman, a highly qualified medical doctor, testified that Janet Lynn's red count was only 1.1 million, indicating rapid progress of the illness and that, if her life was to be saved, she should have an immediate blood transfusion. Otherwise, death would probably occur within a week. She testified that if a transfusion was given immediately, recovery would be complete, but that if done a few days later, her life might be saved but the destruction of brain tissue might result in leaving her mentally defective. Four other doctors, qualified in this field, with whom she had consulted, had opined that blood transfusion was the only remedy for the child's condition. Medical technician Rebecca Henion, who had done or supervised all the laboratory work, testified that Janet Lynn showed every sign of erythroblastic anemia; that the hemoglobin count on that day, 30 per cent, was considered to be about the fatal percent; that it was the procedure at Research Hospital to transfuse all such cases; that the disease always grows either progressively better or progressively worse; that at the Hospital, transfusions will not be given without the parent's consent; and that never before, in her eight years' experience, had parents refused consent for a transfusion in such a case.

The father testified that he was a Jehovah's Witness conservant (minister) and that he based his refusal to consent on Biblical commandments. At the close of the hearing, Justice Cook found Janet Lynn Morrison a neglected child within the meaning of the Missouri statute, adjudged her a ward of the court, and ordered that blood transfusions be administered.

The order and judgment were appealed to the Kansas City Court of Appeals, where, on October 6, 1952, judgment was unanimously affirmed. Commissioner Sperry first commented upon the summary nature of the hearing:

> The cause was heard on the same day the complaint was filed. The father of the child was in court and gave testimony. He was also represented by able counsel. Although the hearing was summary in its nature, no complaint is lodged on that score. Indeed, the urgent need for prompt action, necessary to save the infant's life, permitted of no legal quibbling or unnecessary delay, according to the medical testimony adduced . . .
>
> Appellant, in his brief, vigorously urges that his rights, as guaranteed by the State and Federal Constitution, have been unlawfully invaded because the order complained of violates his right of religious freedom. No such question was raised or presented in the trial court at any time. That being true, the general rule is that it cannot be presented on appeal . . . To that rule there is an exception, namely: Where, on the whole case, some provision of the constitution was either directly or by inexorable implication involved in the rendition of the judgment and decided against appellant . . . That exception is not applicable here.

In the case at bar the question presented is: Does the State have the power . . . to take the custody of an infant child from its parent for the purpose of preserving its life? The question of the right of religious freedom of appellant is in no sense involved. This proceeding in no wise affects the right of appellant to believe, religiously, as he professes to believe, nor does it affect his right to practice his religious belief. It was not ordered that *he* eat blood, or that he cease to believe that the taking of blood, intravenously, is equivalent to the eating of blood. It is only ordered that he may not prevent *another* person, a citizen of our country, from receiving medical attention necessary to preserve her life.

The U. S. Supreme Court has held that the regulation, or suppression of religious *practices,* is not an invasion of religious belief and opinion . . .

Appellant contends that the court lacked jurisdiction, under the statute, to render the judgment that it entered, and that no such power existed at common law, exclusive of the statute. He insists that the relationship of parent and child is sacred, that a parent derives his authority from the natural law; and that it may not be interfered with by the State, even in a case where the child is in need of medical attention, even though its very life may depend upon such interference. His position is that a child cannot be "neglected" within the meaning of the statute merely because its parents fail to provide medical attention. He maintains this attitude in the face of the undisputed medical evidence in this case that, without a blood transfusion, the child would surely die.

As to the parent deriving his authority from natural law, Commissioner Sperry quoted Aristotle's proof that the state also arises from natural law and must be "prior" to the family and the individual. Then:

There is a passage in America's most revered document . . . to wit: "We hold these truths to be self-evident, that all men are created equal, that they are endowed by their Creator with certain unalienable rights, that among these are Life, Liberty and the pursuit of Happiness. That to secure these rights, governments are instituted among Men . . . "

The Declaration is regarded by the American people as expressing their views of the fundamental purpose of Government. We believe that every human being is endowed by God with the inalienable right to live. The fact that the subject is the infant child of a parent who, arbitrarily, puts his own theological belief higher than his duty to preserve the life of his child cannot prevail over the considered judgment of an entire people, in a case such as this. The other rights, liberty, and the pursuit of happiness, are of no benefit to a dead baby . . . Missouri has the power to interfere in the interests of one of its infant citizens, helpless in its own behalf, and to take such steps as may be necessary to preserve its life, over the protest of its father . . . society is not required to stand aside until the child is dead for want of care, but may take direct steps to preserve the life that the parents neglected to cherish . . .

Appellant cites and relies on In re Hudson, where the court reversed a judgment ordering an operation on an infant child, in the face of overwhelming evidence to the effect that, without such an operation, the child would be handicapped and dependent all of her life. The only real difference, in principle, between that case and this, is that in the Hudson case the operation was extremely dangerous to life . . . Such is not the situation here. Appellant would do nothing himself, nor would he consent that others should do anything. The Hudson decision was by a divided court; . . . The dissenting opinion is forceful and well reasoned. We decline to follow that decision . . .

A religious zealot may have the right to fast until death in the sincere belief that, by so doing, God will be influenced to act positively on behalf of a sinful world; but he may not be permitted to abuse his parental authority by denying his children food, freely offered by a compassionate society to relieve their suffering and preserve their lives and mental and physical health.

In January of 1954, in the Children's Court of Erie County, New York, an order was sought to have corrective surgery performed—against the wishes of one Seiferth, the father—on a twelve year old boy who was severely afflicted with a congenital harelip and cleft palate. Judge Wylegala ordered the surgery performed, saying, "The material facts are not disputed. It is conceded that the child is handicapped, that the defect gives him a "hideous" appearance and causes a marked speech defect, and that the child is emotionally and psychologically sensitive to his condition. The objections by the father are that the court should not intervene because 1) The condition is not one where the child's life or health are in immediate danger; 2) The father because of his "religious" beliefs objects to surgery on the human body; 3) That the principal purpose of the operation "to obviate the psychological consequences to the child going through adolescence with a disfigured condition" will be defeated because of the child's fears of doctors, originating in the "religious" beliefs passed on to him from the father; and 4) That when the child gets old enough to decide for himself he may do so."

The effects of emotional and psychological factors during the childhood, adolescence, and later formative years . . . are too well known to . . . require discussion here. The law also is well established that the court has power to interfere not only in matters involving life, health and physical welfare, but also psychological well-being of children . . .

The father's objections are based on a personal philosophy—not a religion—shared with him by a group of ten or fifteen friends, who have the same ideas or thoughts, and who come together, not always at the same time, to discuss the problem. These people, according to the father, have no leader, no literature explaining their theories, believe there are "forces in the universe" which when available to a properly conditioned subject can cure him of disease, including the child's cleft palate and harelip.

No evidence was offered that a cleft palate or harelip was ever cured by these forces—although the father does claim his own tubercular condition was cured by "thought" and that some cases of cancer of the rectum were cured without surgical aid.

Since the beliefs are definitely not claimed to be "religious" and have to do only with the "healing of the human body" in complete defiance of modern science, the objections based on the second ground must be rejected and overruled.

Objections 3 and 4 will be answered together. Had this proceeding been brought before me, shortly after it first came to the notice of the school and medical authorities, in 1948 when the child was seven years old, and had the evidence otherwise been the same, I have no doubt that I would have unhesitatingly signed the order . . .

But we are now dealing with a child over 12 years of age, of normal intelligence, who has been "conditioned" against the physicians tampering in any way with the human body, even in the case of ordinary disease . . .

To arbitrarily force this child to submit to surgery, which he has been "conditioned" to fear, might do more harm than good. Fortunately the beliefs held by the father and passed on to the child are not "religious" and have nothing to do with moral right or wrong. It should, therefore, not strain the child's conscience, to set him right about medical and scientific facts and progress . . .

It is, therefore, the judgment of this court that the father be restrained from in any way interfering with discussions between the child and such reasonable number of persons as this court may designate directed at acquainting the child with the benefits accruing to him from promptly submitting to the recommended operations.

And it is the further judgment that just as soon as practicable after the child consents to submit to the operations and therapy, the same be done at the expense of the father, or in the event that all of such expense cannot be paid by the father, that prompt application be made to this court for financial assistance under the law governing such cases.

The *Minnesota Law Review* has criticized Seiferth:

At the heart of the parent-child relationship lies the proposition that custody and control of the child belong to the parent . . . This premise is of necessity tempered by the doctrine of *parens patriae* under which the state, historically through the chancery court, has the power to interfere with the parents' guardianship if the parents fail to protect the child from abuse, neglect or fraud. The question then becomes whether the court may, in the particular case before it, justifiably encroach upon the relationship of parent and child.

Whether a court may legally order an operation on a child—contrary to the parents' wishes—when the child's life is not in immediate danger is not a new problem, but the opinion . . . declaring that such an operation could have been ordered is apparently a novel solution . . . Although in a jurisdiction which, in contrast to that of the *Tuttendario* case, does not make *malicious* parental intent a prerequisite to judicial intervention, the instant court reached the contrary result by assuming without discussion that it could interfere in matters pertaining to the purely psychological disorders of children as distinguished from situations in which physical ailments of a serious nature threaten life . . . Although the court in the principal case refused to order an immediate operation for fear it would do the child more harm than good while he was still under the influence of his father's beliefs, the right of the court to interfere with the parent-child relationship through persuasion by court appointed agents appears to be just as questionable as would be a decision ordering an operation . . .

In labelling the beliefs of the father "philosophical" rather than "religious" because the group to which the father belonged had no leader, was small, and had no literature explaining its theories, the instant court avoided the issue of interference with the freedom of religion guaranteed by the First and Fourteenth Amendments to the United States Constitution. This type of verbal evasion has been sternly criticized, and its use by a court lends support to the argument that religious freedom exists only for the rich and powerful while the non-conformists, *e.g.,* the faith healing cults, are persecuted because they do not conform to our concept of what a "religion" should be. If the court in the instant case had found that the father entertained a sincere belief in the strange healing "forces in the universe," it should have recognized the belief as being a religious one, and then have gone on frankly to discuss whether or not this was a case in which religious practices need be limited by the demands of society . . . In at least three state jurisdictions the courts have ordered medical care for children in spite of the parents' refusal on religious grounds to seek medical attention [*Labrenz, Morrison* and *Mitchell*]. Each of these cases appears to have been soundly decided, however, for the serious threat to the children's lives outweighed the religious considerations and the comparatively small risk of death involved in the required medical care . . . But it is in the questionable area illustrated by the instant case, where no serious threat to life exists, that courts must face up to their constitutional obligation of safeguarding religious liberties; for by ordering an operation or attempting to persuade children to accept a more "rational" belief than their own or parents' beliefs, they only succeed in tightening the already shrinking boundaries encircling religious freedom.[3]

In comparing the parallel court actions in *Morrison* and *Labrenz,* and considering the failure in the attempted Grzyb action (Ch. 1), we may well ask: In the case of a dying child, why should there have to be a one-day delay between complaint and hearing? Or even an hour?

Professor Robert Keith Larson finds it entirely unreasonable that such a matter of life and death should be delayed by law for 24 hours, while at the same time a writ of *habeas corpus,* for example, concerned with the important but certainly relatively less pressing matter of physical liberty, requires a jailor to produce a prisoner "forthwith"—a word which has been called the strongest in law and which means *right now:*

It was under such a provision [the "neglect" statute] that Illinois authorities ineffectively sought to obtain custody of . . . Thomas Grzyb, Jr. The attempt was rendered useless by the death of the child during normal procedural delays deemed incident to the processes established by law. Although the Illinois statute provided that the summons to the parent should be issued and made returnable "at any time" within twenty days . . . it appeared that a hearing could not lawfully be held that same evening and, since the parents would not waive their apparent right to delay until the following day, there was no alternative but to wait. Presumably, the objection to an immediate hearing was that due process required that the parents be given a reasonable opportunity to prepare and present their side of the case. If this was the reason for the objection, it would seem to have been an entirely unsuitable one in a case where the parents were clearly ready with their reply.

In any event, it may be seriously questioned whether due process requires such a delay for, in analogous emergency situations, certain extraordinary proceedings have been authorized by law. For example, the Habeas Corpus Act provides that the writ shall issue "forthwith," . . . commanding the jailor to bring the prisoner before the judge "immediately." In much the same way, the Mental Health Code provides that, on presentation of a petition and doctor's certificate, a judge may order that a writ shall issue commanding the sheriff to take charge of a mentally ill person and transport him to a mental hospital, leaving the hearing on the petition to come up later so long as it is held within five days after the detention . . . If liberty and safety can be protected in this summary fashion, it is difficult to understand why life itself could not be protected without the need for suffering those delays which cause no untoward harm in less urgent matters."[4]

# 16
# Conclusion

*PREAMBLE*
*We, the people of the United States, in order to form a*
*more perfect Union, establish justice, insure domestic*
*tranquility, provide for the common defense, promote*
*the general welfare, and secure the blessings of liberty to*
*ourselves and our posterity, do ordain and establish this*
*Constitution for the United States of America.*

Just after I came to Massachusetts, in 1945, a friend told me of a tragic experience. Some years before, he had moved to a small New England town. During his first winter there, his neighbors' eight-year-old daughter was taken seriously ill. When he saw the girl he was convinced she had pneumonia. But when he asked the parents if they had called a doctor, they indignantly replied that they had not, and did not intend to. They were "faith healers." They believed their prayers would heal their child.

As the girl weakened, my friend wondered what, if anything, he could do. He had heard of child protection statutes, enforced by juvenile courts. But no juvenile court, to his knowledge, ever had intervened in such a case. Any attempted such action, he was sure, would violate the parents' constitutional right to religious freedom. Afraid of becoming involved in a bitter religious controversy, he said nothing locally. But while in another town he asked a policeman if there was anything that could be done. The policeman drew away and muttered, "That's a touchy business." And while my friend was still wondering what to do, the little girl died.

"What could I or anybody else have done," he asked me, "to save that child's life?"

As I write this, on November 11, 1967, my Boston *Globe* lies unopened beside me. No need to open it: there it all is, again, right on page one—within fifty miles of my own home, it has just happened again. A five-year-old girl died of a lung infection after an illness of three weeks . . .

274

mother relied on Christian Science prayers to cure her . . . doctor testified that if recognized medical aid had been administered within first four or five days, she would have had a 90 to 95 per cent chance of survival . . . the mother's attorney arguing that the elements of involuntary manslaughter were not shown and that the prosecution "is in direct violation of the First Amendment to the Constitution, which guarantees religious freedom" . . . and eventually conviction and probation for five years.

Why didn't *some*body . . .

In 1952, in Chicago's first "Rh" baby case, the Supreme Court of Illinois gave an emphatic answer to my friend's question. The answer: the State most certainly does have the power, over the religious objections of the parents, to step in and save the life of a child.

The practical question is: "Where a child is being denied proper medical attention by its parents, exactly how is the court process set in motion? And by whom? Can *I* start the process?"

As to a child in a hospital and under a doctor's care, but denied the one remedy of a blood transfusion, neither doctor nor hospital is likely to remain silent for long. The chain of events is clear in the case of Cheryl Linn Labrenz: the doctor or hospital authorities appealed to Chicago's Health Commissioner; when Dr. Bundesen's efforts failed to win over the father, he told the office of the State's Attorney for Cook County; this office conferred with the Chief Administrator of the Family Court. As a result, a probation officer of that court prepared a petition alleging the child to be "dependent." And with the filing of that petition, the court process was set in motion. Of course, any one at all could have reported such a matter directly to the Chief Administrator of the Chicago Family Court.

But I am thinking now of the *non*-hospitalized case described by my friend—he, living in a small town, discovering his neighbor's child to be seriously ill, apparently with pneumonia, and with the faith-healing parents refusing to call a doctor.

Today, if the matter had not been so urgent, he could have reported it to the chairman of his town or county welfare board, if there was such a board. Such a board would take proper action, probably beginning with a friendly visit to the parents. And in some cases, such a visit —and from one whose business it is so to inquire—may be enough to bring the parents to their senses. If there is a county Society for the Prevention of Cruelty to Children, with a local office, the matter could be reported there—such societies make their own unofficial investigation and then bring the matter to court if necessary.

But if the matter were truly urgent, and I had direct knowledge of it, here is exactly what I would do. First I would find out the location of the District Court having jurisdiction—some districts take in several towns, while some cities extend over several districts. If I did not know, I would ask a policeman—and, incidentally, except for that one question, I would leave the policeman out of it. Then I would go to the clerk or judge of that District Court and tell him the facts. Afterwards, though it is not likely, if nothing happened within the next few hours, I would go to my attorney (if I did not have one I would get one), tell him the facts, and, if he was in agreement, ask him to apply to the county Superior Court for a writ of *mandamus,* commanding the district judge to perform his public duty.

And that, so far as I know, is all that anyone can do. But if I did not do that much, I would expect to find my conscience heavy when I attended the child's funeral.

That the subject of this book, "denial of medical aid because of religious belief," should become and remain a problem of our democracy was ordained by the above preamble. The Federal government must *insure domestic tranquility,* it must *promote the general welfare,* and it must *secure the blessings of liberty.* These blessings of liberty, as spelled out in the Bill of Rights, include the personal freedoms of speech, press, assembly and religion.

The problem is equally inherent in the states' constitutions, which in varying language ordain the promotion of the public health, safety, order and morals and the prevention of fraud—the state's so-called "police powers"—and at the same time guarantee the liberties of their individual citizens. The resulting clash, for the most part, is resolved within the state. But many times, as in the Jehovah's Witness "handbill" cases, the state would lean heavily toward the peace of the many at the expense of the unpopular religious expression of the few. In such cases, the state is liable to be "called on the carpet" by the Federal government's Supreme Court, and to be held to the Federal Constitution's overriding guarantees of individual freedom.

Clearly, in the state's reasonably necessary exercise of its police power, individual liberty can never be absolute. How far, then, may it be encroached upon? Jefferson, at the one extreme, would hold religious profession and practice beyond the reach of the civil magistrate until "principles break out into overt acts against peace and good order."

But when a man with torch and kerosene sets off for his neighbor's barn, must the state stand idly by until the barn is burning? The "clear and present danger" rule laid down by Holmes in *Schenck* is often applied in cases involving infringement of religious liberty. In such cases, the Supreme Court has laid the burden upon the State not only to prove the greater importance of the interest claimed to justify the infringement, but also to show that there is no way to protect this interest other than by such infringement. In *Barnette,* the Supreme Court held that freedom of worship is "susceptible of restriction only to prevent grave and immediate danger to interests which the state may lawfully protect," and that the aim of the state—to inculcate loyalty and patriotism—could be achieved in other ways than by an enforced flag salute which infringed religious liberty. The same determination to maintain the preferred position of personal freedoms is seen in *Schneider,* where the Supreme Court emphasized that freedom of speech and press were fundamental personal rights, and that there were other ways to prevent littering: "Amongst these is the punishment of those who actually throw papers on the streets." And these would have to be resorted to, rather than a method which, though more efficient, infringed the freedoms of speech and press.

To apply the principle to the problem of this book, let us suppose that a city passes an ordinance (none has, to my knowledge) prohibiting faith healers and Christian Science practitioners from treating sick children. And suppose that a faith healer or Christian Science practitioner is convicted under that ordinance. The highest court of the state upholds the conviction, on the ground that, though the ordinance admittedly infringes upon religious liberty, the infringement is warranted by the need to protect the health and lives of children. The case is then appealed to the Supreme Court, which reverses judgment, holding that there are other, though less efficient, methods available to protect the health and lives of children—for example, statutes requiring parents to furnish proper medical care for their children—so that the ordinance, with its greater restriction of religious liberty, cannot be justified.

The law today, as it applies to "denial of medical aid because of religious belief," can be summarized in question and answer form:

Q. *Can the faith healer or Christian Science practitioner who undertakes to heal a sick adult or child be prosecuted for malpractice?* A. No. He is not hired to perform a medical function. He is only hired to pray.

Q. *Is there no law to prohibit a faith healer or Christian Science practitioner from treating a seriously ill adult or child?* A. No, so long as the healer sticks strictly to prayer. But if the patient must also drink a glass of "holy water," or submit to any other physical treatment, then the "healer" can be prosecuted under medical practice statutes.

Q. *Can a faith healer or Christian Science practitioner be prosecuted for the crime of obtaining money under false pretenses?* A. If he is sincere, no. Furthermore, sincere or not, the truth or falsity of his religious doctrine, no matter how preposterous to others, cannot be tried by a jury. But if a man does *not* believe in a religious doctrine, but deliberately uses it to deceive and to obtain money thereby, and this disbelief and criminal intent can be proved, he can be convicted of fraud.

Q. *Is a sick adult free to submit to treatment by a faith healer or Christian Science practitioner rather than by a licensed medical doctor?* A. Yes, since no statute either requires or forbids that a sick adult submit to *anyone.* Two apparent but not actual exceptions: 1) in a threatened epidemic, the state may require all persons to be vaccinated, and may punish refusal; and, 2) if an ill adult's disease is contagious, the state may isolate him. But in "1" the state still may not forcibly vaccinate the stubborn one, and in "2" it may not forcibly administer treatment. In neither action does the state aim to treat the individual against his will for his own good; it only aims to protect everyone else *from* him.

Q. *Is a sick adult free to refuse a needed blood transfusion?* A. Yes, since no law requires any adult to submit for his own good to any treatment at all.

Q. *Is there any law against counselling a sick adult to submit to a faith healer or Christian Science practitioner or to deny himself a blood transfusion?* A. No. The acts counselled are lawful, and it is no crime to counsel another to a lawful act.

Q. *With all the above religion-motivated acts, which often result in death, permitted, how is it that the faith-proving ritual of handling deadly snakes can be prohibited?* A. At worst, the sick adult's submitting to a faith healer or Christian Science practitioner or refusing a transfusion, amounts to his merely doing *nothing,* good or bad, for himself. And the state tolerates a sick adult's doing nothing for himself. But he who handles poisonous snakes in a religious ritual does *something*—a positive act—which at once endangers not only himself but the other participants and the audience as well. This is against the *public* safety. (So far as I am aware, a man is free to go off alone into the woods, catch himself a rattler and there handle it to his heart's content.)

Q. *May a parent have his seriously ill child treated by a faith healer or Christian Science practitioner instead of a licensed medical doctor, or refuse to allow administration to the child of a necessary blood transfusion?* A. No. If the parent does not furnish his child the proper medical aid required by statute, he can be punished for misdemeanor, or, if the child dies, for manslaughter. Much more importantly, the state, through its courts, will take the neglected child from the parents in a hurry, without any consideration for the parents' religion, and give the child proper medical care.

Q. *But didn't you say, above, that there was no law to prohibit a faith healer or Christian Science practitioner from treating a child?* A. True. But the parent *must* furnish the medical aid required by statute. So long as he does so, he may, if he likes, at the same time hire ten assorted faith healers to pray for the child.

Q. *Can the faith healer or Christian Science practitioner who counsels a parent to the crime of denying statute-required medical aid to his child be punished as an accessory?* A. In Canada, yes. In the United States, only theoretically yes.

Q. *Can a Jehovah's Witness leader who counsels a parent to deny his child a necessary blood transfusion be prosecuted as an accessory?* A. In theory, yes. But I know of no such case.

These answers show both a remarkable restriction on adult religious practices in the interest of insuring that children shall safely reach maturity, and as remarkable a lack of restriction on how the adult shall conserve his own health and life. With the law's status as to children, the majority has no quarrel; indeed, in the last analysis, that status represents nothing more nor less than a successful imposition of the will of the majority upon a dissenting minority. But in tolerating religion-motivated denial of medical aid as to adults, the majority has demonstrated a remarkable restraint. The reason: the majority's realization that, as Justice Jackson puts it, "the price of freedom of religion or of speech or of the press is that we must put up with, and even pay for, a good deal of rubbish."

But if the adult is thus secured "the right to be wrong," there lies in these same guarantees the most obvious of remedies. I refer to Holmes' dissent in *Abrams:* ". . . that the ultimate good desired is better reached by free trade in ideas—that the best test of truth is the power of the thought to get itself accepted in the competition of the market . . ."

Until about fifteen years ago, there was little "free trade in ideas" on faith healing, and the only "competition of the market" was between the various sects. Press, radio, television and screen all seemed committed to a conspiracy of silence against any criticism of religion. It was un-American, and the critic who somehow managed to be heard risked condemnation as an atheist and Communist.

But then a mounting criticism of the faith healers was heard, and this not only from lay writers but from respected religious leaders as well. In September of 1956, on the televised "Frontiers of Faith," the Rev. Carrol R. Stegall, Jr. of Atlanta cited an instance where a faith healer proposed to restore sight to a man who had had both eyeballs removed, and pleaded instead for maximum use of scientific knowledge in aiding health, saying that "God didn't want us to be ignoramuses."[1]

Today, others are daring to question the methods and ethics of the barn-storming healers, to demand medical proofs which such operators always have failed to provide, and to offer eyewitness accounts of fraud and failure. They are explaining the difference between organic disease and hysterical symptoms, the nature of "faith" cures, the grave danger in indiscriminate resort to the method, and are strongly urging that it is no more reasonable to expect God to assume the burden of treating human ailments than it is to sit idle and expect Him to supply one's food and clothing.

It is in this encouraging atmosphere of free trade of ideas, rather than through further attempts to limit religious freedom by law, that we may expect to see dissipated a great deal of the problem of religion-inspired denial of medical aid. Meanwhile, though remaining committed to the widest possible toleration of religious freedom as to adults, we insist that this freedom take second place to the even more basic proposition that a child has the right to live.

# Notes

## CHAPTER 1

1. Twain, Mark (Samuel Clemens): *Christian Science* (N.Y., Harper, 1907). The chapters containing this account first appeared in 1899 in Cosmopolitan Magazine.

2. The "no such subheadings" refer to Dr. Cobb's miracle seeker (Ch. 5); to Cora Sutherland (Ch. 3); and to Thomas Grzyb, Jr. (Ch. 1).

3. Wonders vs. miracles: this distinction is emphasized in *Encyclopedia of Religion and Ethics* (N.Y., Scribner's, 1928) Vol. VIII, p. 676, at "Miracles."

4. For the Canadian item in full (Mrs. Grant) see Ch. 12. For the Philadelphia item in full (Cornelius) see Ch. 3.

## CHAPTER 2

1. General: Haggard, Howard W., M.D.: *Devils, Drugs and Doctors* (N.Y., Harper, 1929).

2. Asklepios: *Encyclopedia of Religion and Ethics* (N.Y., Scribner's, 1929) at "Faith Healing."

3. Peculiar People: *Encyclopedia of Religion and Ethics* (N.Y., Scribner's, 1917) Vol. IX, p. 703; *Encyclopedia Britannica*, 1949 ed., Vol. 17, p. 430.

4. British Medical Journal, June 18, 1910, p. 1471.

5. Sandford: *Time*, Nov. 14, 1938, p. 37; Boston (Mass.) *Globe*, Sept. 25, 1954, p. 3; *Encyclopedia of Religion and Ethics* (N.Y., Scribner's, 1912) Vol. V., p. 320.

6. Gates: Harrington ("Heavenly") Gates came from Saugus, Mass., and apparently was ribbed at Dartmouth for being a pious "Christer." He once tore up a college library copy of Thomas Paine's *Common Sense*. For his Senior year, Gates did not appear for practice, explaining to friends that football was commercialized and Godless and the players swore too much. Before the Yale game, a white-clad figure (a student) entered his room and said: "I am the Lord, and I command you to play football with Dartmouth." Gates reported, and helped beat Yale 24 to 6. But next day he left for the Amherst farm, where he said, "I have found the peace I have been looking for." Four days later he returned to Dartmouth but not to football.

7. Dowie: *Encyclopedia Britannica*, 1949 ed., Vol. 5, p. 631.

8. Heiser, Victor, M.D.: *An American Doctor's Odyssey* (N.Y., W.W. Norton & Co., Inc.) 1936, pp. 190–191.

9. Cartwright: Wallace, Robert: "The Rugged Basis of American Protestantism," *Life*, Dec. 26, 1955, pp. 71–78.

10. Allen: Sacramento (Calif.) *Bee*, April 17, 1956.

11. Miller and Davis: Boston (Mass.) *Traveler*, Aug. 26, 1947.

12. *Lawson v. Com.* (Ky.), *Harden v. State* (Tenn.) and *State v. Massey* (N.C.).

13. Inwood: Texas City (Tex.) *Sun*, April 5, 1956.

14. Morris: " 'Suggestion' in the Treatment of Disease," by Sir Henry Morris, Bart., M.B., F.R.C.S., Ex-President of the Royal College of Surgeons; Consulting Surgeon, Middlesex Hospital. *The British Medical Journal,* June 18, 1910, p. 1459–1460.

15. Holmes: New York (N.Y.) *Herald Tribune,* Dec. 6, 1952.

16. Kaadt: *Time,* May 17, 1948, p. 55.

17. Queen Juliana, Marijke, Hofmans, Yussupov: New York (N.Y.) *Times,* June 14, 16, 22, 25, 30, July 5, 8, Aug. 25, 26, 1956; New York (N.Y.) *Herald Tribune,* June 14, 15, 25, 30, July 1, 12, 13, Aug. 25, 1956; New York (N.Y.) *Journal-American,* June 24, 1956; New York (N.Y.) *World-Telegram & Sun,* July 5, 1956; *Time,* June 25, 1956, pp. 18–19; July 9, 1956, p. 26; Sept. 3, 1956, p. 21.

18. Coe: *Time,* Feb. 13, 1956, pp. 68–70; Henderson (Tex.) *News,* March 30, 1956; New York (N.Y.) *World-Telegram & Sun,* July 14, 1956.

19. Roberts: *Life,* Dec. 26, 1955, p. 53; *Time,* July 11, 1955, pp. 41–42; Feb. 13, 1956, p. 74; New York (N.Y.) *Times,* Feb. 19, 1956 (II, 11:1), March 4, 1956 (II, 9:6); "Oral Roberts—King of the Faith Healers," *American Magazine,* May, 1956, pp. 20–21, 88–91.

20. Large: *Christian Advocate,* April 19, 1956, p. 18.

21. Rev. Ives: *People Today,* May 30, 1956, p. 4.

## CHAPTER 3

1. General: *McClure's Magazine,* articles by Georgine Milmine: Editorial Comment, Dec., 1906, pp. 211–217; Part 1—"Forty Years of Obscurity," Jan., 1907, pp. 227, 242; Part II—"Mrs. Eddy and Phineas Parkhurst Quimby," Feb., 1907, pp. 339–354; Part III, "The Quimby Controversy," March, 1907, pp. 506–524; Part IV—"Six Years of Wandering," April, 1907, pp. 608–627; Part V, May, 1907, pp. 96–116; Editorial Comment, June, 1907, p. 134; Part VI, July, 1907, pp. 333–348; Part VII, Aug., 1907, pp. 447–462; Part VIII, Sept., 1907, pp. 567–581; Part IX, Oct., 1907, pp. 688–699; Part X, Feb., 1908, pp. 387–401; Part XI, March, 1908, pp. 577–590; Part XII, April, 1908, pp. 699–712. Dakin, Edwin Franden: *Mrs. Eddy* (N.Y., Scribner's, 1929). The "popular edition" of 1930 contains valuable added material, as well as a note *re.* the organized attempts to suppress or discredit this carefully documented study.

2. Breech presentation dialogue: Dakin, p. 241.

3. Television programs: Taylor (Tex.) *Press,* March 16, 1956; Waco (Tex.) *Times-Herald,* March 17, 1956; Kerryville (Tex.) *Times,* March 22, 1956; Henderson (Tex.) *News,* March 25, 1956.

4. Cornelius: Berwick (Pa.) *Enterprise,* March 6, 1956; Phoenix (Pa.) *Republican,* March 6, 1956; Camden (N.J.) *Courier-Post,* March 20, 1956; Atlantic City (N.J.) *Press,* March 21, 1956.

5. New Thought: *Time,* Nov. 7, 1938.

6. Workmen's compensation: St. Paul (Minn.) *Morning Tribune,* June 29, 1953.

7. Doubled demand for Eddy writings: *Time,* June 11, 1951, p. 60.

8. Holcomb: *State ex rel. Holcomb v. Armstrong.*

9. Sutherland: *Time,* May 24, 1954, p. 55.

## CHAPTER 4

1. General: Cole, Marley: *Jehovah's Witnesses—The New World Society* (N.Y., Vantage Press, 1955).

2. The resolution is quoted in Waite, Edward F., "The Debt of Constitutional Law to Jehovah's Witnesses," *Minnesota Law Review,* Vol. 28, No. 4, March, 1944, pp. 209–246, at p. 213.

3. 38 out of 45 cases: *Time,* March 23, 1953, p. 72.

4. Justice Jackson's three: *Martin, Murdock* and *Douglas*. Note: Justice Jackson's *Douglas* dissent applies to other cases as well. It begins on page 882 of 63 S.Ct.

5. Czatt, Milton Stacey: "The International Bible Students: Jehovah's Witnesses," Yale Studies in Religion, No. 4, Mennonite Press, Scottsdale, Pa., 1933.

6. Mulder and Comisky: Mulder, John E., and Marvin Comisky, "Jehovah's Witnesses Mold Constitutional Law," *Bill of Rights Review*, Vol. II, No. 4, Summer 1942, pp. 262–268 (published by the Bill of Rights Committee of the American Bar Association).

7. Hoffer, Eric: *The True Believer* (N.Y., Harper, 1951).

8. Larrabee: in *The Humanist,* 1952, No. 5, pp. 240–241.

9. Jehovah's Witness views on faith healing: "Profits Make Miracles Suspect," p. 20; "Capitalizing on the Mind-Body Relationship," pp. 21–24; and "Physical Health by Divine Intervention?" pp. 25–26; all in *Awake!* for May 8, 1954.

10. Odessa and Waxahachie, Texas: New York (N.Y.) *Times,* June 2, 1940 (14:1); June 3, 1940 (9:6).

11. Olliff: New York (N.Y.) *Times,* April 26, 1952 (15:7); April 27, 1952 (17:2); April 28, 1952 (12:7); April 29, 1952 (18:4); *Time,* May 12, 1952, p. 55.

12. Rogers: Rock Hill (S.C.) *Herald,* May 1, 1956.

13. Jones: Toronto (Can.) *Globe & Mail,* Feb. 18, 1956; New York (N.Y.) *Enquirer,* Feb. 27, 1956.

14. Robert Cole: Toronto (Can.) *Star,* March 1, 1956; New York (N.Y.) *Enquirer,* March 12, 1956.

## CHAPTER 5

1. Elyria, Ohio fluoridation: Boston (Mass.) *Globe,* April 29, 1954.

2. "Who Killed Cock Robin?": *American Journal of Public Health,* Vol. 34, No. 6, June, 1944, pp. 658–659.

3. Cobb, Beatrix, M.D.: "Why Do People Detour to Quacks?" *The Psychiatric Bulletin,* Vol. IV, No. 3, Summer, 1954, pp. 66–69; and see summary in *Time,* Aug. 16, 1954, p. 40.

4. Footnote, leukemia victim: Hot Springs (Ark.) *Sentinel-Record,* Feb. 25, 1956; Boston (Mass.) *Record,* Feb. 4, 1957, p. 18.

5. Alvarez, Dr. Walter C.: *Seeing the Doctor,* "Quacks Can Cure Hysteria but Rarely Anything Else," Boston (Mass.) *Sunday Globe,* Sept. 4, 1955.

6. Byrne: *Time,* April 5, 1954, p. 68.

7. Carlson, A. J., Dr.: *Science and the Supernatural,* The Liberal, Vol. 7, No. 11, Nov., 1953, pp. 1–5. Condensed from an article of the same title first published in *Science,* Vol. 73, No. 1887, Feb., 1931, pp. 217–225, and reprinted in the *Scientific Monthly* for August, 1944, pp. 85–95.

8. The argument of this section, the case histories summarized, and the quotations are all from Dr. Laurance Frederic Shaffer's *The Psychology of Adjustment* (Boston, Houghton Mifflin, 1936).

9. Bechet: "Along the Rue Bechet," *Time,* Sept 20, 1954, pp. 83–84.

10. Gentlemen's agreement: Sir Heneage Ogilvie, "The Importance of Leisure," *The Practitioner,* (London) No. 1027, Vol. 172, Jan. 1954, pp. 68–75.

## CHAPTER 6

1. General: Linn, William Alexander, *The Story of the Mormons* (N.Y., Macmillan, 1902; reissued 1963, Russell & Russell, Inc. N.Y.). Bancroft, Hubert Howe, *History of Utah, 1540–1887* (San Francisco, The History Co., 1890).

CHAPTER 7

1. Short Creek: *Time,* Jan. 23, 1956, p. 40; Aug. 3, 1953, p. 16; July 21, 1947, pp. 17–21. *Colliers,* Nov. 13, 1953: "Why I Have Five Wives," by Edson Jessop with Maurine Whipple, pp. 27–30; and "Arizona Raided Short Creek—Why?" by Wiley S. Maloney, pp. 30–31.

2. Bancroft uses the word "jail": see Bancroft, *op. cit.,* p. 683, ff.

CHAPTER 8

1. "Handbill cases": see "The Debt of Constitutional Law to Jehovah's Witnesses," by Edward F. Waite, *Minnesota Law Review,* Vol. 28, No. 4, March, 1944, pp. 209–246.

2. Gobitis: New York (N.Y.) *Times,* Dec. 2, 1937 (1:5); Dec. 3 (25:8); Dec. 4 (19:6); Nov. 11, 1939 (17:3); March 4, 1940 (1:7); Apr. 13 (6:5); June 4 (25:6); June 5 (24:2).

3. Four other flag salute appeals: *Leoles v. Landers, Hering v. State Board of Education, Gabrielli v. Knickerbocker,* and *Johnson v. Deerfield.*

CHAPTER 9

1. Edgar Mortara: *Jewish Encyclopedia* (N.Y., Funk, Wagnalls, 1905) Vol. IX, pp. 35–36.

2. Justice Douglas: *Zorach v. Clauson,* 72 S. Ct. 679 (1952) at p. 684.

3. Pereira: Rec., pp. 5–8. NOTE: Because of the peculiar way in which the appeal was quashed, it will not be found in published case reports. The original case is identified as "Pereira v. Pereira, Bristol County (Mass.) Probate Court, 1954, No. D-16741." As of January 15, 1957, all the papers were on file in the Court House in Pemberton Square, Boston, Room 1407—Reporter of Decisions. These include: (1) "796 F.C., SHIRLEY PEREIRA, Libellant vs. ANTONIO PEREIRA, libelee, PETITION TO MODIFY DECREE NISI, BRISTOL COUNTY," referred to herein as "Rec." (2) "RESPONDENT'S BRIEF." (3) "BRIEF FOR PETITIONER." (4) "MOTION AND AFFIDAVIT TO DISMISS" Oct. Sitting, 1955. (6) Considine's FINDINGS AND DECREE of October 21, 1955 (a bound, typewritten copy). (7) MOTION FOR COSTS presented October 31, 1955. (8) ORDER dismissing appeal as moot, dated Nov. 1, 1955.

4. Rec., p. 12.

5. Resp. Brief, pp. 3–11.

6. Antonio's appeal dismissed: "Order," above.

7. This is the figure stated for her costs by the successful appellant in a comparable case. See McCollum, Vashti, *One Woman's Fight,* Doubleday (and Beacon), 1951, at p. 16.

8. Leo Pfeffer, *Church, State and Freedom* (Boston, Beacon Press, 1953), p. 587.

9. Hildy: *Ellis v. McCoy,* 124 N.E. 2d 266. The voluminous (370 page) printed record of testimony and briefs are in Room 1407, Boston Court House, together with the same for the later (#5549 and #5562) *Ellis v. Doherty* (in the meantime Marjorie had married), 136 N.E. 2d 203. And see *The New York Times* (micro. ed.) Feb. 15, 1955 (1:18), Jul 2 (17:3), Jul 4 (23:1), Jul 7 (12:7), Jul 9 (7:3), Jul 13 (18:7), Oct 6 (18:4), March 17, 1957 (78:8), March 18 (54:2), March 19 (39:4), March 24 (54:6), April 18 (18:5), April 30 (23:5), May 24 (1:2), May 25 (10:6), May 26, IV, (2:7), June 1 (8:7), June 12 (29:6), July 11 (52:1), July 12 (10:3). And Boston (Mass.) *Globe* (eve. ed.) March 5, 1956, p. 6; July 24, p. 1; Sept. 29, p. 3.

10. The 1950 "5B" statute: St. 1950, c. 737, § 3. Now G.L. (Ter. Ed.) c. 210, § 5B.

11. Goldman: New York *Times,* Sept. 29, 1954 (20:3), Feb. 15, 1955 (1:1).

12. Pfeffer, "Religion in the Upbringing of Children," Boston University Law Review, Vol. XXXV, No. 3 (June, 1955), pp. 333–393, at p. 392, note 275; and p. 387, note 260.

13. First Massachusetts adoption statute: St. of 1851, c. 324. For summary see John F. Lombard, *Massachusetts Practice—Vol. 3, Adoption, Illegitimacy and Blood Tests* (Boston: Boston Law Book Co., 1952) p. 19, below note 52.

14. Massachusetts: St. 1905, p. 411, c. 464, § 1.

15. *In re Berry,* R.I. Juv. Ct., No. AD-A-439, decided Feb. 12, 1952; described in Pfeffer, *Church, State and Freedom,* p. 593.

16. Cf. "Religious Factors in Adoption," *Indiana Law Journal,* Vol. 28, No. 3 (Spring 1953) pp. 401–409, at p. 402, Note 6.

17. Paul Blanchard, *The Irish and Catholic Power* (Boston: Beacon Press, 1953) p. 310.

18. *The New York Times,* July 13, 1955 (18:7).

## CHAPTER 10

1. *United States v. Knowles.*

2. 21 Am. & Eng. Enc. of Law 199.

## CHAPTER 11

1. Jessel: *Time,* Sept. 7, 1953, pp. 52–54.

2. *Time,* July 18, 1949, p. 60.

3. Willis Vernon Cole: *The New York Times:* July 11, 1914 (4:6), July 13 (8:4), July 16 (8:5), October 4, 1916 (10:8), Oct. 5 (10:4), Oct. 10 (11:2), Oct. 11 (10:5,6).

## CHAPTER 12

1. Texas, Iowa, Michigan, Ohio: *Grace v. State, State v. Campbell, People v. Roberts, Blackburn v. State.*

2. Newhouse: *Time,* May 12, 1952, p. 55.

3. Ivie: Boston (Mass.) *Globe,* June 9, 1952, p. 1.

4. Justice Holmes' definition of the law: *American Banana Co. v. United Fruit Co.,* 213 U.S. 347, at 356.

5. Grant: Montreal (Can.) *Star,* Feb. 8, 1956; Little Rock (Ark.) *Gazette,* Feb. 9, 1956.

6. Clark, William L., and William L. Marshall, *A Treatise on the Law of Crimes* (Chicago, Callaghan, 1940) §§ 109–111.

7. Volstad-Alvis: Los Angeles (Cal.) *Times,* Sept. 3, Nov. 18, 19, 22, 29, 1938.

8. Clark and Marshall: *op. cit.,* at § 157(d).

9. *Stamper v. Com.;* "later overruled" by *Com. v. Carter.*

## CHAPTER 13

1. The account in this chapter is based upon *U.S. v. Ballard* and the following: *The New York Times,* Jan. 21, 1941 (7:8), Feb. 14, 1942 (22:7), June 22, 1943 (15:5), April 25, 1944 (13:2). "Borden Sues 'I Am' Cult Leaders," *Publisher's Weekly,* Vol. 139, Jan. 4, 1941, p. 42. "The Lunatic Fringe of Religion," by Dr. Frank S. Mead, *American Mercury,* Vol. 52, Feb. 1941, pp. 167–175. "Religious Liberty and Fraud," *Christian Century,* Vol. 61, May 10, 1944, pp. 583–585.

2. After "appropriate ways.": A case footnote at this point reads: "*William James, Collected Essays and Reviews,* pp. 427–8; see generally his *Varieties of Religious Experience* and *The Will to Believe.* See also Burton, *Heyday of a Wizard.*" Jean Burton's book, (N.Y. Knopf, 1944) is the story of the most remarkable medium of modern times, consumptive Daniel Dunglas Home (for a time "Hume") 1833–1886, who traveled in royal circles, never accepted money for his most remarkable and much-documented manifestations, and was

never found guilty of fraud. Elizabeth Barrett Browning became a firm believer in him; husband Robert regarded him with utter revulsion. Home inspired Browning's *Mr. Sludge, the Medium,* and Home's middle name inspired Browning's epithet, "Dung-ball," for him.

3. After "theoretically possible." Case footnote: "William James, *The Will to Believe,* p. 90."

## CHAPTER 14

1. John and Helen Vasko: the account is based upon the case report, *In re Vasko,* and the following *The New York Times* items: April 13, 1933 (1:5), April 14 (21:5), April 15 (15:5), April 16 (15:1), April 17 (15:3), April 18 (17:3), April 19 (36.2), April 20 (5:4), April 21 (38:3), April 22 (15:6), April 23 (2:4), April 24 (2:1 and 14:5), April 25 (11:3), April 26 (17:3), April 27 (19:4), April 28 (19:4), April 29 (15:5), April 30 (16:6), May 1 (17:2), May 7 (6:2), Aug. 7 (15:5), Aug. 9 (20:2), Aug. 10 (9:1), Aug. 11, 1935 (12:4); May 17, 1937 (2:6).

2. Patricia Hudson: *In re Hudson,* and see *The New York Times,* Feb. 22, 1942 (23:7); June 9, 1942 (20:4).

## CHAPTER 15

1. The Labrenz account is based upon the case report, *People ex rel. Wallace v. Labrenz,* and the following: *Time,* April 30, 1951, pp. 84–85; Board of Commissioners of Cook County, Illinois, William N. Erickson, President, 1952 Annual Message; Bangor (Me.) *Daily News,* April 18, 1951, pp. 1, 4.

2. Janet Lynn Morrison: *Morrison v. State.*

3. *Minnesota Law Review* on *Seiferth:* Vol. 39, No. 1, Dec., 1954, pp. 118–122.

4. Larson, Robert Keith, *Child Neglect in the Exercise of Religious Freedom, Chicago-Kent Law Review,* Vol. 32, No. 4, Sept., 1954, pp. 283–297.

## CHAPTER 16

1. Rev. Stegall: *The New York Times,* Sept. 4, 1956.

# Table of Cases

Abrams v. U.S., (1919) 250 U.S. 616, 40 S. Ct. 17, 63 L. Ed. 1173
American Banana Co. v. United Fruit Co., 213 U.S. 347.
American Press: see Grossjean v.
Armstrong: see State ex rel. Holcomb v.
Ash v. Barker, (1915) 2 Cal. I.A.C. 577.

Bailey: see State v.
Baldwin: see Robertson v.
Ballard: see United States v.
Barker: see Ash v.
Barnes: see State v.
Barnette: see West Virginia.
Beardsley: see People v.
Beason: see Davis v.
Beauchamp: see Sturges.
Beck v. State, (Okla. Cr.) 233 Pac. 495 (1925).
Beer: see Reg. v.
Berry: see In re.
Blackburn v. State, 23 Ohio St. 146.
Bradley v. State, (1920) 79 Fla. 651, 84 So. 677, 10 ALR 1129.
Breth: see Com. v.
Bridges v. State of California. Times-Mirror Co. et al. v. Superior
    Court of State of California, in and for Los Angeles County, (1941)
    314 U.S. 252, 62 S. Ct. 190, 86 L. Ed. 192.
Brooks: see Rex v.
Brown: see Reg. v.
Brush: see Matter of.
Buswell: see State v.

Campbell: see State v.
Canfield: see Christian v.
Cantwell v. Connecticut, (1940) 310 U.S. 296, 60 S. Ct. 900, 84 L. Ed.
    1213, 128 A.L.R. 1352.
Carter: see Com. v.
Chaplinsky v. New Hampshire, (1942) 315 U.S. 568, S. Ct. 766, 86 L.
    Ed. 1031.
Chenoweth: see State v.
Christian v. Canfield, (1931) 108 N.J. Eq. 547.
Clauson: see Zorach v.

Cole: see People v.
Com. v. Breth, (1915) 44 Pa. Co. Ct. 56.
Com. v. Carter, 94 Ky. 527, 23 S.W. 344.
Com. v. Dennis, 105 Mass. 162.
Com. v. Hoffman, (1903) 29 Pa. Co. Ct. 65.
Com. v. Pierce, (1884) Sup. Jud. Ct. of Mass., 138 Mass. 165, 52 Am.
  Rep. 264.
  12 Am. St. Rep. 566.
Cook: see Reg. v.
Com. v. Plaisted, (1889) 148 Mass. 375, 19 N.E. 224, 2 L.R.A. 142,
Cox v. New Hampshire, (1940) 312 U.S. 569, 61 S. Ct. 762, 85 L.
  Ed. 1049.

Davis v. Beason, (1890) 133 U.S. 333, 10 S. Ct. 299, 33 L. Ed. 637.
Davis v. Mass., (1897) 167 U.S. 43, 17 S. Ct. 731, 42 L. Ed. 71.
Davis: see Mitchell v.
Debs v. U.S., (1919) 249 U.S. 211, 39 S. Ct. 252, 63 L. Ed. 566.
Deerfield: see Johnson v.
DeJonge v. Oregon, (1937) 299 U.S. 353, 57 S. Ct. 255, 81 L. Ed. 278.
Dennis: see Com. v.
Dent v. West Virginia, (1889) 129 U.S. 114, 9 Sup. Ct. 231, 32 L.
  Ed. 623.
Dickson v. U.S., (1953) 346 U.S. 389.
Doherty: see Ellis v.
Douglas v. City of Jeannette, (1943) 319 U.S. 157, 63 S. Ct. 877, 87 L.
  Ed. 1324; rehearing denied, (1943) 319 U.S. 782, 63 S. Ct. 1170,
  87 L. Ed. 1726.
Downes: see Reg. v.

Elder: see Rex v.
Ellis v. Doherty, 136 N.E. 2d 203.
Ellis v. McCoy, 124 N.E. 2d 266.
Estep: see People v.
Evans: see State v.
Ewer: see People v.

Fealy v. City of Birmingham, (1916) 15 Ala. App. 367, 73 So. 296.
Felton: see Reg. v.
Fort Worth & Denver City Ry. Co. v. Travis, (1907) 45 Tex. C. A.
  117, 99 S.W. 1141.
Frowerk v. U.S., (1919) 249 U.S. 204, 39 S. Ct. 249, 63 L. Ed. 561.

Gabrielli v. Knickerbocker, 306 U.S. 621.
Gitlow v. New York, (1925) 268 U.S. 652, 45 S. Ct. 625, 69 L. Ed.
  1138.
Gobitis: see Minersville.
Goldman: see Petitions of.
Grace v. State, 44 Tex. Cr. R. 193, 69 S.W. 529.
Grossjean v. American Press Co., (1936) 297 U.S. 233, 56 S. Ct. 444,
  80 L. Ed. 660.

Pierce: see Com. v.

Pierce v. Society of Sisters, (1925) 268 U.S. 510, 45 S. Ct. 571, 69 L. Ed. 1070, 39 A.L.R. 468.

Pierson: see People v.

Plaisted: see Com. v.

Prince v. Mass., (1944) 321 U.S. 158, 64 S. Ct. 438, 88 L. Ed. 645. And see 313 Mass. 223, 46 N.E. 2d 755; and 321 U.S. 804, 64 S. Ct. 784.

Purinton v. Jamrock, 195 Mass. 187, 80 N.E. 802; and see 3 Op. Atty. Gen. 124 (Mass. 1907).

Ramsey: see Murphy v.

Reg. v. Beer, (1896) 32 Can. L.J. 416.

Reg. v. Brown, (1893) 1 Terr. L.R. 475, L.N.W. Terr. Sup. Ct. Rep. pt. 4, p. 35.

Reg. v. Cook, (1898) 62 J.P. 712, 58 Alb. L.J. 232.

Reg. v. Downes, (1875) 13 Cox, C.C. 111, L.R. 1 Q.B. Div. 25, 45 L.J. Mag. Cas. N.S. 8, 33 L.T. N.S. 74, 24 Week. Rep. 278.

Reg. v. Felton, (1898) 33 L.J.N.C. (Eng.) 563.

Reg. v. Hines, (1874) 80 Cent. Crim. Ct. Sess. Paper (Eng.) 309, 13 Cox, C.C. 114, note.

Reg. v. Hurry, (1872) 76 Cent. Crim. Ct. Sess. Paper, 63, 13 Cox, C.C. (Eng.) 113, note.

Reg. v. Knights, (1860) 2 Fost. & F. (Eng.) 46.

Reg. v. Morby, (1882) L.R. 8 Q.B. Div. 571, 15 Cox, C.C. 35, 51 L.J. Mag. Cas. N.S. 85, 46 L.T.N.S. 288, 30 Week. Rep. 613, 46 J.P. 422.

Reg. v. Senior, (1889) 1 Q.B. Div. 283, 19 Cox, C.C. 219, 68 L.J.Q.B.N.S. 175, 63 J.P. 8, 47 Week. Rep. 367, 79 L.T.N.S. 562, 15 Times L.R. 102.

Reg. v. Shepherd, (1862) 9 Cox, C.C. (Eng.) 123, Leigh & C.C.C. 147, 31 L.J.Mag. Cas. N.S. 102, 8 Jur. N.S. 418, 5 L.T.N.S. 687, 10 Week. Rep. 297.

Reg. v. Smith, (1837) 8 Car. & P. (Eng.) 153.

Reg. v. Wagstaffe, (1868) 10 Cox, C.C. (Eng.) 530.

Rex v. Brooks, (1902) 22 C.L.T. 105, 9 B.C. 13, 1 B.R.C. 725, 5 Can. Crim. Cas. 372, 22 C.L.T. 105.

Rex v. Elder, (1925) Can., Manitoba Reports, Vol. 35, 161–175.

Rex v. Izod, (1905) 20 Cox, C.C. (Eng.) 690 (as digested in 1 Butterworths' Ten Years' Dig. 1898–1907, col. 834.)

Rex v. Lewis, (1903) 6 Ont. L. Rep. 132, 1 B.R.C. 732, 7 Can. Cas. 261, 23 Can. L.T. Occ. N. 257, 2 Ont. Week. Rep. 566.

Reynolds v. U.S., (1878) 98 U.S. 145, 25 L. Ed. 244.

Roberts: see People v.

Robertson v. Baldwin, (1897) 165 U.S. 275, 17 S. Ct. 326, 41 L. Ed. 715.

Robinson v. Robinson, (1891) 66 N.H. 600, 23 Atl. 362.

Rotkowitz: see In re.

Sadlock v. Board of Education, (1948) 137 N.J. Law 85, 58 A. 2d 218.

Sandford: see State v.

# Index